George Monro Grant

French Canadian life and character

George Monro Grant

French Canadian life and character

ISBN/EAN: 9783742876294

Manufactured in Europe, USA, Canada, Australia, Japa

Cover: Foto ©Thomas Meinert / pixelio.de

Manufactured and distributed by brebook publishing software (www.brebook.com)

George Monro Grant

French Canadian life and character

FRENCH CANADIAN LIFE AND CHARACTER

WITH HISTORICAL AND DESCRIPTIVE SKETCHES OF THE SCENERY AND LIFE IN QUEBEC, MONTREAL, OTTAWA, AND SURROUNDING COUNTRY

EDITED BY
GEORGE MUNRO GRANT, D. D.
QUEEN'S UNIVERSITY, KINGSTON, ONT.

ILLUSTRATED BY WOOD-ENGRAVINGS FROM ORIGINAL DRAWINGS BY F. B. SCHELL, L. R. O'BRIEN, W. T. SMEDLEY, T. MORAN, G. GIBSON, AND OTHERS

CHICAGO
ALEXANDER BELFORD & CO.
1899

CONTENTS

	PAGE
FRENCH-CANADIAN LIFE AND CHARACTER	9
By J. G. A. CREIGHTON, M. A.	
QUEBEC—HISTORICAL AND DESCRIPTIVE	51
By PRINCIPAL GRANT, D. D., and MISS A. M. MACHAR	
SOUTHEASTERN QUEBEC	115
By J. HOWARD HUNTER, M. A.	
MONTREAL	139
By REV. A. J. BRAY and JOHN LESPERANCE, M. R. S. C.	
THE LOWER OTTAWA	179
By R. VASHON ROGERS, B. A., and C. P. MULVANEY, M. A.	
OTTAWA	200
By F. A. DIXON	
THE UPPER OTTAWA	233
By C. P. MULVANEY, M. A.	

FRENCH CANADIAN LIFE AND CHARACTER.

"IF you have never visited the Côte de Beaupré, you know neither Canada nor the Canadians," says the Abbé Ferland.

The beautiful strip of country that borders the St. Lawrence for a score or so of miles below the Falls of Montmorency does, indeed, afford the best possible illustration of the scenery, the life, and the manners of the Province of Quebec, the people of which, not content with naming the Dominion, claim Canada and Canadian as designations peculiarly their own. All that is lovely in landscape is to be found there. The broad sweep of "the great river of Canada," between the ramparts of Cape Diamond and the forest-crowned crest of Cap Tourmente, is fringed with rich meadows rising in terraces of verdure, slope after slope, to the foot of the sombre hills that wall in the vast amphitheatre. In the foreground the north channel, hemmed in by the bold cliffs of the Island of Orleans, sparkles in the sun. Far away across the Traverse, as you look between the tonsured head of Petit Cap and the point of Orleans, a cluster of low islands breaks the broad expanse of the main stream, the brilliant blue of which

GATHERING MARSH HAY.

melts on the distant horizon into the hardly purer azure of the sky. Quaint *batteaux*, with swelling canvas, make their slow way, or lying high on the flats await their cargo. Stately ships glide down with the favouring tide, or announce the near end of the voyage by signals to the shore and guns that roll loud thunder through the hills. The marshes,

LOADING A BATTEAU AT LOW TIDE.

CAP TOURMENTE AND PETIT CAP.

covered with rich grass, are studded with haymakers gathering the abundant yield, or are dotted with cattle. Inland, stiff poplars and bosky elms trace out the long brown ribands of the roads. Here and there the white cottages group closer together, and the spire of the overshadowing church topping the trees, marks the centre of a parish. Red roofs and glistening domes flash out in brilliant points of colour against the fleecy clouds that fleck the summer sky. Rich pastures, waving grain, orchards and maple groves, lead the eye back among their softly-blending tints to the dark masses of purple and green with which the forests clothe the mountains. Huge rifts, in which sunlight and shadow work rare effects, reveal where imprisoned streams burst their way through the Laurentian rocks in successions of magnificent cascades. A glimpse of white far up the mountain side shows one of these, while its placid course through the lowland is marked in silver sheen. As the sun gets low, one perchance catches the flash reflected from some of the lovely lakes that lie among the hills.

The Côte de Beaupré is the oldest as well as the fairest part of the Province. It was settled soon after Champlain landed, the rich marsh hay being utilized at once for the wants of Quebec. In 1633 a fort was built at Petit Cap, the summit of the promonotory that juts out into the river under the overshadowing height of Cap Tourmente. The fort was destroyed by Sir David Kirk—Admiral, the chroniclers call him—in these days he would probably be hanged as a buccaneer—who harried the cattle and then sailed on to summon Quebec to surrender for the first time. In 1670 Laval established here a school for training boys as well in farming and mechanics, as in doctrine and discipline. Among other industries, wood-carving for church decoration was taught, so that the Côte de Beaupré can lay claim to the first Art School and the first model-farm in America. The Quebec Seminary still keeps up this state of things—at least as far as agriculture is concerned. The place is known as "The Priests' Farm," and supplies the Seminary, being thoroughly worked and having much attention given to it. It is also a summer resort for the professors and pupils of the Seminary.

After the restoration of Canada to France by the Treaty of St. Germain-en-Laye, in 1632, this part of the little colony grew apace, so that by the time the seigniory passed into Laval's hands, from whom it came to its present owners—the Seminary—its population, notwithstanding its exposure to attack by the Iroquois, was greater than that of Quebec itself. From its situation it has been less vulnerable than many other districts to outside influences. The face of the country and the character of the people have yielded less to modern ideas, which, working quietly and imperceptibly, have left intact many of the antiquities, traditions and customs that have disappeared elsewhere within the last generation. Here you may find families living on the lands their forefathers took in feudal tenure from the first *seigneurs* of La Nouvelle France. What Ferland says is still to a great extent true: "In the *habitant* of the Côte de Beaupré you have the Norman peasant of the reign of Louis XIV., with his legends, his songs, his superstitions and his customs." He is not so benighted as many people think he is, but here and there you will come across a genuine survival of the Old Régime, and may, perhaps, meet some gray-capoted, fur-capped, brown-visaged, shrivelled-up old man, whose language and ideas make you think a veritable Breton or Norman of the century before last has been weather-beaten and smoke-dried into perpetual preservation.

AN OLD HABITANT.

All the world over your rustic is conservative. The old gods lived long among the Italian villagers, though Rome was the centre of the new faith. Among the *habitans* of the Province of Quebec there yet exist a mode of life and cast of thought strangely in contrast with their surroundings. In the cities a rapid process of assimilation is going on. Quaint and foreign though Montreal, and especially Quebec, seem to the stranger at first sight, their interest is mainly historical and political. To understand the national life of Lower Canada, you must go among the *habitans*.

The word is peculiarly French-Canadian. The *paysan*, or peasant, never existed in

Canada, for the feudalism established by Louis XIV. did not imply any personal dependence upon the *seigneur*, nor, in fact, any real social inferiority. Each *censitaire* was, in all but name, virtually as independent a proprietor as is his descendant to-day. He was and he is emphatically the dweller in the land. He "went up and saw the land that it was good," possessed it, and dwells therein. The term is often used as equivalent to *cultivateur*, or farmer, and as distinguishing the rural from the urban population; but, rightly understood and used as he uses it, nothing more forcibly expresses both the origin and nature of the attachment of the French-Canadian to his country and the tenacity with which he clings to his nationality, his religion and his language.

The persistency of French nationality in Canada is remarkable. The formal guarantees of the Treaty of Paris and the Quebec Act, that language, religion and laws should be preserved, undoubtedly saved it from extinction by conquest. But to the difference in character between the French and English, which is so radical and has been so sedulously fostered by every possible means, not the least effective being an able and vigorous literature which preserves and cultivates the French language; to the political freedom which allowed the realization of the early perception that as individuals they would be without influence, as a body all-powerful; to the inherent merits of their civil law, the direct descendant of a jurisprudence which was a refined science centuries before Christ; and to the ideal of becoming the representatives of Roman Catholicism in America, must be mainly ascribed the vitality that the French-Canadians have shown as a distinct people. Their numerical and physical condition will be dealt with later on, but it may be said here that a great deal is also due to their origin. The hardy sailors of Normandy and Brétagne; the sturdy farmers of Anjou, Poitou, Le Perche, Aunis, Saintonge and L'Ile-de-France; the soldiers of the Carignan regiment who had fought on every battle-field in Europe, brought with them to Canada the spirit of adventure, the endurance, the bravery—in short, all the qualities that go to make successful colonists, and that they inherited from the same source as does the Englishman. In the United States, the second or third generation finds other immigrants completely fused into the common citizenship, but the little French-Canadian colonies in the manufacturing towns of New England and in the wheat regions of the West, keep their language, and, to a great extent, their customs. Canada was a true colony, and has remained the most successful French attempt at colonization. From various causes, Louisiana has failed to keep her nationality intact. In Lower Canada, the spirit of Champlain and La Salle, of the *coureurs de bois*, of the Iroquois-haunted settlers on the narrow fringe of straggling farms along the St. Lawrence—the spirit that kept up the fight for the *Fleurs de Lis* long after "the few acres of snow" had been abandoned by their King—has always remained the same, and still animates the *colons* in the backwoods. The French-Canadians have always fought for a faith and an idea, hence they have remained French.

As one of their most celebrated French orators pointed out at the great national fête of St. Jean Baptiste at Quebec in 1880, that was the secret of it all; while the Thirteen Colonies, which fought for material interests, are American, not English.

Whatever the cause, there is no doubt as to the fact of French nationality. The north shore of the St. Lawrence is more French than is the south, where the proximity of the United States and the influence of the English-settled eastern townships are sensible. In the western part of the Province, the numerical proportion of French is smaller and their characteristics are less marked; but from Montreal downwards—the towns of course excepted—you are to all intents in a land where English is not spoken. Below Quebec, far down to the Labrador coast, is the most purely French portion of all. You may find greater simplicity of life, and more of the old customs, in such a primæval parish as Isle aux Coudres, farther down the river; the people on the coast where the St. Lawrence becomes the gulf, are sailors and fishermen rather than farmers; those along the Ottawa are lumberers and raftsmen; but the Côte de Beaupré is fairly typical of the whole of French-Canada.

HABITANT AND SNOW-SHOES.

The names of its five parishes, L'Ange Gardien, Chateau Richer, Sainte Anne de Beaupré, St. Joachim, and St. Féréol, tell you at once you are in a land with a religion and a history. Nothing, perhaps, strikes a stranger more than the significant nomenclature of the Province. Every village speaks the faith of the people. Ile Jesus, Sainte Foye, L'Assomption, L'Epiphanie, St. Joseph, Ste. Croix, Ste. Anne, St. Barthélémi, St. Eustache, Notre Dame des Anges, are

L'ANGE GARDIEN.

not mere designations. The pious commemorations and joyful celebrations of the patron saint or particular festival show it. Hills, rivers and lakes tell of military achievements, of missionary voyages, of dangers encountered, of rest after peril past, of the hopes that animated the *voyageurs* pushing through the maze of forest and stream in search of the golden West, of grand prospects and lovely landscapes, of quaint semblances and fond reminiscence of home. Take just a few of these names: Calumet, Sault au Récollet, Belange, Carillon, Chaudière, Pointe aux Trembles, Bout de L'Ile, Lachine, Portage du Fort, Beaupré, Beloeil, La Lièvre, La Rose, Chute au Blondeau, Rivière Ouelle, Rivière au Chien, Montreal, Quebec, Joliette, Beauport. Each suggests a story of its own; most of them have their associations of history and tradition, and there are thousands like them. The French knew how to name a country. In point of beauty and significance, their names are unequalled; and they not only described the land as do the Indians they literally christened it. Even where it comes to perpetuating the memories of men, what a sonorous ring there is about Champlain, Richelieu, Sorel, Chambly, Varennes, Contrecoeur, Longueuil and Beauharnois, unapproachable by English analogues. Point Lévis is, in truth, not a whit more aesthetic than Smith's Falls, nor more useful, but there is no denying its superiority of sound. When you know the grotesque and haughty legend that represents the Virgin Mary in heaven telling a Chevalier de Lévis, "Cousin, keep on your hat," you can no longer compare the two names, for you quite understand why the Lévis family should have a Point as well as an Ark of its own.

L'Ange Gardien lies just beyond the famous Falls of Montmorency. Set in trees on the slope of the hills, which here grow close on the river, and standing high over the north channel, the village commands an exquisite view, the placid beauty of which makes "The Guardian Angel" a most appropriate name. The spot has not always had such peaceful associations. Wolfe's troops, those "Fraser's Highlanders", who afterwards turned their swords into ploughshares so effectually that their descendants at Murray Bay and Kamouraska are French even to having forgotten their fathers' language, ravaged this parish and Chateau Richer from one end to the other, destroyed all the crops, and burned almost every house. There is little trace of the devastation now, except in the stories that old *habitans* have heard their elders tell. Two quaint little chapels stand one on each side, a few *arpens* from the parish church. They were originally intended for mortuary chapels during the winter, when the frost prevents graves being dug, and for use at the celebration of the "Fête Dieu" or "Corpus Christi" in June, the procession going to one or the other in alternate years. On these occasions, they would be gay with flowers, flags, and evergreens. Beside one of them is the little plot used for the burial of heretics, excommunicated persons, and unbaptized infants. There is always such a corner in every village cemetery, never a large one, for the people are too good Catholics not to have an intense dread of lying in unconsecrated ground, and too charitable to consign strangers to the fate they fear for themselves. The chapel farthest down the river is now a consecrated shrine of Notre Dame de Lourdes. Before the statue of our Lady burns a perpetual light, and she divides with La Bonne Ste. Anne de Beaupré the devotions of thousands of pilgrims annually.

The course of settlement along the St. Lawrence is well defined. Close to the river, in a belt from two to ten miles wide, on the north shore, lie the old French farms. Back of these, among the foot-hills, is a second range of settlements, for the most part Irish and Scotch. Farther in are the *colons* or pioneers, who, no longer able to live upon the subdivision of their *patrimoine* or family inheritance, commence again, as their ancestors did, in the backwoods. Parallel roads, painfully straight for miles, mark out

FRENCH FARMS.

the ranges into which the seigniories and parishes are divided. These ranges or *concessions* are sometimes numbered, sometimes named, almost universally after a saint. On the south shore, the belt of settlement is much wider. At the westward of the Province it extends to the United States boundary line, but narrows as it approaches Quebec, so that below the city the arrangement is much the same as on the north side. In fact, French-Canada is very truly described as two continuous villages along the St. Lawrence. The succession of white cottages, each on its own little parallelogram of land, has struck every traveller from La Hontan to the present day.

The narrow farms, or *terres*, as they are called, catch the eye at once. Originally three *arpens* wide by thirty deep (the *arpent* as a lineal measure equals 180 French or 191

English feet), or about 200 yards by a little over a mile, they have been subdivided according to the system of intestate succession under the Coutume de Paris, which gives property in equal shares to all the children, until the fences seem to cover more ground than the crops. The division is longitudinal, so that each heir gets an equal strip of beech, marsh, plough land, pasture, and forest. The houses line the road that runs along the top of the river bank, or marks the front of the *concession* if it lies back any distance. This arrangement is but a carrying out of the principle upon which the original settlement was formed, to gain all the advantages of the river frontage. The entire organization of French-Canada depended on it. The system was well adapted for easy communication in the early days of the colony; the river was the highway—in summer, for canoes—in winter, for sleighs; so that the want of good roads was not a serious disadvantage. It was also well suited for defence against the Iroquois, who in their bloody raids had to follow the course of the streams. The settlers could fall back upon each other, gradually gaining strength until the *seigneur's* block-house was reached and a stand made while the news went on from farm to farm, and the whole colony stood to arms. In the district of Quebec you may often hear a *habitant* speak of going "au fort," meaning thereby "au village,"—a curious survival of those fighting days.

In winter the ice is still the best of all roads. Long lanes of bushes and small spruces, dwindling away in distant perspective, mark out the track, to keep which would otherwise be no easy matter at night or in a snowstorm, and point out the "air holes" caused by the "shoving" or moving *en masse* of the ice that usually follows any change in the level of the river.

This universal parallelogramic shape is, however, very disadvantageous to the development of a country, being to no small extent anti-social and particularly unfavourable to a general school system. The geographical, not the mental condition of the *habitant* has militated most against intellectual and social improvement. There were no points of concentration for the interchange of ideas, save the gathering at the parish church on Sundays and fête-days when, after High Mass, the crowd lingers to hear the *huissier's* publications of official notices at the church door; or, once in a while, to listen to electioneering addresses. The villages are, as before noted, for the most part long, straggling lines of houses, with hardly any sign where one begins and the other ends, save the spire of another church, with the neighbouring cottages a little closer together. There are no country gentry. The *seigneur* rarely resides upon his estate, and when he does, his prestige is no longer what it was; he is often merely a *habitant* himself, one of the people, as are the *curé*, the couple of shopkeepers, the village notary, and the doctor, who compose the notables. The judicial terms every month at the Chef Lieu, which in a way corresponds to the County Town, by no means compare with the bustle of the Assizes in an English or Ontarian County. For the *habitans* not close to one of the large cities there is no going to market, as nearly everything they raise is consumed by themselves at home. The isolation of the *curés*, their zeal for their pastoral work and the incessant demands upon their time, used to prevent much study and practice of agriculture as a science, or much attention to the education of their flocks in anything but religious duties. In the old days, when *seigneur* and *curé* both derived their income from imposts on produce, the degree of consideration in which a *habitant* was held by his superiors, and consequently his respectability, was settled principally by the amount of wheat he sowed.

With the energetic development of colonization on the Crown lands, the establishment of agricultural societies, the opening of roads, the construction of the Provincial railway, the liberal aid given by the Government to private railway enterprise, and,

CHATEAU RICHER.

above all, the excellent school system, this state of things is fast disappearing. Though it may require another generation or two to overcome the influence of habits centuries old, originally founded in reason, and still rooted in popular affection by custom and tradition, there is every indication that before long Lower Canada and its *habitans* may become in effect what by nature they are meant to be, one of the most prosperous of countries and intelligent of peoples.

Chateau Richer, which, in natural beauty, equals L'Ange Gardien, is the next parish to the eastward. It gets its name from an old Indian trader, whose chateau near the river is now but a small heap of ruins almost lost in the undergrowth. The hill here advances abruptly towards the river, forming, where the main road crosses its projecting spur, a commanding elevation for the handsome stone church that towers over the cottages which line the gracefully receding curve beyond. Not many years ago the blackened walls of a convent lay at the foot of this same hill, witnesses of the ruin worked at the time of the Conquest. Knox says in his journal, that the priest, at the head of his parishioners, fortified the building and held it against an English detachment and two pieces of artillery, but it was reduced to ashes; the remnant of its brave garrison were scalped by the Iroquois allies of the English. It is far more likely that the brave *curé* stayed with his flock, to comfort them to the last, than that he led them on. However that may be, the convent has been rebuilt, and is now the parish school.

The seigniories or large tracts in which the land was originally granted, varied much in size, but usually corresponded with the ecclesiastical division into parishes. As territorial divisions, they have been supplanted by the modern municipal system. Many of them are still held by the descendants of the grantees; others have passed into the hands of strangers. Some are owned by religious corporations, the principal of these being the Island of Montreal, St. Sulpice and the Lake of Two Mountains all of which belong to the Seminary of St. Sulpice at Montreal and that of the Côte de Beaupré, owned by the Quebec Seminary. Since the abolition of feudal tenure by the Act of 1854, which placed a large sum in the hands of the Government, to be paid to the *seigneurs* in extinction of their rights, their former dignity has sadly dwindled. The title is, in most cases, but a barren honour, though in one instance that of the Barony of Longueuil—it has recently been recognized as carrying with it a patent of nobility. It had been the intention of Louis XIV., in founding a feudal system in Canada, to create a territorial aristocracy, but in avoiding the danger of sowing the teeth of the dragon it had cost the Bourbons so much to kill, he bestowed his favours upon a class unable to support their honours. The consequence was that, in most cases, the *seigneur* made the complaint of the unjust steward, that "to dig he knew not and to beg he was ashamed," and prayed to be allowed to drop his nobility and earn his living the best way he could.

The titles had, therefore, nearly quite disappeared before the Conquest. The seigniorial rights were never very extensive. They consisted principally in the *Cens et Rentes*, or annual ground-rent paid by the *censitaire* for his holding, and in the *Lods et Ventes*, or fine collected on each transfer of a property from one tenant to another. The former were very trifling, something like two sous per acre being the usual amount in hard cash, with a bushel of wheat, a fowl, a pigeon, or a sucking-pig, as payment in kind. On rent-day, in the month of November, the farm-yard of the *manoir* would present a lively scene, in droll contrast to the solemn dignity with which the *seigneur*, seated in his large chair before a table covered with his huge account-books, and in the old days with his sword laid in front of him, received the salutations and compliments, and weighed the excuses of his *censitaires*, who rivalled the Irish peasant in chronic impecuniosity and ingenious devices. The *Lods et Ventes* were a more serious imposition, amounting to one-twelfth of the price of sale. They were a hindrance to the progress of the country, for they discouraged improvements by the tenant, and prevented the infusion of new blood and the spread of new ideas. They seem, however, not to have been considered so by the *censitaires* themselves. In reality, they were an expression of the domesticity of French-Canadians, who dread the breaking up of families, and live for generation after generation upon the same land, with a tenacity and affection equalled only by their industry and endurance, when at length home and kindred have been left. In connection with the motives for the imposition of this fine, one of which, no doubt, was the desire to keep the people bound to the land, and another the wish to profit by the rare chance of a *censitaire* having ready money—though the origin of the *Lods et Ventes* in reality leads back to the earliest feudalism—it is curious to note such conflicting traits in the same people. The contrast is historical. It was hard to persuade the home-loving peasantry of France to emigrate when, in 1663, the King took up so vigorously his dream of an Empire in the West. Once in La Nouvelle France, however, such was the spirit of adventure, that it almost immediately became necessary to issue an edict forbidding their wanderings, and compelling them to make their clearings contiguous and their parishes as much as possible in the form of those in France. Within a hundred years a penalty had to be imposed upon too close settlement and small farms, in order to bring the *seigneurs'* estates all under cultivation. At the present time a great aim of the Government is to discourage emigration, and to aid by every means the repatriation of French-Canadians and colonization in the back country. One of the most potent means of effecting this is found to be their strong family affection.

There was another right incidental to the *Lods et Ventes*—the *Droit de Retrait*, or privilege of pre-emption at the highest price bidden for land within forty days after its sale; this, however, was not much used. The only other right of real consequence was the *Droit de Banalité*, by which the *censitaire* was bound to grind his corn at the *seigneur's* mill, paying one bushel out of every fourteen for toll. This arrangement suited the *habitant* very well. He is saving enough, and manages to accumulate a little capital sometimes, but it goes into the savings bank, not unfrequently into an old stocking. The risk of an investment is too much for him, and he used to prefer that the *seigneur* should make the necessary outlays, while all that he was called upon for would be a sacrifice of part of his crop. In this way, however, all industrial enterprise was hampered and discouraged by the monopoly of the water power. Under the French *régime*, a civil and criminal jurisdiction over his vassals, varying in extent according to the dignity of the fief, was theoretically vested in the *seigneur;* and all the three grades known to feudal law—the *basse, moyenne* and *haute justice*—theoretically existed in

Canada, but its exercise was rare, owing to the expense of keeping up the machinery of a court and the petty amount of its cognizance.

These relics of feudalism have a curious interest to the antiquarian and also a very practical one as regards the progress of the country, existing as they did in the New World and under the protection of the British Constitution, and still living in the memories and language of the present generation.

One of the most interesting aspects of the feudal tenure was the social relation between *seigneur* and *censitaire*. This was nearly always a paternal one, so much so, indeed, that it was quite as much a duty as a right by courtesy of the *seigneur* to stand godfather for the eldest children of his

WAYSIDE WATERING TROUGH.

censitaires. Among his many graphic descriptions of life under the Old Régime, M. de Gaspé gives an amusing account of a friend receiving a New Year's visit from a hundred godsons. The *manoir* was all that "the Great House" of an English squire is and more, for the intercourse between *seigneur* and *censitaire* was freer and more intimate than that between squire and tenant. In spite of the nominal subjection, the *censitaire* was less dependent and subservient than the English peasant. It is impracticable here to go into any detailed description of the seigniorial tenure, its influences and the mode of its abolition; but without some knowledge of it, the actual as well as the past condition of Lower Canada would be impossible to understand. The whole system of colonization originally rested upon two men, the *seig-*

neur and the *curé*. Through them the Government worked its military and religious organizations, while their interests in the soil, from which both derived their income, were identical. "The Sword, the Cross, and the Plough" have been said to explain the secret of French-Canadian nationality. These three came together in their hands. Of course, all around the old French settlements the system of freehold upon which the Crown lands are granted has produced great changes in manners, customs, and ideas, but the influence of the old state of things is still strongly marked. In the face of all the improvements effected and progress made since its abolition, it served its purpose well, and, as the Abbé Casgrain remarks, "The democratic and secularizing spirit of our age is opposed to these feudal and ecclesiastical institutions, but we may be permitted to doubt whether it could have invented a system better adapted to the genius of our race and to the needs of the situation."

There are few drives in the Province prettier than that from Quebec to St. Joachim, as it winds along between the hills and the river through Beauport, past L'Ange Gardien, Chateau Richer, and Ste. Anne, crossing on the way the Montmorency, Sault à la Puce, Rivière aux Chiens, and Ste. Anne, besides a host of smaller streams. Once outside the toll-gates, the rugged streets of Quebec give place to an excellent macadamized road kept in capital order. In summer, wizened old *compères*, too bent and worn out for any other work, salute you from the tops of the piles of stones they lazily hammer between the complacent puffs of their pipes and their comments on passers-by. There is a great deal of work in these old fellows, and their cheerfulness lasts to the end. The French-Canadian is a capital labourer, slow perhaps, but sure. He is docile and willing, and his light-heartedness gets over all difficulties. "Your merry heart goes all the day, your sad one tires in a mile-o," is his motto. In winter you have to turn out to let the snow-plough with its great wings and its long team of six or eight horses go past amid cheery shouts from its guides, whose rosy faces and icicled beards topping the clouds of snow that cover their blanket coats make them look like so many Father Christmases.

There is a great deal to see along the road besides the beautiful scenery that meets the eye everywhere. Springs are abundant in the gravelly soil. They trickle down the bank under the trees, making delicious nooks by the paths where wooden spouts concentrate their flow. Wells, of course, are not much needed along the hillside. If you stop to drink you will probably have an opportunity to appreciate French-Canadian civility. The odds are greatly in favour of some of the host of brown-skinned, black-eyed, merry-looking children that play about the neighbouring house being sent over to ask if "Monsieur will not by preference have some milk?" You like the clear ice-cold water. "*Bien, c'est bonne l'eau frette quand on a soif,*" but "Monsieur will come in, perhaps, and rest, for *sacré il fait chaud cet après-midi.*" Monsieur, however, goes on amid all sorts of good wishes and polite farewells.

It seems strange to see the women at work in the fields. Their blue skirts and enormous hats, however, are fine bits of detail for a picture, and they having been used to such labours all their lives, do not mind it. Young girls of the poorer class hire out for the harvest, together with their brothers. At times you may meet troops of them on their way to church, their *bottes Françaises*—as store-made boots are still called, in contradistinction to *bottes Indiennes*—slung round their necks. This heavy

ST. JOACHIM.

labour, however, has told upon the class, if not upon the individual, and, no doubt, accounts for the ill-favouredness and thick, squat figures of the lower order of *habitans*. Even the children take a good share of hard work, and none of the potential energy of the family is neglected that can possibly be turned to account. One of the most striking sights by the roadside of a night towards the end of autumn are the family groups "breaking" flax. After the stalks have been steeped they are dried over fires built in pits on the hillsides, then stripped of the outer bark by a rude home-made machine constructed entirely of wood, but as effective as it is simple. The dull gleam of the sunken fires and the fantastic shadows of the workers make up a strange scene.

Not the least curious features of the drive are the odd vehicles one meets. Oxen do much of the heavier hauling, their pace being quite fast enough for the easy, patient temperament of the *habitant*, to whom distance is a mere abstraction—time and tobacco take a man anywhere, seems to be his rule. It is impossible to find out the real length of a journey. Ask the first *habitant* you meet, "How far is it to Saint Quelquechose?" "Deux ou trois lieues, je pense, Monsieur," will be the answer, given so thoughtfully and politely that you cannot doubt its correctness. But after you have covered the somewhat wide margin thus indicated, you need not be astonished to find you have to go still "une lieue et encore," or, as the Scotch put it, "three miles and a bittock," nor still, again, to find the "encore" much the best part of the way. Another characteristic mode of measuring distance is by the number of pipes to be smoked in traversing it. "Deux pipes" is a very variable quantity, and more satisfactory to an indeterminate equation than to a hungry traveller.

The "buckboard" is a contrivance originally peculiar to Lower Canada. It has thence found its way, with the French half-breeds, to the North-west, where its simplicity and adaptability to rough roads are much appreciated. It is certainly unique in construction. Put a pair of wheels at each end of a long plank and a movable seat between them; a large load can be stowed away upon it, and you are independent of springs, for when one plank breaks another is easily got. The wayside *forgeron*, or blacksmith, need not be a very cunning craftsman to do all other repairs. The *charette*, or market-cart, is another curiosity on wheels, a cross between a boat and a gig, apparently. The *calèche* is a vehicle of greater dignity, but sorely trying to that of the stranger, as, perched high up in a sort of cabriolet hung by leathern straps between two huge wheels, he flies up and down the most break-neck hills. The driver has a seat in front, almost over the back of the horse, who, if it were not for his gait, would seem quite an unimportant part of the affair.

It is not very long since dog-carts were regularly used in the cities as well as in the country, for all kinds of draught purposes, but this has now been humanely stopped. Along the roads they are a common sight, and notwithstanding the great strength of the dogs used, it is not pleasant to see one of these black, smooth-haired, stoutly-built little fellows panting along, half hidden under a load of wood big enough for a horse, or dragging a milk-cart with a fat old woman on top of the cans. They are generally well-used, however, if one may judge by their good-nature. Out of harness they lie about the doors of the houses very contentedly, and, like their masters, are very civil to strangers.

The signs over the little shops that you meet with at rare intervals in the villages, are touchingly simple in design and execution. An unpainted board, with lettering accommodated to emergencies in the most ludicrous way, sets forth the *"bon marché"* to be had within. The *forgeron*, who is well-to-do—in fact, quite *un habitant à son aise*—has, perhaps, a gorgeous representation of the products of his art. A modest placard in the nine-by-four pane of a tiny cottage window, announces "rafraichissement" for man, and farther on "une bonne cour d'écurie" provides for beast. At Ste. Anne's, where the little taverns bid against each other for the pilgrim's custom, one *hôtellier* bases his claim to favour upon the fact of being "époux de Mdlle." somebody. Whether the Mdlle. was a saint or a publican of renown, the writer knows not. But the oddities of these signs would make an article to themselves, and we must pass on, with the shining domes of convent and church as landmarks of the next village.

Every now and then a roadside cross is passed, sometimes a grand *Calvaire*, resplendent with stone and gilding, covered by a roof, and from its high platform showing afar the symbol of Christian faith. Statues of the Blessed Virgin and St. Joseph sometimes stand at each side of the crucifix, but such elaborate shrines are rare, and as a general rule a simple wooden cross enclosed by a paling reminds the good Catholic of his faith, and is saluted by a reverent lifting of his hat and a pause in his talk as he

ON THE ROAD TO ST. JOACHIM.

goes by. Sometimes you meet little chapels like those at Chateau Richer. They stand open always, and the country people, as they pass, drop in to say a prayer to speed good souls' deliverance and their own journey.

A little off the road you may perhaps find the ruins of an old seigniorial *manoir*, outlived by its avenue of magnificent trees. The stout stone walls and iron-barred windows tell of troublous times long ago, while the vestiges of smooth lawns and the sleepy fishponds show that once the luxury of Versailles reigned here. The old house has gone through many a change of hands since its first owner came across the sea, a gay soldier in the Carignan regiment, or a scapegrace courtier who had made Paris too hot for

A STREET IN CHATEAU RICHER

him. Little is left of it now, save perhaps the tiny chapel, buried in a grove of solemn oaks. A few, very few, of these old buildings have survived.

Ordinary French-Canadian houses, though picturesque enough in some situations, as when you come round a corner upon a street like that in Chateau Richer, are much alike. A *gros habitant*, as a well-to-do farmer is called, will have one larger and better furnished than those of his poorer neighbours, but the type is the same. They are long, low, one-storey cottages, of wood, sometimes of rough stone, but whether of wood or stone, are prim with whitewash often crossed with black lines to simulate, in an amusingly conventional way, courses of regular masonry. By way of variety, they are sometimes painted black or slate colour, with white lines. Square brick buildings with mansard roofs of tin, bare in architecture and surroundings, glaring in newness and hideous with sawed scroll-work, are unfortunately springing up over the country in mistaken testimony of improvement. The artist will still prefer the old houses with their unpretentious simplicity and rude but genuine expressions of ornament. Their high, sharp-pitched roofs spring from a graceful curve at the projecting eaves, over which peep out tiny dormer windows. The shingles at the ridge and over the windows are pointed by way of decoration. Roof, lintels, and door-posts are gaily painted, for the *habitant* loves colour even if the freedom with which he uses the primaries is at times rather distracting to more cultivated eyes. A huge chimney built outside the house projects from the gable end, and sometimes the stairway also has to find room outside, reminding one of the old French towns whose architecture served to model these quaint buildings. A broad gallery runs along the front, furnishing pleasant shade under its vines, but darkening the interior into which small casement windows admit too little light and air. Sometimes a simple platform, with ricketty wooden steps at each end or a couple of stones leading to the door, takes the place of the gallery and affords room for a few chairs. A resting-place of some kind there must be, for in summer the leisure time of the *habitant* is spent at the door, the women knitting, the men smoking the evil-smelling native tobacco, while every passer-by gives a chance for a gossip and a joke. The heavy wooden shutters, a survival of the old Indian-fighting times, are tightly closed at night, giving an appearance of security little needed, for robberies are almost unknown, and in many districts locks are never used. In day-time, the white linen blinds in front are drawn down, which gives a rather funereal look, and the closing of the shutters cuts off the light at night, making the roads very cheerless to the traveller.

In the district of Quebec, the people are very fond of flowers. Even very poor cottages have masses of brilliant bloom in the windows and little garden plots in front neatly kept and assiduously cultivated, for the altar of the parish church is decorated with their growth, and the children present their firstfruits as an offering at their first communion. An elm or two, with masses of beautiful foliage, may afford grateful shade from the intensity of the summer sun. A row of stiff Normandy poplars, brought from old France in Champlain's or Frontenac's time perhaps, is sure to be found bordering the kitchen garden that is fenced off from the road more by the self-grown hedge of raspberry and wild rose than by the dilapidated palings or tumble-down stone wall. A great want, however, in the surroundings of most French farms is foliage, for practical as well as æsthetical objects. The grand second growth of maples, birches and elms that succeeds the primæval forest has been ruthlessly cut away, till the landscape in many districts, especially on the north shore, between Quebec and Montreal, is painfully bare in foreground, while the houses are exposed to the keen north wind and the cattle have no

AN OLD ORCHARD.

shelter from the sun and storm. In the French time the houses were generally surrounded by orchards at once ornamental and profitable. One may even now occasionally come across some descendants of them owing their origin to sunny France. In the Côte de Beaupré you will see them still, but they have in too many cases disappeared, and it is only within a few years past that fruit-growing has been systematically taken up by the *habitans*. The large orchards regularly cultivated on the Island of Montreal, show with what success the beautiful "St. Lawrence," the well-named *Fameuse*, and the golden *Pomme Grise*, a genuine little Normandy pippin, can be grown. Plums, yellow and blue, grow wild in abundance. A small, reddish-purple fruit, of pleasant flavour and not unlike a wild cherry in appearance, is plentiful, as are also cherries, wild and cultivated.

The number and beauty of the waterfalls on the Lower St. Lawrence are astonishing. Every stream must find its way to the river over the immense bank, and must cut its channel through the tremendous hills. In the Côte de Beaupré alone, there are dozens of magnificent falls not known to Canadians even by name, though within a few miles of, sometimes close to, the main road. Those on the Rivière aux Chiens and those from which the Sault à la Puce is named, are only two examples. The Falls of Ste. Anne and those of St. Féréol are sometimes heard of, yet even they, grand as they are and lovely in their surroundings, are rarely visited. Both are on the

Grande Rivière Ste. Anne, which divides the parishes. Its course is nearly opposite to that of the St. Lawrence, and is throughout nothing but a succession of tumultuous rapids and stupendous cataracts.

Leaving the road where the stream crosses, at which point there is a splendid view of Mount Ste. Anne, the highest of the innumerable peaks that break the skyline as you look down the river from Quebec, a drive of three miles through beautiful woods leads within sound of falling water. Another mile over a lovely path through the heart of the forest, and a steep descent into a ravine, brings you face to face with an immense wall of granite, its base a mass of tilted angular blocks. The river narrows here, concentrating all its powers for its tremendous leap into the gorge that forms the main channel, but only the swift rush of the water, the cloud of spray and the deep reverberations that echo from the cliff tell of its fate. A clamber over inclined and slippery rocks, beautiful with lichens of every hue, must be risked before, lying at full length, you can see the perpendicular column of crystal beaten into snowy foam on the rocks over a hundred feet below. Shooting down a second pitch the torrent breaks and rises in plume-like curves. Myriads of glittering gems dance in the play of sunlight upon the spray. Far above, the precipice rises stark and gray, its face seamed with titanic masonry, its crest crowned with huge battlements, like the wall of a gigantic fortress. The trees that banner it above seem no larger than the tufts of grass that cling in the crevices of its perfectly perpendicular front; great buttresses support this mountain wall, polished and bright with perpetual moisture. Other two channels tear their way down the cliff in falls of less volume and grandeur, but of great beauty as they leap from shelf to shelf, uniting at the foot in a large circular basin worn deep into the black basalt. So still and dark, it is well named "The Devil's Kettle."

The chasm through which the main body of the stream flows is narrow enough to jump over; but his would be a steady brain who could face the leap, and a sure fate who should miss his foothold. The island in the centre towers up in a succession of giant steps, each a huge cube of rock. These one may descend, and gain a front view of all three Falls. Down stream one looks through the narrow cleft till the boiling torrent is suddenly shut out from view by a sharply-projecting spur. The rocks seem to jar under the immense weight of the falling water; eye and ear are overpowered. The scene is one of unparalleled grandeur.

Farther up the Ste. Anne, after a beautiful drive along its west bank and round the base of the mountain, the hill-girt village of St. Féréol is reached. Through forest glades, where the moss-festooned spruces mourn over the prostrate trunks of their giant predecessors, and sunlit copses where the golden leaves of the silver birch mingle with the crimson of the dying maples, the delicate emerald of the quivering aspen and the warm russet of the ferns in magic harmonies of autumn hues, the way winds on to

FALLS OF ST. FÉRÉOL.

where the Seven Falls chase each other down the
rocky face of a huge hill in masses of broken water.
Down a narrow cleft in the evergreens which stand in bold relief against the sky,
comes the first and largest Fall. Leaping from step to step, the torrent dashes over

the second shelf in clouds of spray, its snowy fragments uniting again only to be parted by a projecting rock, past which the twin rapids rush, chafing from side to side, as if in search of each other, until they join, and plunge together over the fourth shelf. The fifth Fall pours down a steep decline and whirls in foaming eddies round the inky depths of a rocky basin, upon which looks out through the mist a cave called " Le Trou de St. Patrice." Turning sharply to the left, the stream rolls on in heavy waves of dark water to the sixth Fall, and then sweeping through close walls of rock, plunges into an inaccessible abyss. On both sides of the river deep ravines and high promontories follow each other in rapid succession, and a thick growth of forest clothes the whole.

Within the last fifteen years, agriculture has made great advances in some parts of the Province, much of which, however, yet remains in a primitive enough condition. Long isolation, a fertile soil, simplicity of life and of wants, have combined to keep the French-Canadian farmer pretty much what he was in the middle of the last century. In some respects his ancestors were better than he; they worked on a larger scale and had more energy. The Conquest, with its consequent wholesale emigration, and the unsettled political state of the country down to 1840, nearly extinguished all the spirit and industry that had survived the exactions of officials and the effects of war during the French period. Among the *habitans* farming is decidedly still in its infancy. Tilling, sowing, reaping and storing are all done by hand. In the back parishes the rudest of home-made ploughs, dragged along by a couple of oxen, and a horse who seems to move the oxen that they may move the plough, barely scratch up the soil. A French-Canadian harrow is the most primæval of implements, being at best a rough wooden rake, and often merely a lot of brushwood fastened to a beam. The scythe and the sickle are not yet displaced by mowing machines; all the ingenious contrivances for harvesting, binding and storing, are unknown. Threshing is still done by flails and strong arms, though once in a while you may hear the rattle of a treadmill where the little black pony tramps away as sleepily and contentedly as his master sits on a fence-rail smoking.

Wheat, barley, oats, maize and buckwheat, peas and beans, are the principal grain crops. The beet-root, however, is attracting attention, in consequence of the establishment of beet-root sugar factories, an enterprise cordially furthered by Government aid but yet in its experimental stage. Should this industry be successful, it will give a great impetus to farming, and the undertaking has the merit—no small one, in the people's opinion—of being distinctly French. Hay is abundant and very good. Flax and hemp are raised. Tobacco thrives admirably in the short but intensely warm summer. Patches of its tall, graceful, broad-leaved plants waving in the wind alongside the yellow tassels of the Indian corn, heighten the foreign aspect around some old cottage. Vegetables of every kind grow luxuriantly. Delicious melons are abundant and cheap.

All sorts of garden fruit—strawberries, raspberries, gooseberries and currants—are plentiful. Strawberries are now grown in large quantities for the town markets. Grapes grow wild in abundance. Immense quantities of maple sugar are yearly produced by the "sugar bushes" on the slopes of the hills. Its domestic use is universal among the *habitans*, and in the towns the syrup, sugar and *laitère*—or the sugar in an uncrystallized, pummy state—are in great demand. The processes of tapping the trees, collecting the sap, "boiling down," and "sugaring off," have been described too often to repeat here; but a visit to a sugar camp will well repay anybody who has not seen one, and is a favourite amusement for picnickers. The French-Canadians cling to the most primitive methods in this, as in everything else, the result, if an economic loss, being at least a picturesque gain.

Such fertility as the Province possesses should make it a rich agricultural country. It is really so. A very erroneous impression exists that all the best land has been exhausted; but this is an idea akin to the one that every French-Canadian wears moccasins and is called Jean Baptiste. It is quite true that a couple of hundred years of persistent tillage upon an evil routine, and want of opportunities to see anything better, have run down the old French farms; but even as it is, they yield well. Many an English farmer would be glad to get such land, and would work wonders with a little manure and proper rotation of crops. Then there are millions of acres yet untouched. The state of affairs in the Côte de Beaupré is described only as being an interesting relic of a period almost past. Agriculture is in a state of transition. Already the advantages of rich soil, magnificent summer climate, and cheap labour, are being realized.

At Ste. Anne, history and tradition blend with the life and manners of to-day in a most striking way. The first settlers in the Côte de Beaupré built a little church on the bank of the St. Lawrence, and dedicated it to La Bonne Ste. Anne, in memory, no doubt, as Ferland says, of the celebrated pilgrimage of Sainte Anne d'Auray in Brétagne. The bank, however, was carried away by the ice and the floods. So another building was commenced in 1657 upon the site pointed out by M. de Queylus, the Vicar-General, and given by Etienne de Lessard. It was finished in 1660. The Governor, M. d'Argenson, laid the first stone, and the work was done by the pious labour of the *habitans*. As one of these, Louis Guimont by name, racked with rheumatism, painfully struggled to place three stones in the foundation, he suddenly found his health restored. Thenceforward, La Bonne Ste. Anne de Beaupré became famous throughout all Canada. Among the pilgrims that flocked to celebrate her fête each year, were conspicuous the Christian Hurons and Algonquins, in whom their missionaries had inspired a special devotion for the mother of the Blessed Virgin. To this day their descendants are to be found among the thousands of worshippers whom the steamers carry from Quebec. The pilgrimage is not always such an easy excursion. Those who have special favours to implore, often trudge on foot the long journey to the shrine. A pyramid of crutches, trusses, bandages, and spectacles stands in the church, to attest the miraculous cures worked by faith and prayer.

The site of the old church is marked by a chapel built with the old materials. It is roughly finished within, containing only a few stained seats and a bare-looking altar which stands between two quaint images of Ste. Marie Magdelaine and Ste. Anne,

CHAPEL AND GROTTO AT STE. ANNE DE BEAUPRÉ.

apparently of the time of Louis XIV. By the roadside, close to the chapel, stands a rough grotto surmounted by the image of the sainte set in a niche, over which again there is a cross. Over the stones pours the clear water of a spring; this the pilgrims take away in bottles, for the sake of its miraculous healing power. Near-by is the old presbytery, and farther up the wooded slope, hidden among the trees, is a convent of Hospital Nuns. Their gentleness and kindness to the sick that resort here should suffice to canonize each one of these devoted ladies, whose lives are as beautiful as their surroundings.

A handsome new church was dedicated in 1876. To it were removed the old altar and pulpit, both of the seventeenth century, and the relics and original ornaments of the old church. Among these are an altar-piece by Le Brun, the gift of the Marquis de Tracy; a silver reliquary, and a painting by Le François, both the gift of Mons. de Laval; a chasuble worked by Anne of Austria, and a bone of the finger of Ste. Anne. There are also a great number of *ex-voto* tablets—some very old and

OLD HOUSES AT POINT LÉVIS.

by good masters—to commemorate deliverances from peril at sea, for Ste. Anne watches specially over sailors and travellers. Numbers of costly vestments have also been presented, and Pius IX., in addition to giving a *fac simile* of the miraculous portrait of Our Lady of Perpetual Help, set in a jewelled frame, issued a decree declaring the shrine to be of the first magnitude.

There are many other places in the neighbourhood of Quebec which, if not such exact types of the past nor so varied in natural features as is the Côte de Beaupré, yet afford beauty of scenery, historic association, and opportunity to study the life of the people. It is hard to choose, but a few should be visited, and among these Point Lévis stands first in geographical order and in interest of all kinds.

Landing at Indian Cove, where the descendants of those Iroquois, who got from the English Government so much a-piece for every French scalp, used to build their wigwams, to await the distribution of the annual bounty, one finds a splendid graving dock being built on the very spot where they hauled up their bark canoes. The cliff is a worthy mate for Cape Diamond. From its tree-lined summit rolling hills covered with houses, fields and woods, so that the country looks like an immense park, stretch back to the sky-line, in pleasant contrast with the abrupt outline of the other shore. The main street lies between the river and the jagged face of the rock. At each end it climbs the cliff in zigzags, between old houses whose fantastic shapes, peaked roofs and heavy balconies make the place seem like some old Norman town. At one point where a spring trickles down the cliff, a wooden stairway leads from the lower to the upper town. Close by stand the old and new churches of St. Joseph, the latter a huge stone building of the usual type, the former a rude little chapel, with an image of the saint in a niche over the door. Everywhere there is, as in Quebec, this meeting of the old and the new. The Intercolonial Railway trains shake the foundations of the old houses, and interrupt, with their shrill whistle, the chant of the boys at vespers in the College chapel. Tugs puff noisily along with big ships, where Wolfe's flotilla stole so silently under the cliffs the night before the battle on the Plains of Abraham, and barges of the same pattern as those in which his soldiers crossed lie side by side with Allan steamships. Back of the heights from which his batteries pounded Quebec into ruins, and where Montgomery's men, wasted with their winter march through the wilds, waited for strength to carry out their daring attack, three modern forts dominate the South Channel and the land approaches. Planned with all the skill of the Royal Engineers, their casemates are meant for guns beside which the cannon that last did their work here would look like pop-guns. The view from them is superb. On the east a rolling plateau, densely wooded, stretches to the distant mountains of Maine. Opposite stands Quebec, the lower town in deep shadow beneath the cliff, the upper town glistening in the sun. Up and down the river the eye can roam from Cap Rouge to Grosse Isle, and never weary of the colossal extent of mountain, river and forest.

The forts are in charge of the battery of Canadian artillery stationed at Quebec. Many of the men are French-Canadians, and excellent soldiers they make. In cheerful submission to discipline, respect for their officers, and intelligence, the French militia corps are superior to the English in the rural districts. Among the Field Artillery, the most technical arm of the service,—so much so, indeed, that in England the military authorities have not yet ventured to form volunteer batteries,—the Quebec Field Battery, composed entirely of French-Canadians, is a model of equipment, drill and discipline, and is, after a few days of annual training, quite undistinguishable from the permanently-embodied corps in the Citadel.

About five miles to the northwest of Quebec is the Indian village of Lorette. Every Charter for the settlement of La Nouvelle France repeats in substance the words of that granted by Richelieu to the Company of the One Hundred Associates, the object of which was "to endeavour by Divine assistance to lead the people therein to the knowledge of the true God, to cause them to be disciplined and instructed in the Catholic, Apostolic and Roman faith." In fact the earlier settlements were as professedly missions as trading enterprises. The idea of a regular colony on a large scale did not take shape till the time of Louis XIV., under whom, as his hereditary title of Most Christian Majesty demanded, the interests of religion were by no means a secondary consideration. The Hurons were the first fruits of missionary devotion. In 1634 the Jesuits Brebeuf, Daniel, and Dauost, took up the work begun by the Récollet fathers, Viel and Le Caron, and the Jesuit Sagard, twelve years before. By 1650 the whole nation was professedly Christian. The descendants of these Hurons, only a few hundreds all told, are quite civilized, quiet, orderly, and peaceable. Many of them are well educated, comfortably off and cultivating good farms. The love of the forest and of the chase is, however, too deep in their natures to be totally eradicated, and the younger men are fond of getting away to the woods. You never find an Indian ashamed of his blood; these still call themselves proudly "The Huron Nation," and on official occasions, such as the visit of a Governor or the Indian Commissioner, their chiefs wear full Indian costume. Among them are a few Abenakis and other representatives of the great Algonquin family, to which the Montagnais of the Lower St. Lawrence, the only really "wild Indians" of Lower Canada, also belong. The French term "*Sauvage*," is much more expressive than "Indian," but seems rather a misnomer when applied to some of the fair-complexioned, well-dressed and polished inhabitants of Lorette, among whom there is a great admixture of white blood. They do a large business in all sorts of embroidery, in silk and porcupine quills upon birch-bark and deer-skin, make snow-shoes, bead-work, moccasins, and other curiosities. The old church is shown with much pride, for the Hurons are good Catholics. The school is another of their sights. The children sing with a vigour suggestive of a war-dance rather than a hymn, but their bright, intelligent faces, and the musical name of the performance, reassure one as to his scalp. They get thorough instruction, and are apt pupils. After school some of them are always ready to show visitors the Falls, for a branch of the St. Charles runs through the village, and as has been said before, wherever there is a stream in this country there are Falls. A paper-mill intrudes its dam upon the bed of the river at their head, and spoils what was once a grand sheet of water covering with a crystal curtain the now bare rock; but a sharp turn in the deep gorge soon hides

FALLS OF LORETTE.

this, and the view from below has nothing to detract from its mingled grandeur and loveliness, to which words cannot do justice.

CAP ROUGE.

Following the south shore of the St. Lawrence from Point Lévis all the way up to the Chaudière the same magnificent panorama repeats itself with subtle

CAPE DIAMOND, FROM ST. ROMUALD.

gradations as distance softens down the details of the landscape and new features come into sight. At St. Romuald the view down the river is very grand. The bold outline of Cape Diamond stands clear cut against the sky. Beyond are the purple peaks that close in on the St. Charles, and the misty hills that surround the headwaters of the Montmorency peep through the pass up which the Charlesbourg road winds to Lake Beauport. To the right the conical mass of Mount Ste. Anne towers over the ridge of Lévis. Below runs the river dark under the shadow of banks seamed with leafy coves, but losing itself in the sunshine that makes fairyland of the Beauport shore. Every place in sight has some historic or traditional association to add another charm.

From St. Romuald it is not far to the Chaudière Falls, whose abrupt and tremendous plunge fully justifies their name. There are many Chaudières in Canada, the term being generic, but this "Chaldron" is grand and tumultuous enough to be typical of all, and to name the whole river. It and the Montmorency Falls are probably but miniatures of the unspeakably magnificent cataract that once must have existed at Cap Rouge, that grand promontory seven miles above Quebec, where the great rock cliffs close in and confine the St. Lawrence into river-like dimensions. There are strong indications that the river must once have been dammed up here behind a great barrier, over which, just as its tributaries now find their way into it over the surrounding plateau, it flowed into the sea in a flood compared with which Niagara would be a driblet. In some of the mighty convulsions that heaved the Laurentian rocks—the oldest geological formation of all—from their depths, and shaped their towering peaks, this barrier must have given way and the stream have fallen to its present level.

The rich red rock which gives it its name and the bold outline of its cliff, make Cap Rouge as conspicuous as Cape Diamond. On this "*promontoire haute et raide*," Jacques Cartier built a fort, to guard his ships when he returned to Stadacona on his third voyage, in 1541, and Roberval wintered there the following year, rebuilding Cartier's fort, and naming it "France Roy," in honour of the King. The beauty of the forests that crown the cliffs and the fertility of the soil are still as remarkable as when Cartier wrote of the "*fort bonnes et belles terres pleines d'aussi beaux et puissants arbres que l'on puisse voir au monde.*"

Along the river in the autumn, wild ducks and geese appear in large numbers, while farther back partridges and wild pigeons are abundant, and trout can always be had for the catching. Many of the *habitans* are very skilful with rod and gun, rivalling the Indian half-breeds—wiry, long-haired, black-visaged, wild-looking fellows, who make a regular business of shooting and fishing. Down the Gulf fish is, of course, the great stand-by. Eels, which swarm in the mouths of the streams, are speared in immense numbers. They are a favourite dainty, and are salted for winter use, as are also great quantities of wild fowl.

These peeps at the country about Quebec might be prolonged indefinitely, such is the number of charming spots to be reached by an easy drive. But all this time we

LIGHT-SHIP ON THE ST. LAWRENCE.

have been looking at the *habitant* in a long-cultivated, thickly-settled region, and there is another phase of his life which can only be seen in the wilds. A journey up the St. Maurice gives good opportunity for appreciating it, but to get to the St. Maurice one must go to Three Rivers, and by far the best way of doing this is to make the night voyage up the St. Lawrence by the Richelieu Company's steamer. A moonlight scene on the St. Lawrence is such as to leave a deep impression of the majesty of the great river up which Cartier toiled for a fortnight to reach Stadacona, far beyond which he heard there was "a great sea of fresh water, of which there is no mention to have seen the end." The way is not less well marked in summer than in winter. Light-houses stand at every bend, while buoys and light-ships, moored in midstream, point out the channel. When night has closed in, the twinkle of the far light

HALF-BREED FISHERMAN.

is reflected across the water for miles, broadening out at last into brilliant glare; beneath one gets a momentary glimpse of the black hull and square tower of a light-ship, with weird shadows moving across the cheerful gleam from the cosy cabin. Huge black masses loom up suddenly and glide past in silence. Long, snake-like monsters are left snorting astern. A group of water demons sing in wild chorus round a floating blaze. All manner of strange stars flicker low down on the horizon, changing their lines with sudden flashes. Everything is dim, shadowy and weird, till, suddenly, the moon bursts through the heavy clouds, shows the dull outline of the distant bank, gleams white on the canvas of a passing ship, reveals the long string of deep-laden barges following the sobbing tug, and dims the brightness of the raftsmen's fire.

Three Rivers dates far back in the history of French colonization in Canada. On one of the islands at the mouth of the noble tributary which here enters the St. Lawrence, Cartier, in 1534, planted a cross in the name of the King of France. In 1599 Pontgravé gave it the name of Rivière des Trois Rivières, from the appearance which two of the islands give it of being three separate streams; Cartier had christened it Rivière de Foie, from the Breton family of that name. Champlain and Pontgravé ascended it as far as the first rapids, and a little later Champlain made the mouth of the stream a rendezvous for the Hurons who joined him in his expedition against the Iroquois, the river being the highway of the tribes who came from the interior to barter furs with the French traders, having been driven away from the St. Lawrence by the Iroquois. Traces of an old Algonquin stockade that stood where the upper town is now, and was destroyed before Champlain's time, were found when the boulevard facing the St. Lawrence was made.

One of the Récollet fathers who came with Champlain in 1615, celebrated the first mass. Colonists came two years later, and a mission was founded. In 1634 a regular trading depot was established, as Pontgravé had proposed to do long before, when Tadoussac was preferred by his superior Chauvin. For a long time this was the extreme outpost of the French, and was held only by exceeding vigilance and bravery, which more than once saved Quebec from imminent danger. In 1624 Champlain's diplomacy brought together here one of the greatest assemblages of Indians ever known upon the Continent, and secured a treaty of peace between Hurons, Algonquins, Iroquois, and French. The Mohawks could not long resist the desire to use their newly-acquired fire-arms furnished by the Dutch and English, and then followed the bloody scenes which ended only with the arrival of the long prayed-for troops from France in 1665. The Hurons and Algonquins were almost exterminated, and the French were sore pressed. This was the heroic age of the colony so vigorously described by Parkman. The fur-traders of Three Rivers bore their part in it well, and when there was no more fighting to do their venturesome spirits found outlet in the existing work of exploration, for with the establishment of Montreal the importance of Three Rivers as a trading-post had begun to decline, and the necessity of being farther afield, to say nothing of the half-wild nature of the *coureurs de bois*, led them on. The missionaries whose outpost, in the crusade against Satan and his Indian allies, Three Rivers also was, had set them an example. Jean Nicolet lived and died here, and the old Chateau of the Governors, in which La Verendraye lived, still stands.

Not far from the Chateau is the original parish church, the oldest in Canada

INTERIOR OF PARISH CHURCH.

except the one at Tadoussac. It has the oldest records, for those of Quebec were burned in 1640. They begin on February 6th, 1635, in Père Le Jeune's handwriting, with the statement that M. de la Violette, sent by Champlain to found a *habitation*, landed at Three Rivers on July 4th, 1634, with a party of French, mostly artizans, and commenced the work; that the Jesuits Le Jeune and Buteux came on the 8th of September, to be with them for the salvation of their souls, and that several of them died of scurvy during the winter. The chapel of the Jesuit mission served till 1664, when a wooden church, with presbytery, cemetery and garden, was built. Fifty years

OLD CHIMNEY AND CHATEAU.

later the stone church that yet stands on a corner of the old parochial property was erected; it is an interesting relic of a by-gone time, and its hallowed associations make it for the devout Roman Catholic a place from which the grand new Cathedral cannot draw him.

The beauty of the rich oak carving which lines the whole interior was sadly destroyed by a spasm of cleanliness on the part of the authorities, who a few years ago painted it white, but fortunately this style of renovation has not gone farther, and the old paintings and sculpture, of which there is a profusion, remain intact. The church is dedicated to the Immaculate Conception.

The *curé* and the *marguilliers* form the *fabrique*, or administrative body of the corporation which every parish constitutes. The *curé's* share in temporal mat-

ST. MAURICE FORGES.

ters is, however, limited to the presidency of all meetings, and in this as well as in the keeping of registers of civil status he is a public officer, constrainable by *mandamus* to the exercise of his duties. He appoints the choristers, keeps the keys, and has the right to be buried beneath the choir of the church, even in Quebec and Montreal, where interments within the city limits are prohibited.

The parishes are designated in the first place by the bishop, and are then civilly constituted by the Lieutenant-Governor on the report of five commissioners under the Great Seal, after all parties have been heard. Being corporations, their powers are defined, and exercise of them regulated by the civil law. The revenues are raised and extraordinary expenses defrayed by assessment approved by general meetings. The manner in which the *curés* are paid varies a good deal. They are legally entitled to a tithe in kind, of one portion in twenty-six on all grain grown in the parish by Roman Catholics, except upon lands newly-cleared, which are exempt for the first five years. The tithe must be thrashed, winnowed, and put in the priest's barn. In many parts of the Province, however, what is known as the *supplement*—a money payment—takes the place of, or is combined with, the tithe.

The St. Maurice Forges, on the right bank of the St. Maurice River, about seven miles above Three Rivers, are the oldest smelting furnaces in Canada, and dispute with those of Principio, in Maryland, the right to be considered the oldest in America. The deposits of bog-ore were known very early to the Jesuits. In 1668 they were examined by the Sieur la Potardièn, who reported unfavourably to the Intendant Talon as to their quantity and quality. Frontenac and De Denonville gave a better account of them, and it seems that tests were made before the year 1700. It was not till 1737, however, that a company was found to work them. This company was granted a large tract, including the site where the Old Forges now stand, and erected furnaces, but exhausted its capital, and in 1740 had to surrender its charter. The Government carried on the works very successfully, as a report of the Colonial Inspector Tranquet shows, and must have extended them, as appears by the erection of the old Chateau that stands on a flat bluff overlooking the river. On an iron plate in its chimney are the official *fleurs de lis* and the date 1752. Its walls, some two and a half feet thick, withstood the fire that destroyed its woodwork in 1863.

A brook flows through the ravine immediately below the Chateau. It furnished water-power for the oldest works, remains of which are to be seen near its mouth. The attachments of an old shaft show that a trip-hammer was used, and there are other signs of extensive works for making wrought iron. From 250 to 300 men were employed, under directors who had gained their skill in Sweden. Many of the articles made then—notably stoves—still attest the quality of the iron and of the work. Pigs and bars were sent to France. During the war, shot and shell were cast. When the English came to take possession, the Chateau was occupied by a Demoiselle Poulin, who threw the keys into the river rather than yield them. Legends of mysterious lights and buried treasure cling to the place. After the Conquest the works were leased to private persons, and have passed through several hands before coming into those of the present owners, who use most of the product in the manufacture of car-wheels at Three Rivers.

The original blast-furnace, or cupola—a huge block of granite masonry, thirty feet square at the base—is still used for smelting; the fire has rarely been extinguished, except for repairs, during the past 150 years. In a deep-arched recess is the "dam" from which the molten metal is drawn into beds of sand, to cool into pigs. During the time between "runs" or "casts" glowing slag is continually being drawn off. The cupola is kept filled from the top with ore, broken limestone, and charcoal. The latter is made in immense kilns near the forge, from wood furnished in abundance by the surrounding forests. Against the volumes of white vapour from these kilns the old ironworks stand out, gloomy and black with the smoke and grime of generations. The limestone is obtained a short distance up the river, and the ore—dark-red spongy stuff, yielding forty per cent. of iron—is brought in by the *habitans*, who find it between two beds of sand on land that yields no crops, so that they are only too glad to dig it up.

The works are surrounded by a little hamlet of workmen's cottages. An amphitheatre of wooded hills surrounds the scene. These rise gradually to the left, and over them

FALLS OF THE CHAUDIÈRE—NEAR QUEBEC.

is seen the dark outline of the Laurentian range, against which is set the gleaming spire of St. Etienne Church. The lesser hills, across the St. Maurice to the right, are topped by Mount Carmel, and far up the stream the Shawenegan Mountains consort with the Piles peaks.

There is, perhaps, nothing in Canada that more forcibly strikes the English eye than the wild and silent grandeur of our mighty rivers. Though only ranking third among the tributaries of the St. Lawrence, the St. Maurice is a noble stream. During spring and early summer it becomes a raging flood fed by the melting snow and rains of the great northern water-shed, and even when the parching heat of summer has dried up its sources it remains a navigable stream nearly a quarter of a mile wide far above its mouth.

AND CHARACTER

Far to the north, 220 miles from the St. Lawrence, this river rises in a net-work of lakes and small water-courses, which feed also its elder brothers, the Ottawa and the Saguenay. It pursues its tortuous way in a main direction nearly south, while

HEAD OF SHAWENEGAN FALLS.

the others diverge so widely to the west and east that their several *debouchements* into the St. Lawrence are divided by a space of more than three hundred miles. All the upper part of the St. Maurice's traverses are unbroken wilderness, untrodden by the foot of man, except the few Indians and trappers who yet represent the aboriginal occupants, the Hudson's Bay *voyageurs* and traders who still use this route as a means of access to their remoter posts, and the lumberers whose camps and shanties have been already pushed two hundred miles back into the interior, and the ring of whose axes is heard at the head of every stream down which a saw-log can be floated in the freshets of the

Spring. Nothing can be more lovely than the constantly varied and unexpected beauty of the reaches of river, lake and stream, the water-falls, rapids, wild rocks, densely-wooded hills and forest glades with which this wild region is filled.

One hundred miles from its mouth the river meets civilization at the foot of the wild Falls of the "Tuque" (so called from the fancied resemblance of a hill in the vicinity to the French-Canadian head-gear of that name), in the form of a steamer which traverses a stretch of sixty miles to the "Piles," whence a railway to the front gives the go-by to the formidable but picturesque rapids and falls of the Lower St. Maurice. The first of these is the Grais, so-called because the old portage led across granite rocks now occupied by a saw-mill and all its unlovely litter of lumber, sawdust and slabs. Here the river dashes itself over and through enormous rocks, which cause twin falls and a boiling rapid. A few evergreens cling to the rocks, and a low bench supports a scant growth of bushes, but above the river the tree-clad heights rise in successive steps.

The unlimited water-power has caused the place to be selected as the headquarters of one of the vast lumbering establishments whose chiefs are kings in all but name. The proprietor of this establishment is practically king of the St. Maurice. The farmers, who compose the scant population of the neighbourhood, are dependent upon him for a market and for supplies of all they need from the outside world. Their crops are consumed by his horses and men, and their sons and brothers find employment in his service. The village about the mill is his property and the inhabitants are his servants. Hundreds of men and horses, under the direction of scores of foremen, labour for him through summer and winter,

LITTLE SHAWENEGAN.

undergoing the severest toil and perilling their lives to carry out his behests. His will is their law, his wages are their subsistence, and promotion in his service is their reward. Every foreman is chosen from the ranks of this great family. Should one of them take service with a rival house, he can never return to his allegiance. Great qualities of leadership are required for success in these vast enterprises, but if the rule of the lumber king is despotic, it is also patriarchal and beneficent.

For some distance above the Grais settlements continue on both sides of the river, but the stream itself is generally flanked by forest. High hills rise abruptly from its edge, and the land is a succession of well-defined benches. Good soil is found in the intervales of the tributaries, but some distance from the main river which in its course through the mountains forms many rapids and falls. The grandest of these are the Shawenegan Falls, twenty-four miles from Three Rivers. The river is narrowed between two projecting points, and divided by a rocky island into two channels of equal volume. The twin streams roll placidly for a while. Suddenly a swift rush begins, and their tawny water breaks into tossing foam. The right branch comes down with more direct course, dashed into white masses that rise, like fountains, perpendicularly into the air, and scatter their glittering beads of spray in wild profusion. The left branch sweeps round the island, and far up the narrow channel its stream can be seen, now reflecting the banks like a mirror and now tumbling over steps of shelving rock which stand darkly out of the variously-broken and lighted water. The play of colour from seal-brown to shining white is magnificent, and doubtless suggested the Indian name Shawenegan, or needlework, the "divers colours of needlework finely wrought." The left fall curves till at right angles to the other, when, meeting, they press upon and past a rocky point which stands out full against their united force when the water is low, but is swept by the Spring floods. Recoiling from its impetuous leaps against its adamantine barriers, the torrent sweeps down another long incline between walls of rock into a capacious bay, whose surface heaves as if with the panting of the water resting after its mad rush.

Into this bay enters the Shawenegan River, easily ascended by canoe, first through elm glades and restful flats, and then by sinuous turns between steep banks covered with spruce and birch, till the Little Shawenegan Falls burst on the view in exquisite loveliness.

In the quieter stretches of the St. Maurice there are many islands. These and the banks of the stream are beautifully wooded even up difficult steeps, rising far above the water's edge. Every here and there a mountain wall shadows the river, and breaks the forest greens with the purple and golden glories of the shrubs that alone can find hold upon its rugged face. Deep, gloomy gorges, through which come glimpses of a world of hills, mark the entrances of tributary streams. The grandeur and loveliness intensifies the mysterious solitude of the wilderness. Such is the country to which nearly three hundred years ago the *habitant* first came.

QUEBEC—A GLIMPSE FROM THE OLD CITY WALL.

QUEBEC: HISTORICAL AND DESCRIPTIVE.

QUEBEC

HISTORICAL REVIEW.

COMPARATIVELY speaking, Canada has not much of an historical past, but all that it has from Jacques Cartier's day clusters round this cannon-girt promontory; not much of a present, but in taking stock of national outfit, Quebec should count for something;—indeed, would count with any people. We have a future, and with it that great red rock and the red-cross flag that floats over it are inseparably bound up.

The glowing pages of Parkman reveal how much can be made of our past. A son of the soil like Le Moine, who has an hereditary right to be animated by the *genius loci*, whose Boswell-like conscientiousness in chronicling everything connected with the sacred spot deserves all honourable mention, may exaggerate the importance of the city and the country, its past and its present. But truer far his extreme—if extreme it be—than Voltaire's or La Pompadour's, and their successors' in our own day. The former thought France well rid of "fifteen thousand acres of snow," with an appreciation of the subject like unto his estimate of those "*Juifs miserables*," about whose literature the world was not likely to trouble itself much longer when it could get the writings of the French *Philosophes* instead. The latter heartily agreed with him, for—with Montcalm dead— "at last the King will have a chance of sleeping in peace." To us it seems that the port which for a century and a half was the head-quarters of France in the New World, the door by which she entered and which could be closed against all others, the centre from which she aimed at the conquest of a virgin continent of altogether unknown extent, and from which her adventurous children set forth—long-robed missionaries leading the way, trappers and soldiers following—until they had established themselves at every strategic point on the St. Lawrence, the Great Lakes, the Ohio, and the Mississippi from the Falls of St. Anthony to New Orleans, must always have historical and poetic significance. The city and the Province which for the next hundred and twenty years have remained French in appearance and French to the core, yet have fought repeatedly and are ready to fight again side by side with the red-coats of Great Britain—the best proof surely that men can give of loyal allegiance;—which preserve old Norman and Breton customs and traits, and modes of thought and faith that the Revolution has submerged in the France of their fore-fathers, fondly nursing the seventeenth century in the lap of the nineteenth, must, perhaps beyond any other spot in North America, have an interest for the artist and the statesman.

In the sixteenth century the gallant Francis I. made seven attempts to give France a share in that wonderful New World which Columbus had disclosed to an unbelieving generation, but like his attempts in other directions they came to nothing. In 1535 he put three little vessels under the orders of Jacques Cartier, a skilful navigator, a pious and brave man, well worthy of the patent of nobility which he afterwards received, instructing him to proceed up the broad water-way he had discovered the year before, until he reached the Indies. His duties were to win new realms for Mother Church, as a compensation for those she was losing through Lutheran and Calvinistic heresies, and to bring back his schooners full of yellow gold and rosy pearls. Thus would his labours redound to the glory of God and the good of France. Jacques Cartier crossed the ocean and sailed up the magnificent water-way, piously giving to it the name of the saint on whose fête-day he had first entered its wide-extended portals. For hundreds of miles the river kept its great breadth, more like a sea than a river, till the huge bluff of Quebec, seen from afar, appeared to close it abruptly against farther advance. By means of this bluff thrust into the stream and the opposite point of Levis stretching out to meet it, the view is actually narrowed to three quarters of a mile. Coasting up between the north shore and a large beautiful island, he came, on the 14th of September, to the mouth of a little tributary, which he called the Ste. Croix, from the fête celebrated on that day. Here he cast anchor, for now the time had come to land and make inquiries. It needed no prophet to tell that the power which held that dark red bluff would hold the key to the country beyond. The natives, with their chief Donnacona, paddled out in their birch-bark canoes to gaze upon the strange visitants who had—in great white-winged castles—surely swooped down upon them from another world. Cartier treated them kindly. They willingly guided him through the primeval forest to their town on the banks of the little river, and to the summit of the rock under the shadow of which they had built their wigwams. What a landscape for an explorer to gaze upon! Shore and forest bathed in the mellow light of the September sun for forty miles up and down both sides of the glorious stream! Wealth enough there to satisfy even a king's pilot and captain-general. Between the summit and the river far below he may have seen amid the slate the glitter of the quartz crystals from which the rock afterwards received its name of Cape Diamond. Certainly, on his next voyage he gathered specimens from Cap Rouge. But the great attraction must have been the river itself, flowing past with the tribute of an unknown continent. Its green waters swept round the feet of the mighty Cape. He could cast a stone into the current, for at high tide it rolled right up to the base of the rock. The narrow strip of land that now extends between rock and river, crowded with the houses of Champlain Street, was not there then. The street has been won from the waters and the rock by man, whose greed for land even the boundless spaces of the New

ARRIVAL OF JACQUES CARTIER AT STADACONA.

World cannot satisfy. The ground that sloped down to the Ste. Croix, at the mouth of which his vessels lay at anchor, was covered with the finest hard-wood trees—walnuts, oaks, elms, ashes, and maples—and among these the bark-cabins of Donnacona's tribe could be seen. They called their town Stadacona. To this day no name is more popular with the people of Quebec. Any new enterprise that may be projected, from a skating-rink to a bank or steamship company, prefers Stadacona to any other name.

All the way down to Cap Tourmente and round the horizon formed by the fir-clothed summits of the Laurentides that enclosed the wide-extended-landscape, an unbroken forest ranged. The picture, seen from the Citadel on Cape Diamond to-day, is as fair as the eye can desire to see. The sun shines on the glittering roofs of Quebec, and the continuous village of clean white houses extending miles down to the white riband of

Montmorency, and on cultivated fields running up into still unbroken wilderness, and on the broad river basin enclosing the island, in the forest glades of which wild grapes grew so luxuriantly that Cartier enthusiastically called it Isle of Bacchus. But then it was in all its virgin glory, and Cartier's soul swelled with the emotions of a discoverer, with exultation and boundless hope. Did it not belong to him, did it not almost owe its existence to him? And he was giving it all to God and to France.

Donnacona told the strangers of a far greater town than his, many days' journey up the river. So Cartier placed his two largest vessels within the mouth of the Ste. Croix, or the St. Charles, as the Récollets called it in the next century, and pursued his way, overcoming the obstacles of St. Peter's Lake, to Hochelaga. The natives there received him as if he were a god, bringing fish and corn-cakes, and throwing them into the boats in such profusion that they seemed to fall through the air like rain or snow. Cartier could not help falling in love with the country. The palisaded town nestling under the shadow of Mount Royal was surrounded by fertile fields. Autumn showered its crimson and gold on the forests, turning the mountain into an immense picture suspended high in air, glowing with a wealth of colour that no European painter would dare to put on canvas. The river swept on, two miles wide, with a conquering force that indicated vast distances beyond, new realms waiting to be discovered. All the way back to Quebec the marvellous tints of the forest, and the sweet air and rich sunsets of a Canadian autumn accompanied the happy Frenchmen. Had they now turned their prows homeward, what pictures of the new country would they have held up to wondering listeners! Nothing could have prevented France from precipitating itself at once upon Canada. But the natives, accustomed to the winters, uttered no note of warning to the strangers, and therefore, although Cartier rejoined his comrades at Quebec on the 11th of October, he delayed till the ice-king issued his "*ne exeat*." Then he and they soon learned that the golden shield had another side.

To Canadians, winter is simply one of the four seasons. The summer and autumn suns ripen all the crops that grow in England or the north of France, and in no temperate climate is more than one crop a year expected. The frost and snow of winter are hailed in their turn, not only as useful friends but as ministers to almost all the amusements of the year—the sleighing, skating, snow-shoeing, ice-boating, tobogganning—that both sexes and all classes delight in. The frost does much of our subsoil ploughing. Snow is not only the best possible mulch, shading and protecting the soil at no cost, but its manurial value gives it the name of "the poor man's manure." The ice bridges our lakes and rivers. A good snow-fall means roads without the trouble of road-making, not only to kirk and market, but through thick woods, over cradle-hills, and away into the lumber regions. An insufficient supply of snow and ice is a national calamity; and excess can never be so bad as the pall that covers England and Scotland half the year and makes the people "take their pleasures sadly."

But, we are prepared for winter. Jacques Cartier was not, and very heavily its hand fell upon him, as it did subsequently on Champlain when he first wintered at Quebec. How heavily, we are in a position to estimate from reading the harrowing descriptions of the sufferings endured by the people of London in January 1881, in consequence of a snow-fall of some twelve inches. One periodical describes the scene under the title of "Moscow in London," and soberly asserts that "to have lived in London on Tuesday, the 18th January, 1881, and to have survived the experience, is something which any man is justified in remembering, and which ought to justify occasional boasting of the fact." Another declares that a few more such snow-storms would "render our life and civilization impossible;" that in such a case there could be only "an Esquimaux life, not an English life;" that "a transformation of the rain into these soft white crystals which at first sight seem so much less aggressive than rain is all that is needed to destroy the whole structure of our communications, whether in the way of railway, telegraph, or literature;" and sadly moralises over the fact that this is sure to come about in time from the precession of the equinoxes. Bathos such as this indicates fairly enough the wonderful ignorance of the facts and conditions of Canadian life that reigns supreme in educated English circles. Canadians fancy that their civilization is English. Those of us who are practically acquainted with the conditions of life in England are pretty well agreed that where there are points of difference the advantage is on our side. Not one man in a thousand in Canada wears a fur coat, or an overcoat of any kind heavier than he would have to wear in the mother country. We have ice-houses, but do not live in them. Society shows no signs of approximating to the Esquimaux type. We skim over the snow more rapidly than a four-in-hand can travel in England when the best highway is at its best. A simple contrivance called a snow-plough clears the railway track for the trains, tossing the snow to the right and left as triumphantly as a ship tosses the spray from its bows. We telegraph and telephone, use cabs and busses, and get our mails—from Halifax to Sarnia—with "proofs" and parcels about as regularly in winter as in summer. Incredible as all this must sound to those who have shivered under the power of one snow-storm and a few degrees of frost, there is a certain humiliation to a Canadian in describing what is so entirely a matter of course. He is kept from overmuch wonder by remembering that the people of Western Canada, in spite of practical acquaintance with snow-ploughs, opposed for years the construction of the Intercolonial Railway because they strenuously maintained that it would be blocked up all the winter with ice and snow.

We are accustomed to our environment. Cartier's men were not; and reference has been made to recent experiences in England to help us to understand what horrors those poor fellows from sunny France endured throughout an apparently endless winter, cooped up in the coldest spot in all Canada. "From the middle of November to the 18th of April the ice and snow shut us in," says their captain. Ice increased upon ice. Snow fell upon snow. The great river that no power known to man could fetter, was bound fast.

Everything froze. The breath that came from their mouths, the very blood in their veins, seemed to freeze. Night and day their limbs were benumbed. Thick ice formed on the sides of their ships, on decks, masts, cordage, on everything to which moisture attached itself. Snow wreathed and curled in at every crevice. Every tree had its load. A walk in the woods was an impossibility, and there was nowhere else to walk. Confined within their narrow domain, and living on salted food, scurvy seized upon the helpless

TRIUMPH OF THE SNOW-PLOUGH.

prisoners. What was to be done? Cartier had recourse to heaven, receiving, however, the same minimum of practical answer that was given by Hercules to Æsop's waggoner. A modern writer of scrupulous accuracy describes naïvely the appeal and its bootlessness: "When eight were dead and more than fifty in a helpless state, Cartier ordered a solemn religious act which was, as it were, the first public exercise of the Catholic religion in Canada, and the origin of those processions and pilgrimages which have since been made in honour of Mary, to claim her intercession with God in great calamities. Seeing that the disease had made such frightful ravages he set his crew to prayer, and made them carry an image or statue of the Virgin Mary over the snow and ice, and caused it to be placed against a tree about an arrow's flight away from the fort. He also commanded that on the following Sunday mass should be sung in that place and before that image, and that all those who were able to walk, whether well or ill, should go in the procession—'singing the seven penitential Psalms of David, with the Litany, praying the Virgin to entreat her dear Son to have pity upon us.'" On that day mass was celebrated before the image of Mary, even chanted, Cartier tells us; apparently the first occasion of a high mass in Canada. At the same time Cartier gave another special proof of his vivid and tender trust in Mary—promising to make a pilgrimage in her honour to Roquemadour, should he be spared to return to France. "Nevertheless, that very day, Philip Rougemont, a native of Amboise, twenty years old, died; and the disease became so general that of all who were in the three ships there were not three untouched, and in one of the ships there was not one man who could go into the hold to draw water for himself or the others." Despair fell upon the poor wretches. They gave up hope of ever seeing France again. Cartier alone did not despair, and the dawn followed the darkest hour. One of the Indians told him of "the most exquisite remedy that ever was," a decoction composed of the leaves and bark of the white spruce. He administered the medicine without stint, and in eight days the sick were restored to health. And now the long cruel winter wore away. The icy fetters relaxed their grip of land and river. Under warm April suns the sap rose, thrilling the dead trees into life. Amid the melting snow, green grasses and dainty star-like flowers sprang up as freely as in a hot-house. Cartier prepared to depart, first taking possession of Canada, however, by planting in the fort "a beautiful cross" thirty-five feet high, with the arms of France embossed on the cross-piece, and this inscription, "*Franciscus Primus, Dei gratia, Francorum rex, regnat.*" Then, treacherously luring Donnacona on board ship, that he might present the King of Stadacona to the King of France, he set sail for St. Malo. Nothing came of this, the second voyage of Cartier, and little wonder. What advantages did Canada offer to induce men to leave home! What tales could the travellers tell save of black forests, deep snow, thick ice, starving Indians, and all-devouring scurvy! But Cartier was not discouraged, and six years afterwards Francis resolved to try again. Roberval was commissioned to found a permanent settlement. He sent Cartier ahead and Cartier tried at Cap Rouge, above Quebec, the Indians of Stadacona naturally enough not making him welcome. But the experiment did not succeed. The time had not come. Nearly a century was to pass away before the true father of New France—the founder of Quebec—would appear.

On the 3d of July, 1608, Samuel de Champlain planted the white flag of France on the site of Quebec. The old village of Stadacona had disappeared, and there was no one to dispute possession with the new comers. With characteristic promptitude Champlain set his men to work to cut down trees and saw them into lumber for building, to dig drains and ditches, to pull up the wild grape-vines which abounded, to prepare the ground for garden seeds, or to attend to the commissariat. Every one had his work to do. The winter tried him as it had tried Cartier. The dreaded scurvy attacked his followers. Out of twenty-eight only eight survived, and these were disfigured with its fell marks. The next year he decided to ally himself with the Algonquins and Hurons against the Five Nations. It may have been impossible for him to have remained neutral, though the example of the Dutch at Albany indicates that it was possible. Certainly the step plunged the infant colony into a sea of troubles for a century. It took the sword and was again and again on the point of perishing by the tomahawk.

This man Champlain, soldier, sailor, engineer, geographer, naturalist, statesman, with the heart and soul of a hero, was the founder of New France. He had gained distinction in the wars of the League; in the West Indies he first proposed that ship canal across the Isthmus of Panama which another Frenchman—as unconquerable as he—was later on destined to commence; and subsequently he had spent years exploring and attempting settlements around the rugged Atlantic shores of Acadie and New England. From the day that he planted the lilies of France at the foot of Cape Diamond to the day of his death, on Christmas, 1635, he devoted himself to the infant colony, lived for it and kept it alive, in spite of enemies at home and abroad, and discouragements enough to have shaken any resolve but that of courage founded upon faith. Right under the beetling cliff, between the present Champlain Market and the quaint old church of Notre Dame des Victoires, Champlain determined to build his city. His first work was to prepare the ground for garden seeds, and wheat and rye. He saw from the first, what he never could get any one else in authority to see, that the existence of the colony, as anything more than a temporary fur-trading post, depended on its being able to raise its own food. The Company with which he was associated could not see this, because they had gone into the enterprise with very different motives from those that animated Champlain. When we have no desire to see, we put the telescope to our blind eye and declare that there is nothing to be seen. Every creature acts according to its instincts, and to the rule fur-trading companies are no exception. Give them a monopoly and instinct becomes consecrated by laws human and Divine. The welfare of the Company becomes the supreme law. At the beginning of this century the North-West Company thought it right to stamp out in

CHAMPLAIN

NOTRE DAME DES VICTOIRES.
Site of Original City.

blood and fire the patriotic efforts to colonize Assiniboia made by a Scottish nobleman, who lived half a century before his time. Subsequently the two hundred and sixty-eight shareholders of the Hudson's Bay Company felt justified in keeping half a continent as a preserve for buffalo and beaver. How could better things be expected in the seventeenth century from the monopolies of De Chastes or De Monts, the merchants of St. Malo, Rouen, Dieppe, La Rochelle; or even from the Company of the One Hundred Associates organized by Richelieu? Trading interests were supreme with one and all. Those who clamoured for free trade clamoured only for a share of the monopoly. The empire is perpetually at war, and the soldier gets the blame, perhaps the aristocracy, should Mr. Bright be the speaker; but the real culprit is the trader. Our jealousy of Russia and our little wars all the world over have trade interests as their source and inspiration. In the seventeenth century, Canadian trade meant supplies to the Indians in exchange for peltries, and money spent on anything else seemed to the One Hundred Associates and their servants money thrown away.

Not so thought Champlain. Fortunately, he was too indispensable a man to be recalled, though it was legitimate to oppose, to check, to thwart his projects whenever they did not promise direct returns to the Company. Champlain aimed at founding an empire, and every great empire must be based on farming. Therefore when, in 1617, he brought the erstwhile apothecary, Louis Hébert, to Quebec, he did more for the colony than when he brought the Récollets and Jesuits to it. And let this be said with no depreciation of the labours of the gray robes and black robes. Hébert was the first who gave himself up to the task of cultivating the soil in New France, and the first head of a family resident in the country who lived on what he cultivated. His son-in-law Couillard walked in the same good path, the path first trodden by "the grand old gardener and his wife." No matter how soldiers, sailors, fur-traders and priests might come and go, the farmer's children held on to the land, and their descendants hold it still. They increased and multiplied so mightily that there are few French families of any antiquity in Canada who cannot trace their genealogy by some link back to that of Louis Hébert. Hébert and Couillard Streets, streets quainter and more expressive of the seventeenth century than any to be seen now in St. Malo, commemorate their names. One of their descendants informed the writer that those streets run where the first furrows were ploughed in Canada, probably in the same way that some of the streets in Boston are said to meander along the paths made by the cows of the first inhabitants. Had others followed Hébert's example the colony would not have been so long suspended between life and death, and Champlain could have held out against the Huguenot Kerkts in 1629. But the Company, far from doing anything to encourage the few tillers of the ground, did everything to discourage them. All grain raised had to be sold at a price fixed by the Company, and the Company alone had the power of buying. Of course the Héberts and Couillards ought to have been grateful that there was a Company to buy, for what could farmers do without a market?

Of Champlain's labours it is unnecessary to speak at length. Twenty times he crossed the Atlantic to fight for his colony, though it was a greater undertaking to cross the Atlantic then than to go round the world now. He may be called the founder of Montreal as well as of Quebec. First of Europeans he sailed up the Richelieu, giving to the beautiful river the name of the Company's great patron. He discovered Lake Champlain. He first ascended the Ottawa, crossed to Lake Nipissing, and came down by the valley of the Trent to what he called "the fresh water sea" of Ontario. He secured the alliance of all the Indian tribes—the confederacy of the Five Nations excepted—by treaties which lasted as long as the white flag floated over the castle of St. Louis, and which laid the foundation of the friendship that has existed between every Canadian government and the old sons and lords of the soil. D'Arcy McGee, in one of those addresses that made learned and unlearned feel what is the potency and omnipotency of man's word on the souls of men, thus sketched his moral qualities and amazing versatility:—" He was brave almost to rashness. He would cast himself with a single European follower in the midst of savage enemies, and more than once his life was endangered by the excess of his confidence and his courage. He was eminently social in his habits—witness his order of *le bon temps*, in which every man of his associates was for one day host to all his comrades. He was sanguine, as became an adventurer; and self-denying, as became a

LITTLE CHAMPLAIN STREET,
From head of Break-neck Stairs.

MOUNTAIN HILL.
From top of Break-neck Stairs.

hero. He touched the extremes of human experience among diverse characters and nations. At one time he sketched plans of civilized aggrandizement for Henry IV. and Richelieu; at another, he planned schemes of wild warfare with Huron chiefs and Algonquin braves. He united in a most rare degree the faculties of action and reflection, and like all highly-reflective minds, his thoughts, long cherished in secret, ran often into the mould of maxims, some of which would form the fittest possible inscriptions to be engraven upon his monument. When the merchants of

Quebec grumbled at the cost of fortifying that place, he said, 'It is best not to obey the passions of men; they are but for a season; it is our duty to regard the future.' With all his love of good-fellowship, he was, what seems to some inconsistent with it, sincerely and enthusiastically religious. Among his maxims are these two—that 'the salvation of one soul is of more value than the conquest of an empire;' and that 'kings ought not to think of extending their authority over idolatrous nations, except for the purpose of subjecting them to Jesus Christ.'" The one mistake made by Champlain has already been referred to. He attacked the Iroquois, whereas he should have conciliated them at any cost or remained neutral in all Indian wars. His mistake was not so much intellectual as moral. It was a crime and—*pace* Talleyrand—worse than a blunder. But it is not pleasant to refer to the errors of such a man. Well may Quebec commemorate his name and virtues. Let us not forget, when we walk along the quaint, narrow, crowded street that still bears his name, or clamber "Break-neck Stairs" from Little Champlain Street to reach Durham Terrace, where he built the Chateau of St. Louis and doubtless often gazed, with hope and pride in his eyes, on a scene like to which there are few on this earth, how much Canada owes to him! Well for those who follow him where all may follow—in unselfishness of purpose, in unflinching valour, and in continence of life. No monument points out his last resting-place, for, strange to say, "of all French governors interred within the *enceinte*, he is the only one of whose place of sepulture we are ignorant."* The registers of Quebec were destroyed in the great conflagration of 1640. Thus it happens that we have not the account of his burial. M. Dionne shows that in all probability the remains were first deposited in the chapel of Notre Dame de la Recouvrance; then in a vault of masonry in the chapel built by his successor in the Governorship, whence they were removed by the authorities to the Basilica. Champlain needs no monument, least of all in Quebec. The city is his monument.

PRESCOTT GATE.
Now removed, guarded the approach to the Upper Town by Mountain Hill.

Most religious Quebec was from the first under the influence of Champlain; most religious is it in appearance to this day. There are churches enough for a city with five times the present population. Ecclesiastical establishments of one kind or another occupy the lion's share of the space within the walls. At every corner the soutaned ecclesiastic meets you, moving along quietly, with the confidence of one who knows that his foot is

* "Études Historiques," par M. DIONNE.

on his native heath. It was the same with the cities of France in the seventeenth century: but it is not so now. Things have changed there. The Revolution made the Old World New. In Quebec the New World clings to the garments of the Old. Champlain first induced the Récollet friars to come to his aid. The Jesuits, then at the height of their power in France, followed. The Company disliked missionaries almost as much as it disliked farmers. "They tolerated the poor Récollets," says Ferland, "but they dreaded the coming of the Jesuits, who had powerful protectors at Court and who could through them carry their complaints to the foot of the throne." Consequently, when the first detachment of Jesuits arrived they found every door shut against them, and if the Récollets had not offered them hospitality they would have been obliged to return to France.

Magnificent missionaries those first Jesuits were; more devoted men never lived. The names especially of Charles Lallemant and Jean de Brebeuf are still sacred to thousands of French-Canadian Roman Catholics. Two things the Jesuits felt the colony must have —a school for the instruction of girls, and a hospital for the sick. These institutions they desired for the sake of the colonists, most of whom were poor, but still more for the sake of the Indians. The Fathers had left France to convert the Indians; on that work their hearts were set, and they gave themselves to it with a wisdom as great as their self-sacrifice. Protestant missionaries, as a class, are only now learning to imitate their methods of procedure, especially with regard to the establishment of hospitals and the acquisition of a perfect knowledge of the language and modes of thought of the people whose conversion they seek. What Livingstone did in South Africa when he cut himself loose from all the other missionaries who kept within reach of the comforts of the colony, and plunged into the thick of the native tribes beyond; what the Canadian missionary Mackay did eight years ago in Formosa with such brilliant success, the Jesuits always did. Their first task was to master the language. Grammatical knowledge they knew, was not enough. They lived in the wigwams of the wretched, filthy nomads, travelled with them, carrying the heaviest loads, and submitted to cold and heat to privations, and the thousand abominations of savage life, without a murmur. They cared for the sick, and, expecting little aid from the old, sought to educate the young Charlevoix tells us how they succeeded in establishing in Quebec both the Hotel Dieu and the Ursuline Convent. Madame la Duchesse D'Aiguillon, the niece of Richelieu, undertook to found the first. To carry out her pious project she applied to the hospital nuns of Dieppe "These holy women accepted with joy the opportunity of sacrificing all that they counted dear in the world for the service of the sick poor of Canada; all offered themselves all asked with tears to be admitted to share in the work." About the same time Madame de la Peltrie, a widow of a good family, resolved to found the Convent of the Ursulines. She devoted all her fortune to give a Christian education to the girls of the colonists and of the Indians, and followed up these sacrifices by devoting herself to the

IN THE GARDENS OF THE URSULINE CONVENT.

work. Young, rich, beautiful, she renounced all advantages and prospects for what then must have been a worse than Siberian exile. At Tours, among the Ursuline nuns, she found Marie de l'Incarnation, who became the first Mother Superior of the new convent, and "Marie de St. Joseph, whom New France regards as one of its tutelary angels." On the fourth of May, 1639, she embarked with three hospital nuns, three Ursulines, and Père Vimond, and on the first of July they arrived at Quebec. The length of the voyage, not to refer to its discomforts, reminds us of the difference between crossing the Atlantic then and now. All Quebec rejoiced on their arrival. Work ceased, the shops were shut, and the town was *en fête*. "The Governor received the heroines on the river's bank at the head of his troops with a discharge of cannon, and after the first compliments he led them, amid the acclamations of the people, to church, where Te Deums were chanted as a thanksgiving." From that day till her death, thirty-two years after, Madame de la Peltrie gave herself up to the work she had undertaken. Mère Marie de l'Incarnation, whose fervent piety and spirituality of character gained her the name of the Ste. Theresa of New France, died a year after her. These two women lived in an atmosphere so different from ours, that it is extremely difficult for us to judge them. Both have been condemned, the one as an unnatural mother, the other as a disobedient daughter. They believed they were sacrificing the claims of nature to the superior claim of their Saviour. Certainly, their works have followed them. The great Ursuline Convent of Quebec, to which hundreds of girls are sent to be educated from all parts of the continent, is their monument. The buildings have been repeatedly destroyed by fire, but have always been replaced by others more expensive and substantial, the community apparently delighting to testify its sense of the value of the work done by the devoted Sisters. Within their spacious grounds, in the heart of the city, are various buildings, one for boarders, among whom to this day are daughters of Indian chiefs; another for day scholars; a normal school; a school for the poor; a chapel and choir, and nuns' quarters; with gardens, play and pleasure grounds for the youthful inmates, and summer and winter promenades—all eloquent with the memories of the pious founder, who had not disdained to toil in the garden with her own hand. To each generation of susceptible minds the lives of Mme de la Peltrie and Mère Marie are held up for imitation, and no honour is grudged to their memories.

Not only religious, but charitable and moral, was Quebec under the administration of Champlain and his successors. Ferland cites the registers of Notre Dame of Quebec to show that out of 664 children baptised between 1621 and 1661, only one was illegitimate. Still, the colony did not prosper; again and again it was on the point of extinction at the hands of the Iroquois. The Company sat upon its agricultural and industrial development like the old man of the sea. In 1663 the population of New France consisted of only two thousand souls, scattered along a thin broken line from Tadoussac to Montreal. Of this small total Quebec claimed 800. At any moment a rude breath would have killed the colony, but now favouring gales came from Old France. Louis XIV. determined to suppress the Company, and bring Canada under his own direct authority. He constituted by direct appointment a Sovereign Council to sit in Quebec immediately responsible to himself, the principal functionaries to be the Governor-General, the Royal Intendant, and the Bishop, each to be a spy on the other two. The Governor-General believed himself to be the head of the colony; he formed the apex of the governmental pyramid. But the Intendant, who was Chief of Justice, Police, Finance, and Marine, understood that the King looked to him, and that the colony was in his hands, to be made or marred. The Bishop, again, knew that both Governor-General and Intendant would have to dance according as he pulled the wires at Court. Talon, the first Intendant who arrived in Quebec, was the ablest who ever held the position. Talon was a statesman, a pupil of Colbert, and in some respects in advance

of his great master. He urged immigration as a means of ensuring to France the possession of the New World. Colbert, with the wisdom of the seventeenth century, replied that it would not be prudent to depopulate the kingdom. "Secure New York," Talon urged, "and the great game will be gained for France." When that step was not taken he projected a road to Acadie,—which it was left to our day, by the construction of the Intercolonial Railway, to carry out, and thus to give to Canada indispensable winter ports. He pushed discovery in every direction, selecting his men with marvellous sagacity. Under his direction, St. Simon and La Couture reached Hudson's Bay by the valley of the Saguenay; Père Druilletes, the Atlantic seaboard by the Chaudiere and the Kennebec; Perrot, the end of Lake Michigan and the entrance of Superior; Joliet and Père Marquette, the father of waters down to the Arkansas. In Talon's day Quebec rose from being a fur-trading post into commercial importance. He believed in the country he had been sent to govern, and was of opinion that a wise national policy demanded the encouragement in it of every possible variety of industrial development. His mantle fell on none of his successors. Instead of fostering the industries Talon had inaugurated and defending the commercial liberty which he had obtained, they stifled industry and trade under restrictions and monopolies. Not that the Intendants were wholly to blame; they were sent out on purpose to govern the colony, not with a view to its own benefit, but with a view to the benefit of Old France. Neither the King nor his minister could conceive that Canada would benefit the mother country, only as its material and industrial development increased. Talon had twelve successors. Of all these, the last, Bigot, was the worst. To Bigot more than to any other man France owes the loss of the New World. He impoverished the people, nominally for the King's service, really to enrich himself. That the poor, plundered, cheated *habitans* were willing to fight as they did for the King, an I that Montcalm was able to accomplish anything with the commissariat Bigot provided, are the wonderful facts of the Conquest of 1759. The Intendant's house was by far the most expensive and most splendidly furnished in Quebec. It was emphatically "The Palace," and the gate nearest it was called the Palace Gate. It stood outside the walls,—its principal entrance opposite the cliff on the present line of St. Valier Street, "under the Arsenal;" while its spacious grounds, beautifully laid out in walks and gardens, extending over several acres, sloped down to the river St. Charles.*
It is described in 1698 as having a frontage of 480 feet, consisting of the Royal storehouse and other buildings, in addition to the Palace itself, so that it appeared a little town. In 1713 it was destroyed by fire, but immediately rebuilt in accordance with the French domestic style of the period, two storeys and a basement, as shown by sketches made by one of the officers of the fleet that accompanied Wolfe's expedition. Here, no matter what might be the poverty of the people, the Intendant surrounded himself with splendour. In Bigot's time every form of dissipation reigned in the Palace; while the

* Summary of the "History of the Intendant's Palace," by CHARLES WALKEM, Militia Department.

habitant, who had left his farm to fight for the King, could hardly get a ration of black bread for himself, or a sou to send to his starving wife and little ones at home. Our illustration shows all that is left of the magnificent Palace. It arose out

ST. ROCH'S SUBURBS AND OLD ARSENAL.

of a brewery started by Talon as a part of his national policy, and it has returned to be part of a brewery, and for all the luxury and bravery there is nothing now to show, and the cheating and the gambling are, let us hope, receiving their just recompense of reward.

The Governor's Chateau is not. The Intendant's Palace was destroyed more than a century ago, but the Bishop's house, seminary and cathedral still remain, and the bishop, or archbishop as he is now styled, is yet the most potent personage in Quebec. The early bishop, Laval, is one of the historic figures of New France. Seen by Ultramontane eyes, this first Canadian bishop stands on the highest pinnacle of human excellence and greatness; the only mystery being that the Church has not yet canonized him. He did everything "for the glory of God," the expression meaning to him, as to ecclesiastical fanatics of every creed, the glory of the Church, and in some measure the glory of himself. He cared nothing for money or any form of vulgar greatness. His ambition was loftier. He would rule the souls of men, and woe to the man in his widely-extended diocese, be he Governor-General, statesman, merchant, priest or savage, who ventured to call his soul his own. True, none seemed more ready than Laval to give support to the State. The Church was supreme only in things spiritual. Kings, too, ruled by Divine right. But then the Church was to instruct the King, or the King's representative, as to what matters were civil and what spiritual. For instance, when the bishop decided that the introduction of brandy into the colony was injurious to religion, the importing or sale of brandy became a spiritual matter. In that case the Governor, on pain of excommunication, must punish the vendor of brandy with the pillory, and, if need be, with death. Evidently, General Neal Dow follows, *longo intervallo*, our first Canadian bishop. Always fighting, Laval could say as honestly as the King himself, "It seems to me I am the only person who is always right." The constitution of the Church of New France took its permanent form from him. His clergy were his soldiers. When he said "March," they marched. He established a lesser seminary where they were educated as boys, and the great seminary where they were trained as priests. He assigned their fields of labour, changed them as he saw meet, and provided a home whither, when infirm or exhausted with labour or old age, they might resort, either to recruit or die in peace. Their directory in life and death was every word that proceeded out of the mouth of the bishop. Other directory they desired not. To the seminary a University under Royal Charter was attached in 1852, and to that University Laval's name has been deservedly given. The Charter, which sets forth that the seminary has existed for two hundred years, constitutes the archbishop visitor, and the superior and directors of the seminary a body corporate, with all the privileges of a University, and full power to make all statutes and appoint all professors. "Laval University has nothing more to ask from the civil and religious authorities to complete its constitution," is the announcement of its board of government. Its Royal Charter assimilates it to the most favoured University of the United Kingdom, while the sovereign pontiff, Pius the Ninth, magnificently crowned the edifice by according to it in 1876 solemn canonical honours by the Bull "*inter varias solicitudines*."

From the opposite shore of Levis, Laval University, standing in the most commanding position in the upper town, towering to a height of five storeys, is the most conspicuous building in Quebec. The American tourist takes it for the chief hotel of the place, and congratulates himself that a child of the monster hotels he loves has found its way north of the line. When he finds that it is only a University, he visits it as a matter of course, looks at the library and museum, remarking casually on their inferiority to those in any one of the four hundred and odd Universities in the United States, and comes out in a few minutes, likely enough without having gone to the roof to see one of the most glorious panoramas in the New World. Here

AT THE GATE OF LAVAL UNIVERSITY

he is, at the gate. Blessings on his serene, kindly sense of superiority to all men or things in heaven or on earth! He has seen nothing that can compare for a moment with Slickville. Englishmen, Frenchmen, Sisters, students, Canadian soldiers, civilians, are round about, but he alone is monarch of all he surveys. A strange sight arrests his attention. Young Canada, cap in hand, cap actually off his head, and head reverently bowed while a priest speaks a kind word or perhaps gives his blessing! This is something new, and he is too good an observer not to make a note of it, congratulating himself at the same time that *he* is willing to make allowances. Is it not his "specialty," as John Ruskin hath it, "his one gift to the race—to show men how *not* to worship?"

A Canadian may be pardoned for calling attention to the significance of the grant, by the British Government, of a Royal Charter to Laval University. The trust in an hierarchy that the people trust, illustrates the fundamental principle of its policy in Canada. No matter what the question, so long as it is not inconsistent with the Queen's supremacy, Canada is governed in accordance with the constitutionally expressed wishes of the people of each Province. The success which has attended the frank acceptance of this principle suggests the only possible solution of that Irish Question which still baffles statesmen. What has worked like a charm here ought to work in another part of the Empire. Here, we have a million of people opposed in race, religion, character and historical associations to the majority of Canadians, a people whose forefathers fought England for a century and a half on the soil on which the children are now living; a Celtic people, massed together in one Province, a people proud, sensitive, submissive to their priests, and not very well educated;—this people half a century ago badgered every Governor that Britain sent out, stopped the supplies, embarrassed authority, and at last broke out into open rebellion. Now, they are peaceable, contented, prosperous. They co-operate for all purposes of good government with the other Provinces, do no intentional injustice to the Protestant minority of their own Province, and are so heartily loyal to the central authority that it has become almost an unwritten law to select the Minister of War from their representatives in Parliament. Let him who runs read, and read, too, the answer of D'Arcy McGee to those who wondered that the young rebel in Ireland should be the mature ardent admirer of British government in Canada: "If in my day Ireland had been governed as Canada is now governed, I would have been as sound a constitutionalist as is to be found in Ireland."

The best thing Louis XIV. did for Quebec was the sending to it of the regiment of Carignan-Salières. A few companies of veterans, led by Canadian blue-coats, penetrated by the Richelieu to the lairs of the Iroquois, and struck such terror into them that the colony was thenceforth allowed to breathe and to grow. Still better, when the regiment was disbanded, most of the soldiers remained, and many of the picturesque towns and villages that have grown up along the Richelieu and St. Lawrence owe their names to the officers, to whom large seignorial rights were given by the King on condition of their settling in the colony. From these veterans sprang a race as adventurous and intrepid as ever lived. Their exploits as salt-water and fresh-water sailors, as *coureurs de bois*, discoverers, soldiers regular and irregular, fill many a page of old Canadian history. Whether with the gallant brothers Le Moyne, defending Quebec against Sir William Phipps, or striking terror into New York and New England by swift forays such as Hertel de Rouville led; or with Du Lhut and Durantaye, breaking loose from the strait-jacket in which Royal Intendants imprisoned the colony, and abandoning themselves to the savage freedom of western fort and forest life; or under D'Iberville, most celebrated of the seven sons of Charles Le Moyne, sweeping the English flag from Newfoundland and Hudson's Bay or colonizing Louisiana; or with Jumonville and his brother on the Ohio, defeating Washington and Braddock; or vainly conquering at Fort William Henry and Carillon and Montmorency and Ste. Foye,—the picture is always full of life and colour. Whatever else may fail, valour and devotion to the King never fail. We find the dare-devil courage joined with the gaiety of heart and ready accommodation to circumstances that make the Frenchman popular, alike with friendly savages and civilized foemen, in all parts of the world. Canadian experiences developed in the old French stock new qualities, good and bad, the good predominating. Versed in all kinds of woodcraft, handling an axe as a modern tourist handles a tooth-pick, managing a canoe like Indians, inured to the climate, supplying themselves on the march with food from forest or river and cooking it in the most approved style, fearing neither frost nor ice, depth of snow nor depth of muskeg, independent of roads,—such men needed only a leader who understood them to go anywhere into the untrodden depths of the New World, and to do anything that man could do. Such a leader they found in Louis de Buade, Compte de Palleau et de Frontenac. Buade Street recalls his name, and there is little else in the old city that does, though Quebec loved him well in his day. Talon had done all that man could do to develop the infant colony by means of a national policy that stimulated industry, and an immigration policy, wise and vigorous enough, as far as his appeals to the King and Colbert went, for the nineteenth century. Another man was needed to enable the thin line of colonists to make head against the formidable Iroquois, backed as they were by the Dutch and English of New York, and against the citizen sailors and soldiers of New England; to direct their energies to the Great West; to make them feel that the power of France was with them, no matter how far they wandered from Quebec; and to inspire them with the thought that the whole unbounded continent was theirs by right. Such a man was Frontenac. Of his quarrels with intendants and clergy it would be a waste of time to speak. To defend him from the accusations made against his honour is unnecessary. How could quarrels be avoided where three officials lived, each having some reason to believe, in accordance with the profound state-craft of the Old Régime, that he was the supreme ruler! Frontenac was titular head, and he would be the real head. Neither bishops nor intendants should rule in his day, and they did not, and could not. They could worry him and even secure his recall, but they could not govern the colony when they got the chance. Frontenac had to be sent back to his post, and the universal joy with which the people received him showed that, as usual, the people overlook irritabilities and shortcomings, and discern the man. "He would have been a great prince if heaven had placed him on a throne," says Charlevoix. The good Jesuit forgets that Frontenac was the only man who sought to ascertain by ancient legitimate methods the views of all classes of the people, and that as Quebec was shut out from communication with the throne for half the year, the Governor had to act as a king or to see the country without a head. Frontenac understood the great game that was being played for the sovereignty of this continent. He had almost boundless influence over the Indians, because he appreciated them, and in his heart of hearts was one of themselves. No one understood so well what Indians were fitted to do in the wild warfare that the situation demanded. At the time of his death all signs betokened that France was to dominate the New World. The treaties Champlain had made with the Indians held good. The tribes farther west had allied themselves with the French. At every strategic point the white flag with the *fleurs de lis* floated over a rude fort. The St. Lawrence was linked by lines of military communication with the Gulf of Mexico. Quebec had proudly built the church of Notre Dame de la Victoire to commemorate the defeat of New England, and the power of the terrible Iroquois had been so broken that they could no longer threaten the existence of the colony.

In spite of Frontenac, it was not to be as the signs indicated. In spite of Montcalm's victories it was not to be. History was again to prove that in a contest between peace and war, between steady industry and dashing forays, between the farmer and the soldier, the former is sure to win in the long run. The

HEIGHTS OF ABRAHAM.

corruptions of the Court of France had to do with the issue remotely. Bigot and his vile *entourage* had to do with it immediately. But by no possibility could sixty thousand poor, uneducated Canadians continue to resist the ever-increasing weight of twenty or thirty times their number of thrifty, intelligent neighbours. Wolfe might have been defeated on the Plains of Abraham. When we think of Montcalm's military genius, the victories gained by him against heavy odds in previous campaigns, and his defeat of Wolfe's grenadiers a few weeks before the final struggle, our wonder indeed is that the British were not hurled over those steep cliffs they had so painfully clambered up on that memorable early September morning. Scotchmen attributed the result to those men "in the garb of old Gaul, with the fire of old Rome," whom the British Government had been wise enough to organize into regiments out of the clans who a few years before had marched victoriously from their own northern glens into the heart of England. And Wolfe, had he lived, would probably have agreed with them. For, when he told the grenadiers, after their defeat, that, if they had supposed that they alone could beat the French army, he hoped they had found out their mistake, his tone indicated a boundless confidence in his Highlanders more flattering than any eulogy. But the most crowning victory for Montcalm would only have delayed the inevitable. Other armies were converging towards Quebec. And behind the armies was a population, already counting itself by millions, determined on the destruction of that nest on the northern rock whence hornets were ever issuing to sting and madden. No one understood the actual state of affairs better than Montcalm. He knew that France had practically abandoned Canada, and left him to make the best fight he could for his own honour against hopeless odds. Hence that precipitate attack on Wolfe, for which he has been censured. He knew that every hour's delay would increase Wolfe's relative strength. Hence, too, that abandonment of the whole cause, after the battle, for which he has been censured still more severely. "I will neither give orders nor interfere any further," he exclaimed with emotion, when urged to issue instructions about the defence of the city. He had done all that man could do. He had sealed his loyalty with his blood. And now, seeing that the stars in their courses were fighting against the cause he had so gallantly upheld, and that the issue was pre-determined, he would take no more responsibility. He knew, too, that his best avengers would be found in the ranks of his enemies; that Britain in crushing French power in its seat of strength in America, was overreaching herself, and preparing a loss out of all proportion to the present gain. He appreciated the "Bostonnais;" predicting that they would never submit to an island thousands of miles away when they controlled the continent, whereas they would have remained loyal if a hostile power held the St. Lawrence and the Lakes. Was he not right? And had not Pitt and Wolfe, then, as much to do with bringing about the separation of the Thirteen States from the mother country, as Franklin and Washington?

The story of the campaigns of 1759-60 need not be told here. Every incident is familiar to the traditional school-boy. Every tourist is sure to visit Wolfe's Cove for himself, and to ascend the heights called after the old Scottish pilot "Abraham" Martin. No sign of war now. Rafts of timber in the Cove, and ships from all waters to carry it away, instead of boats crowded with rugged Highlanders silent as the grave. No trouble apprehended by any one, except from stevedores whose right it is to dictate terms to commerce and occasionally to throw the city into a state of siege. No precipice now, the face of which must be scaled on hands and knees. A pleasant road leads to the Plains, and you and your party can drive leisurely up. There, before you, across the common, is the modest column that tells where Wolfe "died victorious." Between it and the Citadel are Martello towers, digging near one of which some years ago, skeletons were found, and military buttons and buckles, the dreary pledges, held by battle-fields, of human valour and devotion and all the pomp and circumstance of war. You must drive into the city to see the monument that commemorates the joint glory of Montcalm and Wolfe; and out again, to see the third monument, sacred to the memory of the braves who, under the skilful De Levis, uselessly avenged at Ste. Foye the defeat of Montcalm.

The red-cross flag floated over the Chateau of St. Louis, and New England gave

OVERLOOKING ST. CHARLES VALLEY

thanks. Fifteen years passed away, and Montcalm's prediction was fulfilled. The "Bostonnais" were in revolt. Wise with the teaching of more than a century, they at the outset determined to secure the St. Lawrence; and they would have succeeded, had it not been for the same strong rock of Quebec which had foiled them so often in the old colonial days. Arnold advanced through the roadless wilderness of Maine, defying swamps, forests, and innumerable privations as hardily as ever did the old Canadian *noblesse* when they raided the villages and forts of Maine. Montgomery swept the British garrisons from the Richelieu and Montreal, and joined Arnold at the appointed rendezvous. Their success must have astonished themselves. The explanation is that the colony had no garrisons to speak of, and that the French Canadians felt that the quarrel was none of their making. In a month all Canada —Quebec excepted—had been gained for Congress; and there was no garrison in Quebec capable of resisting the combined forces that Arnold and Montgomery led. But Guy Carleton reached Quebec, and another proof was given to the world that one man may be equal to a garrison. In a few days he had breathed his own spirit into the militia,

KING NOLTH CHANNEL

native Canadians as well as British born. The invaders established themselves in the Intendant's Palace and other houses near the walls, and after a month's siege made a resolute attempt to take the city by storm. Whatever may have been the result of a more precipitate attack, the delay unquestionably afforded greater advantages to the besieged than to the besiegers. Montgomery set out from Wolfe's Cove and crept along the narrow pathway now known as Champlain Street. Arnold advanced from the opposite direction. His intention was to force his way round by what is now St. Roch's suburbs, below the ramparts, and under the cliff at present crowned by Laval University and the Grand Battery, and to meet Montgomery at the foot of Mountain Hill, when their united forces would endeavour to gain the upper town. Not the first fraction of the plan, on the one side or the other, succeeded. Arnold's men were surrounded and captured. Montgomery, marching in the gray dawn through a heavy snow-storm, came upon a battery that blocked up the narrow pathway. He rushed forward, hoping to take it by surprise; but the gunners were on the alert, and the first discharge swept him and the head of his column, maimed or dead, into the deep white snow or over the bank. The snow continued to fall, quietly effacing all

WOLFE'S MONUMENT

MARTELLO TOWER.
On the Plains of Abraham.

signs of the conflict. A few hours after, Montgomery's body was found lying in the snow, stark and stiff, and was carried to a small log-house in St. Louis Street. No more gallant soldier fell in the Revolutionary War. Nothing now could be done even by the daring Arnold, though he lingered till spring. One whiff of grape-shot had decided that Congress must needs leave its ancient foe to itself, to work out its destinies in connection with that British Empire which it had so long defied.

That decision has ruled events ever since. From that day to this, constitutional questions have occupied the attention of the Canadian people, instead of military ambition and the game of war. No such questions could emerge under the Old Régime. Constitutional development was then impossible. The fundamental principle of the Old Régime was that the spiritual and the civil powers ruled all subjects by Divine right, and therefore that the first and last duty of government was to train the people under a long line of absolute functionaries, religious and civil, to obey the powers that be. A demand for representative institutions could hardly be expected to come in those circumstances from the French Canadians. Their ambition extended no further than the hope that they might be governed economically, on a hard-money basis, and according to their own traditions. Their relation to the land, their disposition, habits and training, their unquenchable Celtic love for their language, laws and religion, made them eminently conservative.

HOUSE TO WHICH MONTGOMERY'S BODY WAS CARRIED.

From the day the British flag floated over their heads, they came into the possession of rights and privileges of which their fathers had never dreamed. The contrast between their condition under Great Britain with what it had been under France, could not be described more forcibly than it was by Papineau in the year 1820 on the hustings of Montreal:—"Then—under France—trade was monopolised by privileged Companies, public and private property often pillaged, and the inhabitants dragged year after year from their homes and families to shed their blood, from the shores of the Great Lakes, from the banks of the Mississippi and the Ohio, to Nova Scotia, Newfoundland, and Hudson's Bay. Now, religious toleration, trial by jury, the act of *Habeas Corpus*, afford legal and equal security to all, and we need submit to no other laws but those of our own making. All these advantages have become our birthright, and shall, I hope, be the lasting inheritance of our posterity." But a disturbing element had gradually worked its way among the *habitans*, in the form of merchants, officials, and other British residents in the cities, and United Empire Loyalists from the States, and disbanded soldiers, to whom grants of land had been made in various parts of the Province, and especially in the eastern townships. From this minority came the first demand for larger liberty. These men of British antecedents felt that they could not and would not tolerate military sway or civil absolutism. They demanded, and they taught the Gallo-Canadians to demand, the rights of free men. At the same time, immigration began to flow into that western part of Canada, now called the Province of Ontario. It could easily be foreseen that this western part would continue to receive a population essentially different from that of Eastern or Lower Canada. A wise statesmanship resolved to allow the Eastern and Western sections to develop according to their own sentiments, and to give to all Canada a constitution modelled, as far as the circumstances of the age and country permitted, on the British Constitution. To secure these objects, Mr. Pitt passed the Act of 1791—an Act that well deserves the name, subsequently given to it, of the first "Magna Charta of Canadian freedom." The bill divided the ancient "Province of Quebec" into two distinct colonies, under the names of Upper and Lower Canada, each section to have a separate elective Assembly. Fox strenuously opposed the division of Canada. "It would be wiser," he said, "to unite still more closely the two races than separate them." Burke lent the weight of political philosophy to the practical statesmanship of Pitt. "For us to attempt to amalgamate two populations composed of races of men diverse in language, laws and habitudes, is a complete absurdity," he warmly argued. Pitt's policy combined all that was valuable in the arguments of both Fox and Burke. It was designed to accomplish all that is now accomplished, according to the spirit as well as the forms of the British Constitution, by that federal system under which we are happily living. In order to make the Act of 1791 successful, only fair play was required, or a disposition on the part of the leaders of the people to accept it loyally. All constitutions require that as the condition of success. Under Pitt's Act the bounds of freedom could have been widened gradually and peacefully. But it did not get fair play in Lower Canada, from either the representatives of the minority or of the majority of the people. The minority had clamoured for representative institutions. They got them, and then made the discovery that the gift implied the government of the country, not according to their wishes, but according to the wishes of the great body of the people. Naturally enough, they then fell back on the Legislative Council, holding that it should be composed of men of British race only or their sympathisers, and that the Executive should be guided not by the representative Chamber, but by the Divinely-appointed Council. On the other hand, the representatives of the majority soon awoke to understand the power of the weapon that had been put into their hands. When they did understand, there was no end to their delight in the use of the weapon. A boy is ready to use his first jack-knife or hatchet on anything and everything. So they acted, as if their new weapon could not be used too much. As with their countrymen in Old France, their logical powers interfered with their success in the practical work of government. They were slow to learn that life is broader than logic, and that free institutions are possible only by the practice of mutual forbearance towards each other of the different bodies among whom the supreme power is distributed. Still, the measure of constitutional freedom that had been generously bestowed had its legitimate effect on the French-Canadians. They learned to appeal to British precedents, and a love of British institutions began to take possession of their minds. Nothing demonstrates this more satisfactorily than the contrast between their inaction during 1775-6, and their united and hearty action during the war of 1812-15. That war, which may be regarded as an episode in the constitutional history we are sketching, teaches to all who are willing to be taught several important lessons. It showed that French-Canadians had not forgotten how to fight, and that according as they were trusted so would they fight. No better illustration can be given than Châteauguay, where Colonel de Salaberry with 300 Canadian militiamen and a few Highlanders victoriously drove back an army 7000 strong. The Canadians everywhere flew to arms, in a quarrel, too, with the bringing on of which they had nothing to do. The Governor sent the regular troops to the frontiers, and confided the guardianship of Quebec to the city militia, while men like Bedard who had been accused of "treason," because they understood the spirit of the Constitution better than their accusers, were appointed officers. Successive campaigns proved, not only that Canada was unconquerable even against a people then forty times as numerous—because of the spirit of its people, its glorious winters, and northern fastnesses, but also because an unprovoked war upon Canada will never command the united support of the people of the States. When the war was declared in 1812, several of the New England States refused their quotas of militia. The Legislature of Maryland declared that they had acted constitutionally in refusing. And all over New England secession was seriously threatened. What happened then would occur again, under other forms, if an effort were made to conquer four or five millions of Canadians, in order to make them citizens of free States. Should either political party propose it, that party would seal its own ruin. A great Christian people will struggle unitedly and religiously to free millions, never to subdue millions. Should momentary madness drive them to attempt the commission of the crime, the consequence would more likely be the disruption of the Republic than the conquest of Canada.

So much the episode of 1812-15 teaches, read in the light of the present day. When the war was over, the struggles for constitutional development were resumed. Complicated in Lower Canada by misunderstandings of race, they broke out in "the troubles" or sputterings of rebellion of 1837-38. The forcible reunion of the two Canadas in 1840 was a temporary measure, necessitated probably by those troubles. It led to friction, irritations, a necessity for double majorities, and perpetual deadlocks. Did not Pitt in 1791 foresee these as the sure results in the long run of any such union, beautiful in its simplicity though it appears to doctrinaires? The confederation of British-America in 1867 put an end to the paralysis, by the adoption of the federal principle, and the ordained extension of Canada to its natural boundaries of three oceans on three sides and the watershed of the American continent on the fourth. Full self-government having now been attained, our position is no longer colonial.

What, then, is our destiny to be? Whatever God wills. The only points clear as sunlight to us as a people are, that Canada is free, and that we dare not break up the unity of the grandest Empire the world has ever known. Annexation has been advocated, but no one has proved that such a change would be, even commercially, to our advantage. We would get closer to fifty and be removed farther from two hundred millions. Politically, Canada would cease to exist. She would serve merely as a make-weight to the Republican or Democratic party. The French-Canadian element, so great a factor actually and potentially in our national life, would become a nullity. We would surrender all hopes of a distinctive future. Strangers would rule over us; for we are too weak to resist the alien forces, and too strong to be readily assimilated. Our neighbours are a great people. So are the French and the Germans. But Belgium does not pray to be absorbed into France, and Holland would not consent to be annexed to Germany. Looking at the question in the light of the past and with foresight of the future, and from the point of view of all the higher considerations that sway men, we say, in the emphatic language of Scripture, "It is a shame even to speak" of such a thing. We would repent it only once, and that would be forever. Their ways are not our ways; their thoughts, traditions, history, are not our thoughts, traditions, history. The occasional cry for Independence is more honourable; but, to break our national continuity in cold blood, to cut ourselves loose from the capital and centre of our strength! to gain—what? A thousand possibilities of danger, and not an atom of added strength. What, then, are we to do? "Things cannot remain as they are," we are told. Who says that they can? They have been changing every decade. The future will bring changes with it, and wisdom too, let us hope, such as our fathers had, to enable us to do our duty in the premises. In the meantime, we have enough to do. We have to simplify the machinery of our government, to make it less absurdly expensive, and to disembarrass it of patronage. We have to put an emphatic stop to the increase of the public debt. We have to reclaim half a continent, and throw doors wide open that millions may enter in. We have to grow wiser and better. We have to guard our own heads while we seek to do our duty to our day and generation. Is not that work enough for the next half century? No one is likely to interfere with us, but we are not thereby absolved from the responsibility of keeping up the defences of Halifax and Quebec, and fortifying Montreal by a cincture of detached forts. These cities safe, Canada might be invaded, but could not be held. But what need of defence, when we are assured that "our best defence is no defence." Go to the mayors of our cities and bid them dismiss the police. Tell bankers not to keep revolvers, and householders to poison their watch-dogs. At one stroke we save what we are expending on all the old fashioned arrangements of the Dark Ages. It has been discovered that the "best defence is no defence!"

It does not become grown men to dream dreams in broad daylight. Wise men regard facts. Here is the Admiral's ship, the shapely "Northampton," in the harbour of

THE CITADEL.
From H. M. S. "Northampton."

Quebec. Come on board, and from the quarter-deck take a view of the grand old storied rock. Whose money built that vast Citadel that crowns its strength? Who gave us those mighty batteries on the Levis heights opposite? What enemy on this planet could take Quebec as long as the "Northampton" pledges to us the command of the sea? And for answer, a charmer says, you would be far stronger, without the forts and without the "Northampton!"

HISTORICAL AND DESCRIPTIVE.

VIEW FROM THE OLD MANOR HOUSE AT BEAUPORT.

QUEBEC—the spot where the most refined civilization of the Old World first touched the barbaric wildness of the New—is also the spot where the largest share of the picturesque and romantic element has gathered round the outlines of a grand though rugged nature. It would seem as if those early heroes, the flower of France's chivalry, who conquered a new country from a savage climate and a savage race, had impressed the features of their nationality on this rock fortress forever. May Quebec always retain its French idiosyncrasy! The shades of its brave founders claim this as their right. From Champlain and Laval down to De Lévis and Montcalm, they deserve this monument to their efforts to build up and preserve a "New France" in this western world; and Wolfe for one would not have grudged that the memory of his gallant foe should here be closely entwined with his own. All who know the value of the mingling of diverse elements in enriching national life, will rejoice in the preservation among us of a distinctly French element, blending harmoniously in our Canadian nationality.

"Saxon and Celt and Norman are we;"

and we may well be proud of having within our borders a "New France" as well as a "Greater Britain."

Imagination could hardly have devised a nobler portal to the Dominion than the mile-wide strait, on one side of which rise the green heights of Lévis, and on the other the bold, abrupt outlines of Cape Diamond. To the traveller from the Old World who first drops anchor under those dark rocks and frowning ramparts, the *coup d'œil* must present an impressive frontispiece to the unread volume. The outlines of the rocky rampart and its crowning fortress, as seen from a distance, recall both Stirling and Ehrenbreitstein, while its aspect as viewed from the foot of the time-worn, steep-roofed old houses that skirt the height, carries at least a suggestion of Edinburgh Castle from the Grassmarket. To the home-bred Canadian, coming from the flat regions of Central Canada by the train that skirts the southern shore and suddenly finds its way along the abrupt, wooded heights that end in Point Lévis, with quaint steep-gabled and balconied French houses climbing the rocky ledges to the right, and affording to curious passengers, through open doors and windows, many a naïve glimpse of the simple domestic life of the *habitans*, the first sight of Quebec from the terminus or the ferry station is a revelation. It is the realization of dim, hovering visions conjured up by the literature of other lands more rich in the picturesque element born of antiquity and historical association. On our Republican neighbours, the effect produced is the same. Quebec has no more enthusiastic admirers than its hosts of American visitors; and no writers have more vividly and appreciatively described its peculiar charm than Parkman and Howells.

Looking at Quebec first from the opposite heights of Lévis, and then passing slowly across from shore to shore, the striking features of the city and its surroundings come gradually into view, in a manner doubly enchanting if it happens to be a soft, misty summer morning. At first, the dim, huge mass of the rock and Citadel, — seemingly one grand fortification, — absorbs the attention. Then the details come out, one after another. The firm lines of rampart and bastion, the

QUEBEC FROM POINT LÉVIS.

shelving outlines of the rock, Dufferin Terrace with its light pavilions, the slope of Mountain Hill, the Grand Battery, the conspicuous pile of Laval University, the dark serried mass of houses clustering along the foot of the rocks and rising gradually up the gentler incline into which these fall away, the busy quays, the large passenger boats steaming in and out from their wharves, all impress the stranger with the most distinctive aspects of Quebec before he lands.

As soon as he has landed, he is impressed by other features of its ancient and foreign aspect. The narrow, crooked lanes that do duty for streets, the grimy, weather-beaten walls and narrow windows on either side, the steep-roofed antique French houses, the cork-screw ascent towards the upper town, the rugged pavement over which the wheels of the *calèche* noisily rattle, recall the peculiarities of an old French town. And before Prescott Gate was sacrificed to modern utilitarian demands, the effect was intensified by the novel sensation—in America—of entering a walled town through a real gate, frowning down as from a mediæval story.

The short, crooked streets of Quebec, diverging at all kinds of angles, make it as difficult to find one's way as in Venice or old Boston. It has grown, like old towns, instead of being laid out like new ones, and its peculiarities of growth have been differentiated to a remarkable degree by the exigencies of its site and fortifications. The "lie" of the place can be best explained by saying that the walls embrace a rudely-drawn section of an ellipse, the straight side of which divides the city from the comparatively level ground of the country in rear (towards the north-west), while the Citadel occupies the western corner of the curve which follows the edge of the precipice abutting on the St. Lawrence, turning an abrupt corner round the Seminary Gardens, and following the line of the high ground till it descends to the valley of the St. Charles. It was on *this* side of the natural fortress, to which Quebec owes its antiquity and its pre-eminence as a capital, that the life of the Old World left its first trace on the history of the Canadian wilderness. For here, a little way up the river, Jacques Cartier anchored his ships, which had so astounded the unsophisticated savages as they came, like things of life, sailing up the river. Here, too, he and his men spent the long, bitter winter, waiting wearily for the slowly-coming spring which so many of them never saw.

But there are pleasanter associations with the side of Quebec which the visitor usually sees first. As we walk or drive up Mountain Hill by the winding ascent which originally existed as a rough gully, the associations are all of Champlain, the Chevalier Bayard of the French *régime* and the founder of Quebec. One cannot but wonder whether there rose before his inner vision a picture of the city which he may have hoped would grow from the oak and walnut-shaded plateau by the river, and up the sides of the rugged hill that now bears its mass of ancient buildings, climbing to the zig-zagged walls and bastions that crown the highest point of what was then a bare beetling rock. As he watched the stately trees falling under the strokes of his sturdy axe-men—where dingy warehouses and high tenements are now densely massed together under the cliff—he may have dreamed of a second Rouen, the queenly capital of a "New France," giving laws to a territory as illimitable as the wilderness of hill and forest that stretched away on every side beyond the range of eye and imagination.

But before ascending Mountain Hill, let us turn aside into the little Notre Dame Place, where stands a small quaint church with high-peaked roof and antique belfry, one of the oldest buildings in Quebec, for its walls date back at least before 1690 when the fête of Notre Dame des Victoires was established to commemorate the defeat of Sir William

Phipps. It was close to this spot that Champlain built his first fort and warehouse for stores and peltries. A little farther to the left—where the Champlain Market, built out of the stones of the old Parliament buildings, presents on market days a busy and picturesque tableau—stood the first "Abitation de Quebecq," perpetuated for us by Champlain's inartistic pencil, with its three tall, narrow wooden houses set close together, its store-house and dove-cote, its loop-holed gallery running round the second storey, its moat and surrounding wall. Just above frowned the dark-brown rock; the blue waters of the St. Lawrence almost washed its outer wall; while the gardens which Champlain delighted to lay out and plant with roses, lay on three sides, to grace the wilderness abode. Now there are no gardens and no roses,—only a busy market-place that blooms out periodically, to be sure, with flowers and fruit; masses of buildings, narrow streets and crowded docks, where the tides of the St. Lawrence washed the shingly beach; huge piles of wharves driving the river still farther to bay; loaded wains carrying the produce of the Old World from the great ocean vessels or the produce of the New World to them; light French *calèches* dashing by the primitive carts of the market-folk, their drivers exchanging gay *badinage* as they pass; grave, long-robed priests, or jaunty French clerks or lads in the Seminary uniform hurrying to and fro and replying in French if you ask them a question in English; all the busy life of a complex civilization, combined with an air of antiquity which makes it difficult to realize that even three centuries ago the scene was one unbroken wilderness.

Pursuing Champlain Street a little farther, the lower town presents not a few characteristic studies. A quaint old street —"Sous Le Cap"—lies so close under the precipice surmounted by the Grand Battery and Laval University that no casual passer-by would think of penetrating its obscurity. Its dilapidated old houses, with their backs to the cliff, are braced against their opposite neighbours by cross-beams of timber to keep them upright, and even the narrow French carts can with difficulty pass through what looks more like a Scottish wynd than a Canadian street; while the old red-capped *habitant* who sits calmly smoking at his door might have stepped out of a French picture. If we pass down to the docks, we may see ocean vessels preparing for departure, perhaps, out in the stream, a timber ship loading her cargo,—the piles of fragrant wood suggesting the distant forests where, in the clear, sharp winter days the men from the lumber camp were busy hewing down and squaring the giant pines, the growth of centuries of summers.

But it is time for us to retrace our steps from this region of shipping and docks and piers, of warehouses and offices, stretching along the ledge underneath the Citadel. We may follow back Champlain Street into Little Champlain Street, and pass on to the foot of Break-neck Steps, a shorter and more direct route than the circuitous one of Mountain Hill, though there is a still easier mode of ascent provided in the new elevator, which transports you to the terrace above without any exertion. On a market day, the steps are alive with the good folks of the upper town going down to market or to business; and the busy scene below—the crowd of people

SOUS LE CAP.

and conveyances in the market-place, with the old houses built close against the cliff, the background of steamboats and shipping, and the terrace with its light, graceful pagodas against the sky above—affords one of the many bits of contrast in which Quebec abounds.

A few minutes bring us to the top of the stairs and out on what was old Durham Terrace, which, extended at the suggestion of Lord Dufferin to the foot of the glacis of the Citadel, has appropriately taken its present name and, supplied with light pavilions at the points commanding the most striking views, now bears the name of the popular Governor who so warmly appreciated the old city. It affords one of the noblest promenades that a city could possess, from the magnificent view it commands; while the old portion which, as Durham Terrace, perpetuated the name of one of the ablest British Governors of Canada, is also the centre of the most romantic and heroic memories that cluster round Quebec. For, close by, in the time of Champlain, was built the rude stockaded fort, within which he and his men were fain to take refuge from the incursions of the fierce Iroquois; while here, also, rose the old Chateau St. Louis which, for two centuries, under the *Fleur de Lis* or the Union Jack, was the centre of Canadian government and the heart and core of Canadian defence against Iroquois, British or American assailants. The Chateau of St. Louis—burned down at last, its stones helping to build this broad terrace—might furnish material for half a dozen

LOOKING UP FROM THE WHARVES.

DUFFERIN TERRACE.

romances. Looking across from the busy mass of swarming life below, and the flitting steamers and stately ships with which the river is studded, you see, first, the picturesque heights of Lévis, on which rise, tier after tier—from the busy town of South Quebec and the Grand Trunk buildings, a town in themselves,—village after village, glittering church spires, massive conventual buildings gleaming out of embosoming foliage, till the eye follows the curve of the height down again to the river. Thence it follows still the line of the lower hills that bound the receding shores of the widening expanse—the bold outline, looming perhaps, through one of the frequent sea-mists, of the richly-wooded, hamlet-sprinkled Isle of Orleans,—the old Ile de Bacchus,—then northward, across the soft gray expanse of river, with its white sails or dark steam-craft, to the hither shore, with the light mist of Montmorency on the distant woods, and the grand outlines of the Laurentian Hills that here first meet the river whose name they bear; while nearer still, the Grecian front and dome of the Custom House, the mass of Laval University and the towers and steeples of the upper town fill in a varied foreground. To the right, the terrace stretches away in a promenade, till it is cut short by the steep slope of the Citadel crowned by rampart and bastion, while behind lie the shady walks of the Governor's Garden, surrounding the pillar dedicated to the joint memory of Wolfe and Montcalm. It is a view to which no artist's pencil could do justice, since no picture could give it in its completeness, and it would take many to

CUSTOM HOUSE.

fully illustrate its ever-varying aspect from sunrise to sunset, or when the moonlight enfolds it in a serener and more solemn beauty.

One might dream away a summer day or a summer night on Dufferin Terrace; but the present claims attention as well as the past. Passing to the rear, you can wander through the shady walks of the Governor's Garden or sit on the iron seats near the "Ring," and call up before the imagination the stirring, martial scenes so often enacted on the *Grande Place* before the chateau. There the remnant of the unfortunate Hurons pitched their tents after the butchery of thousands of their number by the Iroquois on the Isle of Orleans, and there they were allowed to build a small fort. Thither, too, came a deputation of forty Iroquois, tattooed and naked, vociferating an appeal for peace to the *Ononthio* or Governor, in the summer of 1666, when the gallant regiment of Carignan-Salières had at last succeeded in instilling fear into their savage breasts. Here, also, many a French Governor, as the representative of His Most Catholic Majesty, surrounded by a bewigged and plumed retinue, received with due circumstance the keys of the Castle of St. Louis.

But it is time that we ascended to the Citadel, at which we have been so long looking from below. A flight of steps takes us up from the western end of Dufferin Terrace to the glacis. Here we again stop to look down. It is the view from the terrace, expanded in every direction. At our feet lies the busy panorama of river and docks; the Grand Trunk ferry-boat, like a tiny *batteau*, is stealing across the river in a wide curve, to avoid the pressure of the tide. On the other side we see trains arriving and departing, steaming along the rocky ledge of the opposite height upward towards Montreal or downward on the way to the sea. Just below the Citadel stretches the long massive dock of the Allan Steamship Company, at which, if it is Saturday morning, the Liverpool steamer is lying, getting ready for departure. Vans loaded with freight or luggage are discharging their contents into the hold. Passengers are stepping on board to take possession of their cabins, accompanied by friends reluctant to say the final adieu. One looks with a strange interest, never dulled by repetition, at the black hull about to bear its precious freight across the wide ocean to "the under world," unwitting of the peril it is going to brave.

From the terrace we climb by a flight of some two hundred and fifty steps to the top of the glacis. A path round its grassy slope leads to the entrance of the Citadel itself—ascending from St. Louis Street, built up on each side by solid stone walls. Passing through the celebrated chain gates, we find ourselves in the spacious area made by the widened ditch and retiring bastion, the level sward being used for a parade-ground. On the green sides of the earthwork above the ditch goats are peacefully grazing, giving an aspect of rural tranquillity that presents a picturesque contrast to the massive portals of Dalhousie Gate, with its guard-rooms built into the thickness of the arch on either side. Entering through it, we are at last within the Citadel itself, which, spreading over forty acres its labyrinth of ditch and earthwork and rampart and bastion, impresses us at once with the appropriateness of its proud title of the Canadian Gibraltar. Ascending to the broad gravel walk on the top of the bastion, we retrace our steps toward the river by the parallel line of wall on the inner side of the ditch, pierced with embrasures for the cannon that command every avenue of approach. Passing on, we take in glimpses of the ever-glorious view which bursts upon us at last in all its magnificence, as we stand on the King's Bastion beside the flag-staff,—a view which, take it all in all, it is not too much to say is unsurpassed in North America. Quebec — with its quaint contrasts of old and new—lies at our feet, the fringe of buildings and wharves at the foot of Cape Diamond literally so, the remainder of the city clustering about and up the height, like Athens about her Acropolis. Across the river, studded with craft of all imaginable variety—from the huge primitive raft that hardly seems to move, to the swift, arrowy steam-tug or the stately ocean-ship that spreads her sails to catch the breeze —the eye ascends the heights of Lévis, beyond the masses of railway buildings to the undulating curves in which nestle the clusters of tiny French houses, with their great protecting churches; then it follows the widening river, studded with sails, to the dim blue woods and distant hamlets of Orleans; on, still, to the bold mountains that form so grand a background to the cultivated slopes which descend to the long village street of the Beauport road, with its church towers guiding the eye to the Montmorency cleft or *embouchure*, in which, on a very clear day, you can just discern the faint white spray ascending from the Fall, and farther on, to Cap Tourmente and the blue mountain of St. Anne. Nearer, the glance returning takes in the winding St. Charles, the outlying suburbs of St. John and St. Roch and St. Sauveur, the crooked line of the city wall, the green turf and poplars of the Esplanade, the shady grounds and Officers' Quarters of the Artillery Barracks, the Hotel Dieu, Laval University with its belfry, the towers of the Basilica, the Gothic turrets of the English Cathedral, while, just below, we have a bird's-eye view of Dufferin Terrace and its pavilions; of the Governor's Garden, with the top of Montcalm's monument rising above the trees; of the line of Champlain Street and Champlain Market, and the rows of tall French houses that rise up against the dark, slaty cliff, with its fringe and tufts of scanty vegetation; of the line of wharves and docks, steamboats and steamships, till the field of view is suddenly curtailed by the abutments of the cliff on which we stand.

But there are other points of view, so we pass on along the entrance front of the Officers' Quarters, a portion of which is set apart for the summer residence of the Governor-General. It is not a very imposing vice-regal abode, but the simplicity of the accommodation and the restricted space are more than atoned for by the noble vistas of river and height and mountain commanded by the deeply-embrasured windows.

In a line with the Officers' Quarters are the hospital, the magazines and the Observatory, where the falling black ball gives the time daily, at one o'clock, to the shipping below. Outside the Governor-General's Quarters, and extending towards the King's Bastion, a platform has been erected which, on summer fête-nights, serves as a promenade unique and wonderful, from which "fair women and brave men" look down five hundred feet into the dark abyss below, sparkling with myriads of lights gleaming from city, height and river.

At the Prince's Bastion, on the western angle of the fortress, where the "Prince's Feather," carved in stone, commemorates the

GATES OF THE CITADEL.

visit of the Prince of Wales, the view is still more extensive. Westward, we look up the river, to the green bluff curving into Wolfe's Cove and Sillery, while across we still have before us the varied line of the opposite heights, with their long street of old French houses creeping just under its wooded sides, and a little farther to the right you catch the gleam of the steeples of New Liverpool.

After the eye has been partially satisfied with gazing on this grand panorama, we may stroll leisurely along the wall, taking in the ever-shifting views from the various

VIEW FROM THE CITADEL.

points, and observing the massiveness of the bastions and earthworks, that with many a bewildering zigzag, encompass the central fortification. As we pass back through the chain gates, let us stop to look into the casemates, or rooms built in the interior of the massive earthwork. One catches a glimpse, through the intervening darkness, of a lighted interior, reminding us of a Dutch picture, throwing a bit of domestic life into strong light and shade. Here are rooms where the soldiers and their families reside, the solid earthwork above and around them, deep windows letting in the light and air. Before leaving the precincts of the Citadel, take a look at the rock on which it is built—an uneven, circular surface of light gray rock bearing the *soubriquet* of " Hog's Back." No French or ancient associations attach to the Citadel, except to one magazine near the Prince's Bastion, the inner portion of which seems to belong to the French *régime*, being built of rubble, the outer casing only being modern. The plans for the present Citadel were supervised by the Iron Duke, though he never saw the place. The chain gates let us out into a sort of extension of the ditch, from which we emerge by the sally-port. From thence, a path leads over the broken ground of the "Plains" to the ball-cartridge field. As we pass we shall not fail to note the broken grassy curves and mounds that preserve the outlines of the old French earthworks—the predecessors of the present fortifications,—a prominent and interesting object. Approaching the Martello tower we are obliged to go out on the St. Louis road, or the *Chemin de la Grande Allée*, as it was called in the old French period. Following this still westward, a turn to the left, between the turnpike and the race-course, takes us down to some barren and neglected-looking ground on which stands Wolfe's monument, and a little farther on, a road leads downwards to the Cove where Wolfe landed his troops the night before the battle, when even Montcalm at first refused to attach importance to what he thought was " only Mr. Wolfe, with a small party, come to burn a few houses, and return."

MONUMENT TO WOLFE AND MONTCALM.

A road now winds down the face of the cliff among the straggling pines where, in Wolfe's time, there was only a rough gully up which he and his soldiers scrambled, dragging with them a six-pounder — their only gun - which played no mean part in gaining the victory. Now the quiet bay, with its rafts and lumber-piles and passing craft, is peaceful enough, and in the soft purple light of a summer evening, seems to harmonize less with martial memories than with the association with Gray's *Elegy* bequeathed to it by Wolfe, who, on the night before the decisive

TIME-BALL, FROM THE PRINCE'S BASTION.

WOLFE'S COVE.

action, repeated here, with perhaps some sad presentiment of impending fate, the stanza—

> "The boast of heraldry, the pomp of power,
> And all that beauty, all that wealth e'er gave,
> Await alike the inevitable hour—
> The paths of glory lead but to the grave!"

Retracing our steps to the St. Louis road, we follow it straight back to the city, noting the fine new pile of buildings erected for the Houses of Parliament, just beyond which we pass through one of the old gates of Quebec, the St. Louis Gate, now massively rebuilt with embrasures and Norman towers—one of the three still to be preserved to the city. But it is not the old St. Louis Gate, with its weather-beaten superstructure and zigzag approach. When the excessive newness has somewhat worn off, it will doubtless be much more imposing than its predecessor, and more fitted, like its neighbour, Kent Gate, built at her Majesty's expense, to hold up its head in a progressive age, which does not appreciate dilapidation, however picturesque.

Passing through St. Louis Gate, with its new Norman turrets, we have to our right the winding ascent to the Citadel and to our left the Esplanade; while at the corner of the St. Louis Hotel we are again in the business centre of the upper town, and soon come to the open area of the Place d'Armes, whence we pass into Buade Street, on which stands the new Post-Office, a handsome building of gray cut-stone, plain but in good taste, with two short Ionic pillars at the entrance. The old Post-Office which preceded it had a history, symbolized by a French inscription under the sign of the Chien d'Or, or Golden Dog, which legendary animal still retains his post over the entrance of the present building. This inscription was the expression of the wrongs suffered by the original owner a merchant named Philibert—at the hands of the Intendant Bigot of unsavoury memory. It ran, in old French—

> "JE SVIS VN CHIEN QVI RONGE L'OS,
> EN LE RONGEANT JE PRENDS MON REPOS,
> VN TEMS VIENDRA QVI N'EST PAS VENV
> QVE JE MORDRAY QVI M'AVRA MORDV."

The legend may be freely translated, "*I bide my time.*" Poor Philibert was never able to put his threat into execution, his life and his plans for revenge being suddenly brought to an end one day on Mountain Hill, by a sword-thrust from a French officer, no doubt at the Intendant's instigation. The story had a sequel, however. Philibert's brother, who came all the way from Bordeaux as his executor and blood-avenger, tracked the assassin to his refuge in the East Indies, and slew him there. Champlain's bust, and the symbolic dog over the entrance, with the sign of "The Golden Dog" on an inn close by, connect the new Post-Office with the memories of old Quebec, while the name of one of the streets at the corner of which it stands—Buade Street—recalls the palmiest days of the French régime, under Louis Buade, Count de Frontenac. From here Mountain Hill begins its circuitous descent, and on the opposite side is the old-fashioned-building, originally the Archbishop's Palace, which has been used for many years as the Parliament Buildings.

Going down Mountain Hill from hence, we come to the dilapidated stairway, the antique, gambrel-roofed buildings beside it being very characteristic of the old city. But we will not descend to the lower town, but walk back up Buade Street till we come to what, until recently, was the market-place of the upper town, now transferred, however, to the open space in front of St. John's Gate. On one side of the wide, open square,

KENT GATE

ST. JOHN'S GATE.

stands the Basilica, as the French Cathedral is called, linked with some of the oldest memories of the settlement of Quebec. It hardly looks its age, and is not by any means so imposing as Notre Dame, of Montreal. It was begun by Bishop Laval in 1647, and was consecrated in 1666, under the name of the Church of the Immaculate Conception. Its massive façade, with its tower on one side and its tall spire on the other, gives an impression of a rare solidity within, and the lofty arches of the nave would have a fine effect, if it were not finished in a cold and dead florid Renaissance style, which looks quite out of keeping with the homely antiquity of the "gray lady of the North." But the main charm of the building lies in its long association with the religious life of French-Canada, from the days of Le Jeune and De Jogues,

Madame de la Peltrie and Marie de l'Incarnation. Within these walls many an agonized vow and prayer has gone up from the early martyrs and heroes of the Canadian Mission for the conversion of Huron and Iroquois, and for safety from the murderous attacks of their savage foes. Here, too, have echoed the Te Deums of a grateful colony, in the joy of some signal deliverance or decisive victory. The somewhat gaudy decoration of the present interior seems to fade away as we go back, in thought, to the days when the bare rafters over-arched the self-exiled worshippers whose needs and enthusiasm mingled in prayers of pathetic earnestness to Him in whose cross and sufferings they deemed themselves sharers.

It is a natural transition from the Basilica to the Seminary, and a few steps lead through the massive open iron gates of Laval University, along the narrow passage that brings us to the door of the Seminary chapel. This chapel is over a hundred years old, Mr. Le Moine tells us, and its chief historic association is that of having served as a military

ST. LOUIS GATE.

THE BASILICA.
From Fabrique Street.

prison for American officers taken prisoners of war in the attack by Arnold and Montgomery. But the Seminary was founded by Bishop Laval in 1663, about the time that the Basilica was completed. Laval University is a secular off-shoot of the Seminary proper, which was founded for theological education only,—this being still the object of the *Grand Séminaire*. The buildings of the Seminary enclose the site of the first house built by the first French settler Hébert, and its garden, with the neighbouring streets, occupies the land first cleared for agricultural purposes. The University building, with its spacious new wings, extends to the very edge of the promontory, and from its tower another view can be obtained of the city and its surroundings.

There is not much to see in the University itself, so we pass out again and retrace our steps to the Little Market Square in front of the Basilica, where stands the long row of *calèches* whose drivers, French and Irish, have a keen eye for any passer-by who seems to wear the tourist's air of observation. Just opposite the Cathedral stood until recently the large pile of the Jesuit Barracks—originally the Jesuit College—with its yellow, stuccoed front and grated windows, and a high portal with the time-worn letters "I. H. S." still visible as the mark of its early owners.

Turning back we pass down St. Famille Street, which extends along the eastern side of the Seminary Gardens and leads to the opening in the wall where but recently stood Hope Gate. From this point there used to be a continuous promenade round the ramparts, which, when the present work of pulling down and rebuilding is completed, will again exist in a greatly improved state, in fulfilment of one of Lord Dufferin's plans for the adornment of Quebec. But now we will retrace our steps to the Cathedral Square, and crossing it at its upper end, pass in front of the English Cathedral, a sombre-looking building, with a substantial turret, standing within an old-fashioned, shady enclosure. A little farther on we come to a gray, ecclesiastical-looking cluster of buildings around a small green "close," consisting of the old Scottish church, dating from 1810, with its substantial manse and school-house. The group seems to belong to a Scottish landscape as naturally as the greater part of Quebec does to a French one.

Just opposite the church stands what was the old gaol, associated with some grim memories of the days of political imprisonments, now, through the generosity of Dr.

LOOKING ACROSS THE ESPLANADE TO BEAUPORT.

Morrin, one of Quebec's old citizens, converted into a Presbyterian College, a part of it being devoted to the rooms of the Literary and Historical Society.

Passing along St. Ursule Street, we come back to St. Louis Street, and, turning the corner of the long range of massive gray stone convent buildings, we reach the entrance to the chapel, at the end of Parloir Street. The Ursuline Convent and gardens occupy no small portion of the space within the walls, and they deserve it by a well-earned right. The chapel of the convent has various interesting reminiscences and associations, religious and artistic, and martial as well. One interesting and suggestive object is a votive lamp, lighted a hundred and fifty years ago by two French officers, on their sisters taking the veil, and kept burning ever since, except for a short time during the siege of 1759. There are paintings sent from France at the Revolution—one said to be by Vandyke and one by Champagna—and wood carvings, the work of the first Canadian School of Art, at St. Ann's, early in the eighteenth century. Montcalm, taken thither to die, was buried within the convent precincts in a grave dug for him by a bursting shell; and his skull, carefully preserved, is still shown to visitors to the chapel.

From the Ursuline Convent a short walk brings us back to the Esplanade, between the St. Louis and Kent Gates. Turning into its quiet area, faced by a row of rather sombre-looking private residences, we ascend the slope to the walk that runs along the line of wall. Looking city-ward, from one point in our promenade we take in the idyllic view of the tranquil Esplanade, with its poplars and disused guns, the ancient little Jesuit church and the old National school immediately in front; while across the ramparts and the abrupt descent beyond, we catch the blue strip of river between us and Beauport, with white sails skimming across, and the white houses scattered along the green slopes opposite, that end again in a grand mountain wall. Proceeding on from the Esplanade, we walk across the top of Kent Gate and then follow the line of the ramparts to the massive arched portal of St. John's Gate, whence we look down on the busy Montcalm Market immediately below, with its primitive French market-carts and good-humoured French market-women, who will sell you a whole handful of bouquets for a few cents. We have to leave the ramparts soon after passing St. John's Gate, the promenade, which will be continuous, not being yet finished.

Taking our way back, we return to the square, and engage one of the eager *calèche*-drivers to take us out to Montmorency Falls, a nine-mile drive. Ascending to the high-perched seat in the little two-wheeled vehicle, we are soon rattling over the not very smooth thoroughfare of the St. John suburbs, among modern and uninteresting streets—for these suburbs have been again and again laid waste by fire. We pass near the ruins of the old Intendant's Palace, and are soon on Dorchester Bridge, the gray rock of the city rising behind us, the valley of the St. Charles winding away to the north-west. "There," our driver will say, looking up at the river where the tide is rising among some ship-yards, "is where Jacques Cartier laid up his ships." Near that point, also, Montcalm's bridge of boats crossed the river, in 1759, and in a large entrenchment, where once stood the Jesuit Mission House, the remnants of his scattered army rallied after the battle of the "Plains." Even the *calèche*-drivers are antiquarian and historical in Quebec, and take pride in acting the part of cicerone to the venerable associations of the place.

The memory of Montcalm is associated with many points along the pleasant road that leads through long-stretching French villages, between the green meadows that slope up to the hills on the one side and down to the St. Lawrence on the other. The burning sun of our Canadian summer, softened here by the frequent mists and fogs from the sea, does not parch the verdure, as it too often does in regions farther inland. The velvety green of the low-lying meadows, dotted and fringed with graceful elms and beech and maple, would do no discredit to the Emerald Isle; and if the villas and fields were surrounded by hedges instead of fences, the landscape might easily be taken for an English one. About three miles below Quebec we pass the Beauport Asylum, a fine, substantial building, with a good deal of ornamental statuary and other decoration in front, in which a large number of lunatics are cared for under Government supervision. Here and there other residences and grounds attract the eye. The most notable in bye-gone times was the manor-house of old Beauport, recently destroyed by fire, and occupied in 1759 by Montcalm as his head-quarters. An old leaden plate was lately found in the ruins, bearing an inscription, interesting to antiquarians. The date of its first erection, as given in the plate, proves the ruined mansion to have been older than any existing in Canada to-day, since it preceded by three years that of the Jesuits' residence at Sillery. Robert Giffart, physician and founder of the Seigniory, figures in a curious old story told by the Abbé Ferland, of the enforced penitence and submission of a rebellious vassal—Jean Guion, or Dion—a lettered stone-mason, who thought fit to refuse the homage he owed to Giffart, his feudal lord. The vicinity of the ruined chateau bearing such interesting associations, is called *La Canardière*, preserving, in this cognomen, a reminiscence of the time when this Giffart, a keen sportsman, was wont to bag wild duck in large numbers along the marshy bank of the stream, the "*Ruisseau de l'Ours*," on which he erected his rude stockaded mansion.

One or two other *chateaux* are still inhabited by the representatives of the French families of the Old Régime. By degrees the scattered mansions, in their settings of green turf and foliage, merge into the long lines of Beauport village, its neat, quaint houses, generally of substantial stone, steep-roofed and dormer-windowed, and often completed with the little balcony; some of them old and weather-worn, others spick and span in gay new paint, and most of them bright with a profusion of flowers in a little plot before the door or in the windows. Behind each little house is its riband-like strip of ground, seemingly narrowed down to the smallest space within which a horse could turn; and here and there may be seen a man at work with the primitive cart and single horse—all his little farm will support—which carries to market the vegetables that are his chief dependence. Altogether, the light-hearted, open-air life of the simple folk carries a pleasant suggestion of that so vividly sketched in "Evangeline" and of "*la belle Normandie*," without its Gothic churches

WAYSIDE CROSS, AND BEAUPORT CHURCH.

and its peculiar costume. The massive stone building that lifts its gleaming, protecting spires high above the humble dwellings at its feet, is of no old Norman type, but a plain, straightforward substantial structure, of the same model on which the French-Canadian churches are generally built. It looks large enough to contain the whole population of a village seven or eight miles long, and doubtless on fête-days it does so.

Much more quaint and picturesque are the tiny wayside chapels and crosses which we occasionally pass—the former sometimes relics of the days when the long village was a hamlet, and glad to have a chapel of the smallest, of its very own; while the wayside cross, close by, with its sacred symbol of suffering casting its pathetic shadow on the life and brightness around, would be quite in place in a landscape of France or of Southern Germany.

At last the village of Beauport is left behind, and we skirt an open stretch of field and woodland on either side. Towards the St. Lawrence, which lies broad and blue between us and the richly-wooded Isle of Orleans, is seen a white mansion on a commanding point, just above the Montmorency Falls, which was once occupied by the Duke of Kent. Beyond the river and the Isle of Orleans the low blue hills appear, while before us to the left rise the noble outlines of the Laurentians, flecked with passing gleams of soft light and violet shadow. If we choose to alight, and walk a mile or so across the fields to our left, we come to the "Natural Steps," a succession of rocky ledges, exactly like steps cut in the rock, between which the narrow river sweeps silently on, fringed by a fragrant wood of low spruce and hemlock, soon to brawl and foam over the brown-gray rocks in tiny cascades, before its final plunge. Returning again to the road, and driving on, we come to the wooden bridge across the river, where it dashes itself over its rocky bed, which the advancing summer leaves half uncovered and dry. Crossing the bridge, we drive some few hundred yards to the little country inn, where carriages put up to await the return of their passengers, who must go the rest of the way on foot. A little farther on is the gate to the pathway leading to the Fall, winding along the top of a high bank, fringed with foliage and wild flowers. Following this path we gradually catch a glimpse of slender, snowy streams of foam descending over the dark, rocky precipice. These are the outlying stragglers of the great Fall, and are as beautiful in themselves as some Swiss cascades, one of them looking like braided threads of molten silver as it falls over the jutting rocks, and another reminding the traveller of the Geissbach. By the time the top of the strong wooden stairs leading down the rapidly-descending bank is reached the upper part of the main Fall is in full view; though not till we descend two-thirds of really dizzying stair, can it be realized in its entire majesty, as it makes a sheer plunge, a mass of snowy foam in mad, headlong rush, down the precipice of 250 feet. The illustration, excellent as it is, can hardly convey a true idea of its majestic height as seen from one of the resting-places, about one-third of the distance from below, where we can best appreciate the full sweep and volume—partly cut off, in the illustration, by the intervening rocks. Higher than Niagara, yet on account of its comparatively small volume, it has nothing like the stupendous grandeur of that mighty cataract, but much more of picturesque beauty in its setting—while its greater height is emphasized by its narrower limits.

At the head of the Fall, on either bank, stand massive stone piers, memorials of a tragedy which occurred there many years ago. A suspension bridge, built across the

LOOKING TOWARDS QUEBEC,
From Montmorency.

top of the Fall, had been too slightly constructed, and had not stood very long before it broke asunder while a *habitant* and his wife were crossing it in their market-cart. They were swept at once over the cataract, never to be seen again. The bridge was not rebuilt, the two piers still standing, mute monuments of the tragedy. The house already seen above the Fall—associated with the father of our gracious Queen—is a conspicuous object from the top of the stair, and the paths laid out in the grounds must command noble views. A part of one of the small cascades is used for turning the machinery of a saw-mill near by, but the mill itself is kept well out of sight. Rafts and lumber piles, however, are prominent features along the shore of the river as it enters the St. Lawrence.

At the foot of the Fall the famous "Cone," an irregular mound of ice and snow, is gradually formed, in winter, by the freezing spray. It grows till it attains a height so considerable that it serves as the favourite tobogganning ground of the gay people of Quebec, who make regular sleighing expeditions to the locality to enjoy this exhilarating though somewhat dangerous Canadian sport. When the "Cone" and its vicinity are alive with tobogganners—the ladies dressed in bright, becoming costumes, some of them making the dizzy descent in a light cloud of snow, others slowly drawing

MONTMORENCY RIVER ABOVE FALLS.

their toboggans up the "Cone" the scene, in its winter attire of pure, sparkling snow, crusting the dark evergreens and contrasting with the rushing Fall, is at once a grand and pleasing one.

We turn away reluctantly from the beautiful picture, and in a few minutes are rattling back along the road to Quebec. The city, as we draw near it, in the evening light, appears to blaze out in a glittering sheen, every tin roof giving back the afternoon sunshine till the whole rock seems irradiated with a golden glory, in strong contrast to the deep tones of the hills beyond. Gradually the glory resolves itself into roofs and houses, and soon we cross Dorchester Bridge again, when, turning by a side street to the right, we pass through the deserted market-place outside St. John's Gate, and are once more within the city, driving along St. John Street, the chief thoroughfare.

One of the points of interest in the immediate vicinity of Quebec, is the site of the old hunting-lodge of the Intendant Bigot, beyond the village of Charlesbourg. Leaving the main road, we penetrate through a tangled thicket and reach an open glade beside a stream where some weather-worn walls, the remains of what is popularly called the Chateau Bigot, stand amid lilac and syringa bushes which still show traces of an old garden. There the wicked Intendant was wont to hold his carousals with his boon companions of the hunt, after the fashion described in the "*Chien d'Or*." It has its legend of a buried hoard of silver and of a beautiful Huron girl who loved Bigot and died a violent death. But apart from legend, it has a wild grace of its own, with its hoary vestiges of a long-past habitation, and the pine-crowned mountain rising as a noble background behind the surrounding trees.

Sillery is among the sacred places of Quebec, and a pilgrimage thither is one of the pleasantest little excursions one can make from the old city. From the deck of the "James," which plies on the river between Quebec and Sillery, we can look up, first to the old, steep houses massed under the scarped rock that shoots aloft on to Dufferin Terrace, with its watch-towers, and thence to the crowning height of the Citadel. We steam slowly past the brown shelving precipice of Cape Diamond, with its fringe of French houses and shipping; past lumber vessels lifting huge logs from rafts in the stream, beyond the point where, high up on the red-brown rock we can easily read the inscription, "Here Montgomery fell—1775." Then we pass the green plains, with their broken ground and old earthworks and Martello towers and observatory, and the grim gaol a conspicuous mass; then a stretch of ground, covered with low vegetation, gives place to high-wooded banks and shades, opening, through masses of pine and oak and maple foliage, glimpses of pleasant country-seats. Opposite, from the curving point of Lévis, the eye follows height after height, rich, rounded, wooded hills, at the foot of which, just opposite, lies the busy village of New Liverpool, with its massive and finely-frescoed church.

But we must leave Sillery, with its sacred and stirring memories, and drive up the foliage-clad height which makes so effective a background. A gradual ascent above the residence, soon brings us to the level ground above, to the pretty, foliage-embowered St. Louis road, where we pass the pine-shaded glades of Mount Hermon Cemetery. Spencer Wood is one of the charming country residences of which we catch a passing

ON THE ROAD TO SILLERY.

glimpse, and its bosky recesses and bright gardens are the scenes of many a pleasant fête for the *beau monde* of Quebec, under the hospitable auspices of the Lieutenant-Governor of the day. As we draw nearer the city, cross-roads give us glimpses of the grand mountain landscape to the north, and of the Ste. Foye road, which leads by an extremely pretty drive to the Ste. Foye monument, on an open plateau on the brow of the cliff overhanging the valley of the St. Charles. The monument, a slender Doric pillar crowned by a bronze statue of Bellona, presented by Prince Napoleon on the occasion of his visit to Canada, commemorates the battle of Ste. Foye, between Lévis and Murray—the final scene in the struggle between French and English for the possession of Canada—and also marks the grave of those who fell. It bears the inscription, "*Aux braves de* 1760, *érigé par le Société St. Jean Baptiste de Québec*, 1860."

About two and a half miles along the Ste. Foye road lies the Belmont Cemetery, the burying-place of the great Roman Catholic churches—the Basilica and St. Jean Baptiste. There, under the solemn pines, sleeps, among many of his compatriots, the noble and patriotic Garneau, the historian of French-Canada. With a visit to his tomb we may appropriately close our wanderings about this historic city.

AUX BRAVES.

FALLS OF MONTMORENCY.

ROUGEMONT AND VALLEY.

SOUTH-EASTERN QUEBEC.

STRETCHING away south-easterly from the St. Lawrence to the New England frontier, and on other two sides bounded by the Rivers Richelieu and Chaudière, lies one of the fairest tracts of Old Canada. Forming the core of it, lie the freeholds of the Eastern Townships; and they are fringed on three sides by the old fiefs of Louis XIV. Altogether, there may be ten thousand square miles in the tract. A land of river and plain; of mountain, and tarn, and lake, and valley; but first and chiefly a river-land. Along its northern shore sweeps the mighty St. Lawrence, now deploying nto a lake ten miles wide, and then calling in his battalions for that majestic, resistless march to the sea. And down to the swelling tide of the St. Lawrence hasten—besides brooks or streams innumerable—half a dozen goodly rivers, the Richelieu, Yamaska, St. Francis, Nicolet, Bécancourt, Chaudière. Were we to climb these rivers through their beautiful winding glens, we should meet foaming rapids and dizzy cascades; then quiet pools within lofty walls of verdure, and delightful shadowed reaches where speckled trout still linger; yet higher among the mountains we should find such romantic lakes as Brome, Memphremagog, Massawippi, and Megantic.

Throughout this land, the strata have been much shaken and changed by some Titanic force,—seemingly steam heated beyond the scale of any pyrometer, and tortured under pressure which would be inadequately gauged by thousands of tons to the square inch. Sir William Logan traced a line of dislocation from Missisquoi Bay on Lake Champlain to Point Lévis, along which the wrenching asunder of strata is equivalent to a vertical displacement of many thousands of feet. Westward of this line of rupture,—which we shall call Logan's Line,—the sedimentary rocks that were directly exposed to incandescent steam softened, rearranged their elements, and ran to a glassy or stony paste. Under the enormous pressure below, the surface strata presently cracked and sometimes opened wide. Instantly, into the cracks and fissures rushed the pasty rock, forming dykes of trachyte or diorite. In places, the very granite foundations of the world seem to have softened, and followed the sedimentary rocks to the surface. Where the ground yielded most, stately pyramids of mountain-protoplasm were born. It is to such throes of Mother Earth we owe the beautiful sisterhood of Belœil Mountain and Yamaska, Rougemont and Mount Monnoir; the Boucherville Mountains, and Mont Royal itself. Eastward of Logan's Line, more intense still must have been the energy that girdled Lake Memphremagog with such soaring peaks as Mount Orford, Owl's Head, and Elephantis. Within historic times, some severe earthquakes have shaken this area, but even the most violent were gentle pastime compared with the elemental wars of geological antiquity. To be sure, every one was frightened by these earthquakes, but then no one was killed. From the records of the old Jesuit Mission on the St. Francis, we learn that on the fifth of September, 1732, the Indian Village was so rudely shaken as to destroy its identity; of this "bouleversement," traces are still discernible on both sides of the river. More general, and far more violent, was the famous earthquake of 1663. On the fifth of February, began a series of convulsions which did not quite disappear till midsummer. Land-slides occurred all along the river-banks, and the blue St. Lawrence ran white as far down as Tadousac. Every one explained the phenomenon in his own way. At Montreal, not a few consciences were smitten for having sold fire-water to the Indians. The Indians, however, declared that the shades of their forefathers were struggling to return to the earthly Hunting Grounds; and, most undutifully, they kept firing off their muskets to scare their

BELŒIL MOUNTAIN, FROM RICHELIEU RIVER.

unquiet sires; for, quoth the musketeers, it's plain to see there's not game enough on earth for both of us!

Some ancient hurly-burly of the rocks has here brought within convenient reach a vast variety of things useful or ornamental. If you are house-building, you have limestone for the foundation, clay for bricks, and sand and lime for mortar; granite for the lintels and window-sills, or for the whole house if you like; magnesite for cements; slate for your roof; serpentine and verd-antique for your mantles. Then, as for metals, we find chromic iron at Melbourne, and in Bolton and Ham; manganese in Stanstead; the copper ore of Acton has long been famous; and gold has been found in notable quantity on the upper course of the Chaudière, and around its fountain, Lake Megantic. Not even are gems altogether absent: jasper is found at Sherbrooke; and beautiful little green garnets, like miniature emeralds, have been picked up in Orford.

This land was first seen of Europeans three centuries and a half ago. Let us for a little view it through the keen, searching eyes of Captain Cartier, the famous St. Malo seaman. He had a few days ago reached Stadacona, the Indian precursor of Quebec. Donnacona, the Indian lord of the soil, tried to dissuade him from going farther; but, laughing aside all fears and obstructions, Cartier would explore for himself the great river of Hochelaga, and would see that Indian metropolis of which the fame had reached him down by the Gaspé shore. On the 19th of September, 1535, leaving the two largest of his three vessels in the River St. Charles, the explorer pushed up stream with two boats and the *Émerillon*. This ship was named from the little falcon that in England was called the Merlin:—indeed, a craft of forty tons would seem to us a land-bird, rather than a bird of the ocean. Over the St. Lawrence now hover great sea-fowl, of more than a hundred times the *Merlin's* tonnage; but pray remember it was the *Merlin* led the way. The staunch little ship had bravely ridden the violent storms of the outward passage; outliving one of her consorts, she would return to France; and, six years hence, she would again be put in commission for Cartier's third cruise to Canada.

In the discoverer's party were not only weather-beaten tars of Normandy and Brittany, but some of the young *noblesse* of the court of Francis the First. There were Claude du Pont-Briant, Chief Cup-bearer to the Dauphin,—Charles de la Pommeraye, and others of the *jeunesse dorée* of that gay epoch. Their dreams were of romantic adventure, and, at the farther end, rich Cathay, or, as they called it, *La Chine*; to these Argonauts La Chine was the land of the Golden Fleece, and now they were surely on the road thither. If you ascend the St. Lawrence on a sunny afternoon in the autumn, the chances are that you, too, may fall into some such day-dream. As the rock of Quebec faded from sight, the river-banks became clothed with such loveliness as stirred the St. Malo seaman. There were park-lands wooded with "the most beautiful trees in the world"; and the trees were so trellised with vines and festooned with grapes that it all seemed the work of man's hand. Indeed, human dwellings now became numerous, and fishermen were seen taking frequent toll of the river. With great heartiness and good-will the natives brought their fish to Cartier's little squadron. Presently a sharp current was felt on reaching the river-elbow that now bears the classical name of *Pointe Platon*. Just above was a *sault*, as yet only known or named of Indians, but a century later its hurrying waters would reflect the unquiet spirit of the time, and be called the Richelieu Rapid. It is still the custom with our sailors to wait for the flood-tide in taking this dangerous gateway. The little *Merlin* wisely dropped anchor.

> "Scarce could Argo stem it: wherefore they,
> It being but early, anchored till mid-day,
> And as they waited, saw an eddy rise
> Where sea joined river, and before their eyes
> The battle of the waters did begin.
> So, seeing the mighty ocean best therein,
> Weighing their anchor, they made haste to man
> Both oars and sails, and therewith flying, ran
> With the first wave of the great conquering flood
> Far up the stream, on whose banks forests stood
> Darkening the swirling water on each side."

While the French explorers still lay at anchor they were encompassed by a flotilla of canoes. One brought the *Grand Seigneur*—as Cartier calls him—of the country, which is now occupied by the Eastern Townships and the enclosing seigniories. His village on Pointe Platon was called Ochelay. By signs and gesticulations the Indian chief pictured the dangers of the rapid. As a conclusive proof of his sincerity, the lord of Ochelay offered the French commander two of his children for adoption; and Cartier chose a little girl of seven or eight years. The poor mother's heart seems to have been ill at ease; for, when the explorers returned to Quebec, she went down the river to see how it fared with her child.

Cartier's journal and description of the Ste. Croix River were, two centuries and a half ago, read to mean that the discoverer spent the woful winter of 1535-6 under Pointe Platon, and that his vessels lay in the estuary of the river which enters the St. Lawrence from the opposite bank. So that to this day the parish on the south bank is called Ste. Croix, and the opposite river is called Jacques Cartier. But Champlain, in 1608, cleared up this question by finding near Quebec the remains of Cartier's winter encampment, and three or four cannon-balls. When, despite the Convention of Susa, Admiral Kirkt pounced on Quebec, it set Champlain thinking that if ever he got Canada back, the country would have more than one bastion for its defence. Restoration having been made by the Treaty of St. Germain, the Governor set to work, in 1633, and fortified the little island that commands the gateway of Pointe Platon,—calling island and fort "Richelieu," in honour of the great Cardinal who had just chartered the "New Company of One Hundred Associates." More than two centuries ago, Champlain's Fort Richelieu had already mouldered into oblivion, but river pilots still call the swirling water here the Richelieu Rapid. In early days the island produced such a profusion of grapes, that Cartier's description of Orleans Island was misapplied to Isle Richelieu, thus completing the confusion in the discoverer's narrative. And this brings us back to 1535.

After passing the rocky gateway of Pointe Platon the St. Lawrence widened, and then the country seemed to our Jason and his Argonauts a very land of enchantment.

No wonder. The genial September sun, the cloudless skies, the blue waters of the mighty river here gently drawing the shores miles apart; and then the towering forests on either bank with their long vistas of verdure and romantic gloom,—the St. Malo seaman might well declare it "as fair a land as heart could desire!" Cartier and his brother-in-law, Mark Jalobert, were practised pilots. With their yawls and sounding-lines they would speedily find that the channel lay half a league off the south bank. At times they were near enough to distinguish our native trees. There were seen lordly oak-forests, the memory of which is still preserved in the two *Rivières du Chêne*. As the *Merlin* climbed the river, the south bank fell, and then there were stately elms whose long tresses swayed in the breeze and toyed with the laughing water. Within recesses of the shore were descried wild swans swimming among the willows. From the marshes beyond rose cranes and the great blue heron, disturbed in their dreams by this inauspicious Merlin, startled from their ancient haunts by the spectre of civilization! The young "*gentilz hommes*" must go ashore and spy out this Land of Promise; and like those who in the ancient days spied out Canaan, our adventurers returned from this Valley of Eshcol fairly borne down with a load of grapes. In their excursions they thought they had seen the sky-lark soaring from the meadow-land. While within the shadow of the walnut-trees, day-dreams of dear Old France came strong upon them, and they declared that in this New France there were the same sweet warblers as they many a time heard—but, alas, some of them, poor lads, would never hear again—in the royal parks of St. Germain and Fontainebleau,—linnets, and thrushes, and blackbirds; aye, and *roussignolz*,—"nightingales"! Our melodious song-sparrow was mistaken for a nightingale; so to this hour you may hear in old French Canada, and in the Eastern Townships, the sweet notes of the "rossignol."

Nine of these delightful September days were loitered away in exploring the St. Lawrence from the rock of Quebec to the foot of a lake into which the river now opened. But to many, if not most, of those gallant fellows,—"*les principaulx et bons compaignons que nous eussions*," says Cartier, brushing away a tear,—this would be their last summer upon earth; then why begrudge them a few sunny hours? Their commander called the water into which they now glided *Lac d'Angoulême*,—doubtless after the ancestral earldom of Francis the First. Sixty-eight summers later, Champlain was exploring the river anew, and, as he then supposed, for the first time. He reached this point on St. Peter's Day,—29th June, 1603,—and so from that hour to this the water has been called Lake St. Peter.

What the earlier navigator viewed from the top of Mont Royal, Champlain explored in detail. And first, that arrowy river which, after shooting past the towering Belœil, entered Lake St. Peter. When the great Cardinal-Duke of Richelieu became "*Chef, Grand Maistre, et Sur-Intendant General*" of French Commerce and Navigation," the River of the Iroquois and the archipelago at its mouth took his name; but in 1603, and all through Champlain's narratives and maps, this water-course is *Rivière des*

CHAMBLY—THE OLD FORT, AND CHAMBLY RAPIDS.

BASTION OF FORT.

MONUMENT TO DE SALABERRY.

lieu and St. Lawrence. It formed a kind of naval depôt, and thus anticipated by nearly three centuries the present river-fleets and ship-yards of Sorel.

Yrocois. It led directly to the land of the Mohawks, the most easterly of the Five Nations; and, as the most easterly, the Mohawks were, in Indian metaphor, the "Door" of that "Long House" which stretched from the Hudson to the Niagara.

But these sprightly doorkeepers were not content to stand at their arms. In 1603, Champlain found that they were preparing an invasion of Canada, and that, by way of precaution against them, an inclosure had been strongly stockaded by the Algonquins at the junction of the Richelieu. As he ascended the Richelieu, Champlain, finding the current too strong for his boat, attempted to make his way along the banks:

> "Through woods and waste lands cleft by stormy streams,
> Past yew-trees, and the heavy hair of pines,
> And where the dew is thickest under oaks,
> This way and that; but questing up and down
> They saw no trail."

With the aid of a light skiff, Champlain got two leagues farther, but here met violent rapids, which have since been levelled up by the great dam at St. Ours. For the present his exploration must be abandoned; but six years later he was here again. He must meantime content himself with questioning the Indians as to the undiscovered country to the south and west. In language that he but imperfectly understood they told him of a chain of lakes; and sounding through these lines of his narrative, we, in 1603, for the first time recognize the mighty voice of the distant Niagara. (*Il descend un grandissime courant d'eau dans le dict lac.*)

At his second visit, (1609,) Champlain coasted in a more leisurely way the south shore of Lake St. Peter. He explored for some little distance the rivers Dupont (Nicolet), and Gennes (Yamaska), admiring their scenery and the luxuriant vegetation of their banks. The Dupont we take to have been named, seventy-four years before, as a compliment to Dupont-Briant, whom Cartier mentions among the young *noblesse* of his Hochelaga expedition. More than a century afterwards—probably in 1643—this beautiful and romantic river was named anew; this time, "Nicolet," after a much nobler and more serviceable fellow than the Chief Cup-bearer to his Highness the Dauphin. By the way, our Most Serene Dauphin found a sudden death in his cups.

Francis the First declared that his son had been poisoned by the contrivance of his great adversary, the Emperor Charles V; but the cooler view of the matter is that the young man took cramps from gulping down ice-water. So pass off the stage Dauphin, his Ganymede, and our River Dupont!

At his second visit Champlain rested two days at the mouth of the Richelieu. The Iroquois of the Mohawk Valley were making determined efforts to regain their ancient control of the St. Lawrence. To the Algonquin tribes now in possession the arrival of a few French warriors was a lucky windfall. Champlain above all things desired to explore the country, and was thus beguiled into leading an Algonquin foray into the undiscovered land that lay to the south. After his party had heartened themselves for coming toils by abundant venison, fish, and game, he began the ascent of the Richelieu. It was early in July, 1609. On the lower river-islands oaks and walnuts towered aloft, and groined out into great domes of foliage. Into their shadows glided the flotilla; then

OLD CHURCH AT IBERVILLE.

ST. JOHNS.

into the deeper shadows of Beloeil, which Champlain marked on his map as *mont fort*. Now Chambly Basin was discovered with its parquet of meadows and a rising amphitheatre of woods. At the farther end the river entered then, as now, with foaming current, throwing the beautiful lake into gentle undulations, and on its heaving bosom islets of brilliant verdure shimmered like emeralds. With infinite fatigue a portage was made through the forest around Chambly Rapids, which are now so easily surmounted by the Chambly and St. Johns Canal. Above the rapids, in mid-river, was the island since called Ste. Thérèse. It is now a sunny pasturage, but at its discovery, in 1609, it was all a grove of what Champlain declares the noblest pines he had ever beheld. Thence past the site of the future St. Johns; and past the afterwards historic Île aux Noix; then, rounding Rouse's Point, Champlain led his flotilla of twenty-four canoes into the lake-fountain of the Richelieu. Altogether, a sight to stir one's blood on a bright July morning: the new-found lake with its glittering waters and its diadem of mountains; the wooded islands and shores in the full glory of their summer leafage; the teeming life of lake and forest. And mark the arrowy flight of the canoes under the sweeping stroke of those swart athletes! They have already bounded over the water-front of Canada, but in the wake of yonder canoes is following a perilous surf of border-wars. Into the undertow will be drawn all who approach these waters;—not alone Indians, but French, Dutch, English, Americans; and more than two centuries will pass over before these shores enjoy a lasting peace. But of all this our old Governor had no thought. He had just made his first acquaintance with a gar-pike; was remarking on its "bill" and vicious teeth; was thrusting at its armour with his poniard. As he coursed down the lake he was much engrossed with the magnificent scenery on either hand. To the west lay the Adirondacks, the ancient homestead of the Algonquin warriors who were his companions. Their forefathers deserted that picturesque wilderness for the gentler shores of Hochelaga, driving before them the then unwarlike Iroquois, whom Cartier had found fishing, corn-planting, and road-making. Contrasting their own better fare with that of improvident and often famished Algonquins, the Iroquois had nicknamed them *Adirondacks*,—" Bark-Eaters." Once in Canada, the Adirondacks became fused into the other Algonquin tribes that occupied the banks of the Ottawa; but the ancient nickname still happily adheres to their old mountain home. Through Emerson's muse those peaks have won a name in literature, as well as on maps; but on that morning, and long afterwards, they were "Titans without muse or name." Then away on his left Champlain saw the soaring peaks of the Green Mountains, which, through the French *verts monts*, have given name to the State of Vermont. The discoverer remarked, though a July sun was shining, that their summits were white with snow. His Canadian warriors sighted the Iroquois one night at ten o'clock, and dawn brought an encounter on the headland which afterwards became historic as Crown Point. Champlain and his two French soldiers shared the fray, and then, for the first time, these solitudes heard the sound of firearms. Loaded with four slugs and fired into a crowd at thirty paces, their *arquebuses* scattered the Mohawks like wild pigeons. While the panic lasted Champlain hurried down the lake, and back to the St. Lawrence. To commemorate his discovery and adventure, the lake was by himself named Champlain. He was by no means of the mind to give alms to oblivion: his wife's name is preserved in St. Helen's Island; and the river St. Francis once bore his father's name, Antoine, though by 1685 the old sea-captain had already lost his grip on fame, and the river had passed over to the patron saint of the Abenakis Indians.

Among Champlain's contemporaries was Jean Nicolet, who never rose to be archon, but yet became *eponymus* of lake, river, town, and county in the tract we are describing. A native of Cherbourg, he emigrated to Canada when young to become an interpreter. Utterly devoid of fear, he lived eleven years among the Indians, and took a full share of every danger and hardship. Of this life nine years were spent among the Nipissings, that nation of wizards. Henceforward, Nicolet himself was a wizard. By the sorcery of fair dealing, and by the enchantment of truthful words, he gained a most extraordinary ascendancy over the native races, and became the great peace-maker of his time. He composed for the remainder of his life the old deadly feud between Algonquin and Iroquois. He had given these wild men "medicine" to make them love him; it was his limpid honesty of speech and purpose. In only one extraordinary emergency did he add scenic effects; and, mark you, he was then on a foreign embassy. The Hurons had become embroiled with a tribe on the

OWL'S HEAD, FROM MOUNTAIN HOUSE.

farther shore of Lake Michigan, and all the horrors of savage warfare were impending. To heal the breach, Nicolet was sent to that undiscovered land where dwelt the "Gens de Mer," as the French then

OWL'S HEAD, FROM LAKE MEMPHREMAGOG.

MOUNT ELEPHANTIS.

called them. Full of the dream of the time, Jean thought "Mer" must be the Chinese Sea; and to caparison himself for an interview with the Mandarins, he bought a robe of Chinese damask, embroidered in colours with a wild profusion of birds and flowers. Father Vimont's description of this droll outfit was evidently written after a near view; and, between the lines, you can hear the worthy father chuckling at the bare thought of it. Arrived on the farther shore of Lake Michigan, honest Jean set up, as an earnest of peace and good-will, two Christmas-trees, laden with gifts. He then harnessed himself into his Chinese flower-garden and aviary. But, doubting how the Mandarins of Green Bay might receive him, he took in each hand one of the tremendous pistols of that era, and, sending forward his Huron companions, advanced towards the yet unseen metropolis. The nerves of the Winnebago ladies were unequal to the strain thus cast upon them; they ran from wigwam to wigwam, screaming, "A bogie is coming, thunderbolt in each hand!" This startling prelude over, Nicolet got together the chiefs, and soon won them over to friendship with the Hurons. After "planting the Tree of Peace," and throwing earth on the buried tomahawks, he returned to his home at Three Rivers. Though Nicolet did not reach the Chinese Sea, he had found the Wisconsin River, and *all but found the Mississippi*. Indeed, Mr. Gilmary Shea awards him the honour of first discovery.

Seven or eight years after this, Nicolet, then at Quebec, received urgent word from Governor Montmagny that the Algonquins at Three Rivers had captured a Sokoki Indian, and were about to burn him alive. A storm was raging on the St. Lawrence, but instantly Nicolet was down to the river, entreating the owner of a shallop to put out. They had passed the mouth of the Chaudière, and were abreast of Sillery when the craft was blown over, and Nicolet was swept down the river. The survivor reported that the drowning man's thoughts were not of himself, but of his wife and daughter. So, onward! thou simple, heroic soul, past the River of Death and the Great Gulf, to the Shoreless Ocean!

To a modern tourist who enters Canada for the first time by the route of Lake Champlain, there is something very startling in the sudden change of names as he passes from New York or Vermont to the valley of the Richelieu. With his usual artistic vividness, Thoreau expresses the effect produced on his mind: "To me coming from New England it appeared as Normandy itself, and realized much that had been heard of Europe and the Middle Ages. Even the names of the humble Canadian villages affected me as if they had been those of the renowned cities of antiquity. To be told by a *habitant*, when I asked the name of a village in sight, that it is *St. Fereol* or *Ste. Anne*, the *Guardian Angel*, or the *Holy St. Joseph's*; or of a mountain that it was *Belange* or *St. Hyacinthe*! As soon as we leave the States these saintly names begin. St. Johns is the first town you stop at, and henceforth the names of the mountains,

MOUNT ORFORD.

and streams, and villages reel, if I may so speak, with the intoxication of poetry: Chambly, Longueuil, Pointe-aux-Trembles, Barthélemi, etc., as if it needed only a little foreign accent, a few more liquids and vowels perchance in the language to make or locate our ideals at once. I began to dream of Provence and the Troubadours."

So far the Hermit of Walden. But underlying what he calls "saintly names," there was in the Richelieu Peninsula a fervent military feudalism. Through this cassock gleamed a steel cuirass. Though the splendid illusions of the Old Régime have long since faded, the haughty names of that epoch still kindle with an afterglow. By the mere names of these villages, towns, and seigniories, you may conjure back Louis Quatorze and Versailles; the state-craft of Colbert; the soldiers of Turenne and Vauban. Picketed around the ancient rendezvous at the confluence of the Richelieu and St. Lawrence are the officers of the Carignan-Salières, as though still guarding the Iroquois River-Gate and the approaches to Montreal:—Captain Berthier, Lieutenant Lavaltrie; Boucher, Varennes, Verchères, Contrecœur. Twilight in these ancient woodlands awakens sleeping echoes and dead centuries; with the rising night-wind the whole place seems

"Filled as with shadow of sound, with the pulse of invisible feet."

Through the forest aisles ring out elfin trumpet-calls; we hear the *réveillé* of ghostly drums beating; the prancing of phantom horses; the clinking of sabres; the measured tread of Louis the Fourteenth's battalions. At roll-call we hear officers answer to familiar names: "Captain Sorel?"—"Here!"—"Captain St. Ours?"—"Here!"—"Captain Chambly?" "Here!" And in good truth most of them are still here. In the soft grass of God's Acre they are resting, surrounded by those faithful soldiers who in death, as in life, have not deserted them. Together these veterans fought the Turk in Hungary, and drove him into the Raab; together they chased the Iroquois up the Richelieu, and down the Mohawk Valley; and, after van and rear had passed a darker valley and an icier flood, they mustered here at last in eerie bivouac together.

During the summer and autumn of 1665 the soldiers of the Carignan-Salières may have been seen working like beavers along the banks of the Richelieu, cutting down trees and casting up earthworks. By the following year a line of five forts had been completed,—Richelieu (Sorel), St. Louis (Chambly), St. Thérèse, St. Jean, St. Anne. The first, occupying the site of the Chevalier Montmagny's old fort, commanded the mouth of the river; the last commanded the outlet of Lake Champlain, and stood on the island still called La Motte after the Captain who directed the work. With this bridle of forts well in hand, Louis XIV hoped to rein in the wild Iroquois, just as the Wall of Severus was meant as a snaffle for the wild Caledonian.

Settlements of the legionaries and their captains were formed behind the Roman Wall; so our centurions and their soldiers occupied seigniories and fiefs under cover of these river-forts.

The officers' sons and daughters inherited the high spirit of their race, and were often remarkable for adventurous and heroic qualities. Lieutenant Varennes married little Marie Boucher, daughter of a brother officer, who was then Governor of Three Rivers. One of their sons was that Ensign Varennes de Verendrye, who, fighting like a lion under Marshal Villars at Malplaquet, was left for dead on the field, but revived nevertheless, and was consoled for his nine wounds with a lieutenancy, and returned to Canada; next we hear of him on Lake Nipigon; then on the Kaministiquia; now he has reached Lake Winnipeg, is building a fort, and is floating the first *fleur de lis* on those waters; is the first to explore the Saskatchewan; is the first to behold the Rocky Mountains. And what school-child in Canada has not read or heard of Madeleine Verchères, who, at fourteen years of age, beat off the Iroquois from her father's fort, and for a whole week maintained her vigil on the bastion until help came up from Quebec?

The first commandant and *seigneur* of Chambly seems to have left his heart in France, for he made over his whole estate to Mademoiselle Tavenet,—to be hers at once if she shared his fortunes in Canada; in any case, to become hers after his death. The charming Tavenet preferred to wait; but it is doubtful whether the estate ever reached her. A few words more will dispose of the gallant Jacques Chambly, appointed by Frontenac to the chief command "as a most efficient, and as the oldest officer in the country"; promoted by Louis XIV to the Governorship of Acadie; captured one hot August day at the mouth of the Penobscot, after being shot down in defending Fort Pentagouet against a St. Domingo pirate; held for ransom at Boston; ransomed by Frontenac at his private charge; appointed to Martinique, where, let us hope, Governor Chambly recovered from his St. Domingo acquaintance the amount of Frontenac's bill of exchange. A little more than a century later, there was serving at Martinique another *seigneur* of Chambly, who was to become the most distinguished of them all,—Charles de Salaberry. In the West Indies he early exhibited the courage and resource which afterwards won for him and his Canadian Voltigeurs such renown at Chateaugay. Yet with might, mercy; and here he had before his mind not only the family motto, but the example of his old Basque ancestor whose feats on the battle-field of Coutras were so tempered with mercy, that Henry of Navarre gave him that chivalrous device, *Force à superbe; mercy à faible*,—" Might for the arrogant; mercy for the fallen!"

But, besides the Richelieu, there were other water-ways leading over to the St. Lawrence, any one of which might serve the Mohawk raider. If the Yamaska approached too near the soldiers' homes of the Richelieu Valley, there were still other rivers in reserve,—notably the St. Francis. To close at a stroke all these flood-gates of Iroquois invasion, Frontenac conceived the bold project of throwing across the whole country, from the Yamaska to the Chaudière, the warlike Algonquin tribe of Abenakis, who, while close friends of the French, were, from their very lineage, at deadly feud with the Iroquois. Though once lords of nearly ten thousand square miles, and the terror of New England, the Abenakis are now almost extinct. A mere handful—descendants of the few that escaped Rogers' Rangers—still linger near the mouth of the St. Francis. Within their former domain, the Abbé Maurault, who has devoted nearly a lifetime to these Indians and their annals, can discover but three words of Abenaki origin:—*Coaticook,* "The Stream of the Pine-Land"; *Memphremagog,* "The Great Sheet of Water"; *Megantic,* "The Resort of Fish." A movement of the Abenakis into the region west of the Chaudière began in December, 1679, and embraced Indians of two contiguous tribes,—the Etchemins and Micmacs,—all three being described by the French as *Nations Abenakises.* Henceforth the Abenakis remained close allies of France. Ghastly reprisals were made on New England for the scalping-raids of the Iroquois into Canada. Horror succeeded horror. The Massacre of Lachine was more than avenged by the atrocities of Schenectady, Deerfield, and Haverhill.

At Haverhill these avenging furies were led by J. B. Hertel de Rouville, who regarded his father's hand mutilated and burnt by Iroquois torturers—as his sufficient commission. He was the first lord of Belœil Mountain, and of that lovely mountain-lake which Fréchette calls *un joyau tombé d'un écrin fantastique,*—" a sapphire dropped from fairy casket." His seigniory included the romantic Rougemont Valley which separates Rougemont Mountain from Belœil. Swooping from his eyry, Rouville's beak and talons were at the heart of New England before the approach of a war-party was dreamt of. Iberville, the *vis-à-vis* of St. Johns on the Richelieu, takes its name from him who not only became a distinguished navigator, and the founder of Louisiana, but who, in earlier life, had unhappily been foremost in the midnight attack on Schenectady. For nearly a century this merciless and revolting border-war continued, until in the end the battle-field was shared by England and France, and the armies of Amherst and Montcalm were at each other's throats. The old war-trail of the Richelieu, which conducted Champlain, and Courcelles, and De Tracy against the Iroquois, now led French regiments up to Crown Point, Ticonderoga, and William Henry; or, with a different fortune of war, might lead English troops down to Montreal. Even the pacification of 1763 brought but brief rest to this border-land. With the outbreak of the Revolutionary War came Montgomery's invasion by the Richelieu, and the capture of Forts St. John and Chambly. Simultaneously, Arnold undertook his memorable winter-march of nearly 600 miles up the Kennebec and down the Chaudière.

LAKE MASSAWIPPI, AND VALLEY

With the Peace of 1783, the pioneer's axe began once more to ring out among these river-valleys. Within a romantic bend of the Yamaska, "The Rush-floored River," as the Indian name is interpreted, — a hamlet took root which has grown into the very pretty cathedral-town or city of St. Hyacinthe. Notre-Dame of Montreal has here been reproduced in miniature, together with Hôtel-Dieu and other ecclesiastical foundations. The Jesuit College is remarkable for its equipment as well as extraordinary size. Academies under Protestant auspices are also in full activity. Indeed, this beautiful river-nook, with its shadowy pine groves and the restful murmur of the water, seems to have been by Nature set apart for study and contemplation. Matins and even-song here pealed through the rood-loft of great pines, ages before the swelling organ of church or cathedral was heard. Even now the Genius of the Forest lingers despite the rumble and outcry of two railways. Still ascending the river, we pass Mount Yamaska, and, after resting at the village of Granby, climb to a dark valley walled in on the north by Shefford Mountain, and by the Brome Mountains on the south. In Brome Lake the fountain-head of the Yamaska is reached,—a romantic sheet of water, with the village of Knowlton near the south end.

Here leave the basin of Yamaska, and cross over to Memphremagog and Massawippi, lake-fountains of the St. Francis. A mountain-road clambers through Bolton Pass, and then races down to the shore of Lake Memphremagog. From the heights we look out upon scenes of many a wild expedition, romantic or tragic. Yonder is the lake-gateway through which the fierce Abenakis so often carried desolation to the heart of Massachusetts. It was through those maple woods, on our west flank, that Rogers' Rangers, in 1759, swept like a whirlwind of flame, to exterminate the whole brood of tigers that had so long harried the homes of New England. Many the lawless adventure of love and war in the old days of Partizan and Ranger, who often helped out the glamour of romance by picturesque finery or Indian costume. Now you may wander at will amid the wildest of this magnificent scenery, without other adventure than the rough salute of the mountain-air, that "chartered libertine":—

> But here how often rides the Ranger-Wind!
>   To trembling aspens he now lisps of love,
>   Or grieving balsam-firs to tears will move;
> Tragic his tale the pallid birches find;
> He, envious, sees the wooded peaks reclined
>   On the sweet bosom of the Lake; nor frown
>   Of darkling Orford heeds, but blusters down
> The echoing pass, a plume of mist to bind
> On scowling brow, carbine with lightning fill;
>   He decks him in rain-fringes tagged with hail,
>   In ribbons of flying cloud; then whistles shrill,—
>   Snorting leaps forth the war-horse of the gale!
> Wild Centaur-clouds in wheeling squadrons form,
> And o'er the border sweeps the Ranger-Storm!

Lake Memphremagog is brought within three hours of Montreal by the South-Eastern Railway. After six minutes of darkness in the great tube of Victoria Bridge, we recover speed with sunlight, and strike away for the Richelieu, which is crossed

SOUTHEASTERN QUEBEC

BOLTON PASS.

SHERBROOKE.

COMMERCIAL STREET.

within view of Chambly Basin and the old Fort. Touching the Yamaska at West Farnham, we climb the water-shed of Brome. Thence, descend the valley of the Missisquoi River, winding through its lovely glens and past the southern Pinnacle Mountain, and Hawk and Bear Mountains, to Newport at the Vermont end of Lake Memphremagog. A third of the way down this most romantic water the boat-whistle apprises us that we are crossing the 45th parallel, our International Boundary. Then, for twenty miles northward, a perspective of noblest scenery. The west shore is embossed with lofty cones—Canadian kindred of the Green Mountains—the highest of the coves being Mount Orford, 4,500 feet. Owl's Head springs from the water's edge 2,700 feet into the air. Between this venerable owl-haunt and the sculptured profile of Elephantis you sail over a still unsounded abyss, which baffled Sir Hugh Allan and his sea-line of 1,200 feet. Yonder, on the opposite headland, is that old sea-king's Château; for, in the swelter of summer, it was his custom to rest here from the care of his fleets, and brace his nerves with "the wine of mountain air." When we reach the lake-outlet at Magog we seem to be in the immediate presence of Orford, though the mountain stands back a few miles from the shore. From the summit, in clear weather, a most magnificent view is had: Mount Royal, and all the mountain-peaks from the Richelieu to the Chaudière; Lake Memphremagog, its beautiful sister, Massawippi, and a score of other lakes; the Arcadian landscape of the Eastern Townships; and, beyond their southern frontier, the Green Mountains of Vermont, and the White Mountains of New Hampshire.

Not the least delicious bits of scenery in the Eastern Townships lie in the valley of the St. Francis. Among the farmsteads and rich herds of Compton and Stanstead winds the deep chasm of the Coaticook. Of Compton you would say,—" Just the nook that a contemplative naturalist might choose for writing a *Shepherd's Calendar!*" So thought Philip Henry Gosse before you, and settled here amid the "martial alarms and stormy politics" of 1837-8. It will soon be a half-century since he haunted these glens and woodlands. In an excursion to Sherbrooke we need no longer hope to find a moose, nor fear to meet a gigantic gray wolf; mill-wheels and factories on the Coaticook and Magog have frightened away many of the fish of pioneer days; but in bird, insect, and wild-flower, and in the Spring ferns, flushing with sweet verdure, may be seen the descendants of those which sat to the gentle naturalist for their portraits, and, "amid the fatigues of labour, solaced him with simple but enchanting studies."

Rising in Lake St. Francis, and expanding into Lake Aylmer, the St. Francis is joined at Lennoxville by the Massawippi, which brings the tribute of the Coaticook and other streams, as well as the overflow of Lake Massawippi. Overlooking this meeting of waters at Lennoxville, and surrounded by a landscape of rare loveliness, is the University of Bishop's College, with its pretty Chapel and Collegiate School. The friends of Bishop's College, undisheartened by repeated fires, have not only restored the buildings, but extended them, and provided anew a good working library. Among literary donations is a sumptuous *fac-simile* of the *Codex Sinaiticus*, from the Emperor of Russia. Above and below Lennoxville, the St. Francis lingers among

SPRING FERNS.

some sweet scenery; the stillness of the river here is in striking contrast to the rude concourse at Sherbrooke, where the Magog dashes wildly down a steep incline, bringing the overflow of Lakes Magog and Memphremagog.

The hill-slopes of Sherbrooke are conspicuous several miles off, and glitter in the sun with their Cathedral, College, and Church-spires. To the early Jesuits the site was familiar, for the St. Francis was the old water-way from New England to Three Rivers and Quebec. The local annals have been collected by Mrs. C. M. Day and by the Rev. P. Girard, Superior of the *Séminaire St. Charles-Borromée*.

Just above its confluence with the St. Francis, the river Magog descends a hundred and fourteen feet in little more than half a mile. The inevitable saw-mill, and grist-mill, and carding-mill appeared at the beginning of the present century; and around this nucleus a hamlet gathered, which, in 1817, was visited and paternally adopted by the Governor, Sir John Sherbrooke. A distinct impulse was given to its growth when Sherbrooke became headquarters for the British-American Land Company, which, chartered in 1833, was a prime instrument in opening out the beautiful wilderness of the Eastern Townships. In its boundless water-power, and in the fertility of the district, Sherbrooke has enduring resources. Its manufactures are already very extensive, some of the factories reaching the size of villages. The educational institutions are well-equipped and efficient. Commercial Street is the chief thoroughfare. At the farther end, the street fades into a perspective of pretty villas. Melbourne Street makes a delightful promenade, with its fine residences and flower-gardens, and its charming river-views.

Throughout the Eastern Townships, but most of all in Missisquoi, Stanstead, and Compton, there is a robust strain of the early Massachusetts pioneer. At the epoch of the Great Divide, not a few Loyalists followed the old flag, and settled a little beyond the "Province Line." Picking up the disused axe with a sigh—often with a secret tear—they once more hewed out for themselves homes in the forest. They brought across the frontier, with their old Hebrew names, the pith and industry, and intense earnestness of the Puritan. They transplanted to Canadian soil that old farm-life of New England, which, by its quaint ways, has stirred so many delightful fancies in American novelists and poets. Such fire-light pictures and winter-idylls as Hawthorne and Whittier love to paint, were here to be seen of a winter evening in every snow-bound farmstead. Among the dusty heirlooms of these Township homesteads may still be found andirons that stood on early New England hearths. Burned out and fallen to ashes are the last forestick and back-log; and so are that brave old couple who, in their gray hairs, wandered into the Canadian wilderness, and, with trembling hands, hung the old crane over a new hearth.

LAKE MEMPHREMAGOG, FROM OWL'S HEAD.

A GLIMPSE FROM THE MOUNTAIN

MONTREAL

THERE is no more beautiful city on the continent of America than the commercial metropolis of the Dominion of Canada. The geographical features of the place at once suggest a city. Ocean-going steamers can navigate the river St. Lawrence no farther inland, but here where insuperable difficulties stop navigation, nature has made it possible for human skill to produce a magnificent harbour. Lying between the

MONTREAL FROM THE MOUNTAIN.

river and Mount Royal, rarely has it been the good fortune of any city to have so fine a background. The flat part, situated at the base by the river side, makes it easy for business; the sloping sides of the mountain are intended, perhaps, to meet the modern idea that prosperity shall build in the west end, and abundance in some overlooking heights. That which was natural happened; the city has extended westward and along the mountain side—that is to say, wealth used its undoubted right to erect its dwelling-places up the river where the water is clear, and up the mountain where the air is pure.

Reaching the city by way of the St. Lawrence, the eye rests upon a scene of rare beauty; three miles of river frontage turned into wharves; shipping of every kind and description, from the enormous steamship to the tiny pleasure yacht; back of that, long lines of warehouses; then, great public and private buildings, church spires and towers asserting their right to be higher than all other structures, and thus bid the busy world pause at times and look up. But the finest view of the city can be had from the mountain.

L'ESCALIER.

The top is reached by a winding path or, if the traveller choose, by steps suggestive of lungs and nerves, and a swimming head and death by falling. The view from the summit, however, is well worth the climb, whichever way may be chosen. The city lies at the base; the majestic St. Lawrence may be traced for miles. Just opposite it is spanned by the great Victoria Bridge, one mile and three-quarters long, built by Stephenson and Brunel, and opened by the Prince of Wales in 1861. Beyond the river is a vast stretch of land absolutely flat, bounded by ranges of hills among which, conspicuous, rise the twin mountains of St. Hilaire.

Montreal abounds with striking contrasts. The city is comparatively small— less than one hundred and fifty thousand inhabitants—as what was called "the census" has declared. It has had only one or two hundred years of history; and yet everything is here—the antique and the modern—while hostile oddities lie cheek-by-jowl on every hand. Here are frame houses, some of them scarcely better than an Irishman's hovel on his native bog, and ignorance and squalour and dirt; close at hand are great streets of great houses, all of fine-cut stone. Here are thousands of French who cannot speak one word of English, and thousands of English who cannot speak one word of French. Unthrift and thrift come along the same thoroughfares. Some are content with a bare existence and some are not content with colossal fortunes. In social life we have the old French families with their Old World refinement pressed upon and almost pushed out of existence by the loud manners of the *nouveaux riches*. The older houses have their heirlooms of gold trinkets and silver plate; the new houses have their art galleries of elaborate picture-frames, the meanest of which would honour Cellini, and gladden the eyes and heart of a solid Manchester man.

We have the same striking contrasts in the appearance of the people on the streets. Here are unmistakable descendants of the ancient Iroquois Indians; at a turn we come upon a company who, by their dress and talk, take us back to the peasant classes of older France; while crowding everywhere are ladies and gentlemen of the most approved modern type, according to the fashions of London, Paris, and New York. The business of the place shows the same quaint differences. At one market we are in an exclusively agricultural district; there is nothing to suggest a ship, a warehouse, or a factory; buyers and sellers are country people with country ways, except that now and then a lady from the more aristocratic parts ventures to go a-marketing in the interests of economy. Our illustration represents what may be seen in one of the principal squares of the city on a market day. All the streets round the Bonsecours Market are crowded with carts filled with country produce, and the overflow finds its way into Jacques Cartier Square. The horses feeding peacefully as they would beside a country hostelry, primitive carts and harness, the *habitant* piously committing his horse or his basket to the care of God while he slips into the old church to say a prayer, are not the pictures one expects to find in a great city

COMMISSIONERS WHARF, AND BONSECOURS MARKET.

BONSECOURS CHURCH.

in the restless New World. A very little way to the west, you are in a different latitude. Signs of commerce and modern taste and industrial life abound. Here is a corner where we look into Victoria Square. The crowded streets, the magnificent cut-stone shops, hotels and warehouses, the well-appointed hall and rooms of the Young Men's Christian Association—the oldest Association of the kind in America,—the beautiful Kirk, Salisbury Cathedral in miniature, the bronze statue of the Queen by Marshall Wood, all reflect the nineteenth century. What surprises the visitor is the sharp distinction so long maintained. The new does not shoulder the ancient out of the way—does not even modify it. They move along parallel lines, neither affecting the other. There is no fusion of races in commer-

MARKET SCENES IN JACQUES CARTIER SQUARE.

McGILL STREET.

cial, social or political life; the differences are sharply defined, and appear to be permanent. It must be confessed that this adds to the interest of the city, and enables the curious to study human life and work under a variety of aspects. But we must turn now to a closer description of people and places and their history.

The history of Montreal is an eventful one, and full of interest. The site was first visited by Jacques Cartier, the discoverer of Canada, on the 2d October, 1535. The Algonquin village of twelve hundred inhabitants was then named Hochelaga, and the Frenchman was well received, supplies of fish and maize being freely offered in return for beads, knives, small mirrors and crucifixes. Hochelaga was, even in those days, a centre of importance, having eight or ten settlements subject to it. Nothing more was heard of it, however, till 1611, when Champlain left Quebec for Hochelaga, with the intention of establishing there a trading-station. Temporary structures were erected, ground was cleared and seeds were sown, in order to test the fertility of the soil. Before returning to Quebec, Champlain held conferences with many Indians—Hurons and Algonquins—who had come to meet him in the neighbourhood of the present Lachine Rapids. Two years later, Champlain visited Hochelaga again, and pushed forward up the river Ottawa as far as Lake Nipissing. It was not, however, till 1640 that a permanent establishment was attempted on the island of Montreal. In that year a society, designated "La Compagnie de Montreal," was formed in Paris for the promotion of religion in the colony. This Company consisted of about thirty persons of wealth, who proposed to build a regular town and protect it against the Indians by means of fortifications. Maisonneuve, a distinguished and pious soldier from Champagne, was chosen to lead the expedition and direct the Company. The sanction of the King of France having been obtained, priests and families were sent out, and on the 17th of May, 1642, Villemarie was solemnly consecrated. The spot chosen for the ceremony was near the foot of the mountain.

Maisonneuve was a great man, knightly in bearing, brave as a lion and devout as a monk. Among his most efficient colleagues was d'Aillebout, who was subsequently twice Governor of New France. During the first few years the colony of Villemarie barely managed to subsist, being constantly exposed to the incursions of Indians. On one occasion, in 1652, a small band of Frenchmen defeated a body of two hundred Iroquois in the immediate neighbourhood of Montreal. The following year Maisonneuve returned from France with three vessels and upwards of a hundred soldiers. In 1663, an important event occurred, the "Company of Montreal" having sold their rights to the Seminary of Montreal, who have ever since been the seigniors of the island and associated with every incident of its history. In 1672 the population of Montreal had reached the figure of 1500, and a few years later the place began to be laid out into streets within a quadrangular space surrounded by a wall. About the same time the village of Laprairie, on the opposite side of the river, was founded by a number of converted Iroquois, and later they migrated a little farther up to Caughnawaga, where their descendants survive to this day.

The Iroquois were the allies of the English of the New England Colonies and the Dutch on the Hudson, as the Hurons were of the French of Canada; and the wars between these two savage nations naturally involved their white friends. In 1690 an expedition, consisting of two hundred French and Indians, set out from Montreal on snow-shoes, and fell upon a Dutch settlement at Schenectady, putting all therein to fire and sword. In retaliation, a force of thirteen hundred men, under General Winthrop and Major Schuyler, was equipped for a movement upon Montreal, by the way of Lake Champlain, while a fleet was dispatched against Quebec under the command of Sir William Phipps. The former accomplished nothing, owing to the difficulties of the march, and were easily repulsed; while the defeat of the latter by Frontenac is one of the most brilliant pages of the history of New France. In 1700-01 a great peace was concluded at Montreal between the Iroquois on the one hand, and the Hurons, Ottawas, Abnakis, and Algonquins on the other. This did not prevent works of defence being carried on, and in 1722 a low stone wall was erected, with bastions and outlets, extending all around the town. The population of Montreal at that time was three thousand. The fortifications, however, were available only against the Indians, and were not calculated to withstand artillery, as the events of fifty years later clearly proved. In 1760, after the fall of Quebec and the unsuccessful attempt of Lévis to recover that stronghold, Montreal became the last station of French power in America, and it is therefore indissolubly connected with the closing events of the Conquest. The British plan of campaign was to hem Montreal in from every side. With that view, General Murray moved up from Quebec, while Colonel Haviland advanced his army, composed of three thousand regulars and provincials, with a small body of Indians, from Crown Point on Lake Champlain, and up the Richelieu. On his side Sir Jeffrey Amherst, the Commander-in-Chief, set out from Albany and passed through the Iroquois country, now the State of New York, as far as Oswego, where he took boats to transport his men across the lower part of Lake Ontario and down the St. Lawrence. When he reached Lachine, Haviland had already occupied the south shore of the river opposite the city, and Murray was master of the territory extending to the foot of the island. Lévis had fired his last musket, Vaudreuil had exhausted all his diplomacy, and there only remained to be enacted the final scene of Capitulation whereby the fairest colony of France was transferred to Great Britain. It has never been definitely ascertained at what particular spot this impressive historical event took place. Most historians locate it at the Château de Ramezay, on Notre Dame Street, the official residence of Marquis de Vaudreuil, Governor and Lieutenant-General. There is a local tradition, however, that the Articles of Surrender were signed in a small frame house, on the Cote des Neiges road, behind the mountain, which was unfortunately destroyed by fire only a few years ago. It is not necessary to trace the general history of the city from this point of the Conquest down to our day. It will suffice to say that from 1760 to 1810, Montreal was little better than a frontier outpost, and an emporium of the trade of peltries with the Indians. In the succeeding decade, the North-West was explored by a number of hardy adventurers—the Selkirks, MacTavishes and others penetrated into the wilderness; the North-West Company multiplied its stations throughout the Red River valley, and Montreal became the headquarters of all these mighty traders. There are episodes in this period of the history of Montreal, up to 1830, which have the charm of romance, reminding one of its ancient days. The famous *voyageurs* and *coureurs de bois* are indissolubly associated with the city. All the canoes that went up the Ottawa, thence to French River and Georgian Bay, to Lake Superior and on through innumerable portages, to Lake of the Woods and the Winnipeg River and Lake to Fort Garry, set out from the village of Lachine, it is true, but they were all laden with Montreal freight and propelled by the stalwart arms of Montreal oarsmen. Then came the great development of the lumber trade, which gave additional importance to Montreal and increased its wealth. This trade brought the whole back country of the Upper Ottawa into commercial union with the city, and the profitable connection has continued down to the present time. Toward 1840, steamboat navigation was introduced, first from Montreal to Quebec, and afterwards from Montreal to the principal towns of Upper Canada. This was the dawn of the era which was gradually to enlarge into the system of railways and steamships whereby the standard position of Montreal as one of the chief cities of the continent was permanently assured.

It is easy to trace the two main divisions of the population of Montreal. Taking St. Lawrence Main Street as a dividing line, all that is east of it is French, and all that is west of it is English-speaking. The two nationalities scarcely overlap this conventional barrier, except in a few isolated cases. And other external characteristics of the French population are as distinct as their language. The houses are less pretentious, though quite comfortable, and there is a general absence of ornament or of surrounding plantations. The extreme eastern portion is designated the Quebec suburbs, and there the native people can be studied as easily as in the rural villages, from which the majority hail. They are an honest, hard-working race, very gay and courteous, and of primitive simplicity of life. Their thrift is remarkable, and they manage to subsist on one half of what would hardly satisfy the needs of people of other nationalities. The old folks speak little or no English, but it is different with the rising generation. These use the two languages indifferently, and herein possess a marked advantage over the English, Scotch and Irish. Within late years also, they have learned to husband their resources. They have in their midst a flourishing branch of the City and District Savings Bank, a number of building societies and two or three benevolent guilds. Their poor are cared for by the St. Vincent de Paul Association, which has several ramifications, and the Union St. Joseph is devoted to the relief of artisans during life, and of their families after death.

There is a great deal of hoarded wealth among the French inhabitants, but as a rule they do not invest it freely. They have among them some of the richest men in the city who, however, are modest in their wants, and make no display either in the way of sumptuous mansions or gaudy equipages. Although extremely hospitable and fond of society, they are not in the habit of giving balls or fancy entertainments, their evenings being spent mostly in mutual visits, where a quiet game of cards

MOUNTAIN DRIVE.

predominates. As in Paris so in Montreal, it is not easy to obtain access into the inner French circles; but once initiated, the stranger is agreeably surprised at the amount of grace and culture which he meets. It is a current mistake that higher education is uncommon among these people. The gift of conversation is almost universal; the best topics of art and literature are freely discussed, and ladies are familiar with political questions.

The western part of the city is English. By this term is meant all those whose vernacular is our mother-tongue. Numerically, the English portion is not so great as the Scotch, who unquestionably take the lead in commerce, finance and public enterprise generally. In perhaps no section of the Colonies have Englishmen and Scotchmen made more of their opportunities than in Montreal. There is an air of prosperity about all their surroundings which at once impresses the visitor. Taken all in all, there is perhaps no wealthier city area in the world than that comprised between Beaver Hall Hill and the foot of Mount Royal, and between the parallel lines of Dorchester and Sherbrooke Streets in the West End. Sherbrooke Street is scarcely surpassed by the Fifth Avenue of New York in the magnificence of its buildings. The grounds include demesne and park, the charms of the country amid the rush and roar of a great commercial centre. In winter the equipages present a most attractive spectacle. It has been said that in this respect only St. Petersburg can claim precedence over Montreal. A favourite drive on a Saturday afternoon in winter is from Victoria Square to Nelson's Column and back, the sumptuous sleighs of every description, drawn by high-steppers, and bearing lovely women ensconced in the richest furs of the Canadian forest, following each other in endless succession. There is also a winter driving club, which periodically starts from the iron gates of McGill College and glides like the wind along the country roads to a hospitable rendezvous at Sault aux Récollet, Lachine or Longue Pointe, where a bounteous repast and a "hop" are provided. The return home under the moon and stars is the most enjoyable feature of the entertainment, and many a journey through life has been initiated by these exhilarating drives.

The extreme south-western portion of the city is occupied almost exclusively by the Irish population. It is called Griffintown, from a man of that name who first settled there and leased a large tract of ground from the Grey Nuns for ninety-nine years. Over sixty years of this lease have already expired, so that in about twenty-five or thirty years the ground rent of this immense section will revert to the nuns. Griffintown comprises a little world within itself—shops, factories, schools, academies, churches and asylums. The Irish population of Montreal take a high stand in business, politics and society. They number in their ranks many successful merchants and large capitalists, and have leading representatives in all the learned professions.

The island of Montreal is the most fertile area in the Province of Quebec, and is specially renowned for its fruit, the *Pomme Grise*, queen of russets, and the incomparable *Fameuse*, growing with a perfection obtainable nowhere else. It is thickly settled, being studded with thriving villages and rich farms. It is about thirty miles long and ten broad, and is formed by the confluence of the Ottawa with the St. Lawrence at Ste. Anne's, in the western extremity, and by the meeting of the same rivers at Bout de l'Isle, on the eastern verge. The Ottawa behind the island is called Rivière des Prairies by the French, while the English have adopted the more prosaic title of Back River. About the middle of its course is a rapid known as Sault aux Récollet, so called from a Récollet missionary who perished there in the days of the Iroquois.

The city is bountifully provided with summer resorts and retreats within easy distance by rail and river. Lachine and Ste. Anne's have long been favourites among these, being admirably fitted by nature for boating and fishing purposes. They contain many charming villas and country houses. St. Lambert, immediately opposite the city, is growing in estimation from year to year. An old stopping-place is Longueuil, a little below St. Lambert, which has long had a considerable English colony, and is still a favourite resort in summer. No institution pays so well as the Longueuil Ferry, for a great deal of the traffic from the fertile counties of Chambly and Laprairie comes by it to the city. The quiet bay in front of the village is the roadstead for the craft of the Longueuil Yacht Club, whose record stands high in aquatic annals. Within an hour's ride is Chambly, situate on a basin of the same name, which forms part of the beautiful Richelieu River. Directly opposite tower the basaltic pillars of Belœil Mountain, one of the most picturesque spots in Canada, on whose summit a lovely

THE LONGUEUIL FERRY.

lake mirrors the sky—a spot resorted to by scores of families whose heads are able to come and go, to and from the city, without detriment to their business.

In the way of parks and pleasure-grounds Montreal is singularly fortunate. There is a Mountain Park and an Island Park, both of which may fairly claim to be unrivalled. The former cost the city nearly half a million of dollars, but is well worth the money. The drive round it is a favourite afternoon recreation for citizens and visitors. It ascends from the south-eastern base of Mount Royal, by curves that are sometimes like corkscrews, to the highest altitude, whence a magnificent panorama is outspread, including the whole island of Montreal, the fair Richelieu peninsula, the blue waters of Lake Champlain, and the undulating line of the Green Mountains of Vermont. Our illustration on page 149 shows the Nuns' Island above the Victoria bridge, a beautiful islet that owes its name to its ownership. This Mountain Park is

MONTREAL FROM ST. HELEN'S ISLAND.

THE ISLAND PARK.

still in its native ruggedness, and it will take years before it is completed, according to a scientific plan embracing tracts of landscape-gardening, relieved by spaces of woodland, glade and primeval forest. It is intended also to have preserves for game and wild animals. The Island Park is St. Helen's Island, in the middle of the river, and in it, within reach of sling or arquebuse, Montreal possesses a pleasure resort nowhere excelled. St. Helen's Island has a romantic history. Champlain's wife, Helen Bouillé, took a fancy to it, bought it with the contents of her own purse, and in return Champlain gave it her name. Later, it fell into the hands of the Le Moyne family, and became incorporated in their seigniory of Longueuil. Finally, it was purchased by the Imperial Government for military purposes, and barracks were erected thereon. After

MONTREAL: HISTORICAL AND DESCRIPTIVE

the departure of the British troops from the country, the property was passed over to the Federal Government, who leased it, on certain conditions, to the city for park purposes. Looking at it from the city one has no idea of its height in the centre. It slopes upward from the water's edge, and thus affords a capital military position, as may be seen at a glance in our illustration of the Old Battery. The same feature makes it one of the best possible points from which to get a view of the city, especially of the harbour and long-extended line of wharves and docks, with the mountain towering up in the back-

OLD BATTERY, ST. HELEN'S ISLAND.

ground. In the fall of 1760, the island was the scene of a dramatic incident. The Chevalier de Lévis, who defeated Murray at the battle of Ste. Foye in the summer of that year, and would have recaptured Quebec and retrieved the disaster of the Plains of Abraham, had not a British fleet suddenly arrived under the shadow of Cape Diamond, was obliged to retreat towards Montreal, whither he was soon followed by Murray and Amherst. The French had to bow to the inevitable, and Vaudreuil signed the articles of capitulation. Meantime Lévis, who had retired to St. Helen's Island, sent a flag of truce to Murray, to request the surrender of his troops with the honours of war. For some inexplicable reason this demand was not granted, and the high-minded Frenchman construed the denial into an insult. When the shadows of night had fallen, and the foliage of the great trees intensified the darkness, he gathered his men in the centre of the island around a pyre of blazing wood. At the word of command the colours were trooped, the staffs broken, and the whole thrown into the fire, while the drums beat to arms, and the veterans cried "Vive la France!" with the anguish of despair. The next morning the remnant of the French army filed before their conquerors and piled their arms, but never a shred of the white flag was there, to deepen their humiliation.

Chief among the public squares and gardens of Montreal, in size and in historic interest, is the Champ de Mars. In 1812, the citadel or mound on the present site of Dalhousie Square was demolished, and the earth of which it was composed was carried over and strewn upon the Champ de Mars. This fact, within the memory of the oldest inhabitants, has led some people to suppose that the Field of Mars dates only from that comparatively late period. Such, however, is not the fact. No doubt the dumping of so much new earth, with proper levelling and rolling, was a great improvement; but the site and general outlines of the ground itself belong to a higher antiquity. The Champ was a scene of promenade in the old French days, and many is the golden sunset that fired the leafy cylinders of its Lombardy poplars, as beaux, with peaked hats and purple doublets, sauntered under their graceful ranks in the company of short-skirted damsels. The chief glory of the Champ de Mars is its military history. With the single exception of the Plains of Abraham, there is no other piece of ground in America which has been successively trodden by the armies of so many different nations in martial array. First, it witnessed the evolutions of the blue-coated Frenchmen—probably such historical regiments as those of Carignan and Rousillon—and its sands were crunched by the hoofs of chargers that bore Montcalm and Lévis. Then the serried ranks of red-coats paraded from the days of Murray and Carleton. It were worth while to know how many regiments of the British army have, at one time or another, turned out on the Champ de Mars. Next, for about six months, the ground was used by

> "The cocked-hat Continentals,
> In their ragged regimentals;"

many of whom went forth therefrom to defeat and death under the cliffs at Quebec, with the heroic Montgomery. And now it is the parade-ground of our Canadian Volunteers. The illustration gives us a specimen of the Victoria Rifles, one of Montreal's crack regiments. The buildings shown are the rear of the Hôtel de Ville and of the Court House; then the twin towers of the parish church, which are seen from almost every point of view; and next to them the side of the modest little Presbyterian Church called St. Gabriel's, which is given below in its full dimensions. This is the oldest

THE CHAMP DE MARS.

Protestant Church standing in Montreal, and long may it stand, for it preserves the memory of Christian courtesies between three leading Christian communions. While the church was being built, the good old Récollet Fathers offered the congregation the use of their chapel to worship in. The sturdy Scotchmen accepted the offer, and when they moved into their own kirk presented the Fathers with a hogshead of Canary wine and two boxes of candles. Subsequently, when the Anglican church was burnt, the Presbyterians—doubtless remembering how they had been indebted to others—came forward promptly and put St. Gabriel's at the entire disposal of the Anglicans for the half of every

150 FRENCH CANADIAN LIFE AND CHARACTER

FROM THE TOWERS OF NOTRE DAME, OVERLOOKING THE PLACE D'ARMES.

Sunday, until their church could be rebuilt. This offer was accepted as graciously as it was made, and thus St. Gabriel's is, in itself, a monument equal in interest to anything in Montreal.

Historically, the Place d'Armes is even more interesting. As it stands at present, there are few more charming spots in Canada, framed in as it is by the Corinthian portico of the Montreal Bank, the Ionic colonnade of the City Bank—now the buildings of the Canada Pacific Railway Company—and the towers of Notre Dame. Our view is taken from Notre Dame, so that we get only a portion of the Place d'Armes; but while we lose part of the Place, we gain a glimpse of the city as a whole, extending away to the foot of the mountains. Next to the Bank of Montreal, with its beautiful portico, stands the Post Office. Between it and the mountains the most prominent buildings are St. Mary's College and the Church of the *Gesu*, which attracts Protestants to its services by good music. Farther west the unshapely pile of St. Patrick's Cathedral bulks largely on the slope of Beaver Hall. The garden of the Place d'Armes is very beautiful in summer, with its young trees and central pyramidal fountain; but in winter it is invested with a particular glory—for the place is the coldest spot in Montreal at all seasons of the year—the north-west winds streaming from the mountain in that direction as through a Colorado cañon. Its history goes back to the early history of the city. In 1643 and 1644, the Colony of Villemarie—the beautiful ancient name of Montreal - was practically in a state of siege, owing to the incursions of Indians. The noble Maisonneuve kept on the defensive for a time, until he was remonstrated with, and several of his more influential followers openly charged him with cowardice. This stirred his martial spirit; he determined on changing his tactics. With a train of dogs accustomed to scent the trail of the Iroquois, and at the head of thirty armed men, he marched out in the direction of the mountain, where he was met by upwards of two hundred savages, who fell upon him and compelled his forces to retreat. Maisonneuve formed the rear-guard. With a pistol in each hand, he walked slowly back, and never halted until he reached the present site of the Place d'Armes. There, when the French had repulsed the foe and gathered their dead and wounded, they understood both the valour of their commandant and the wisdom of remaining behind the shelter of their fortifications.

There is no city in America which has a greater number of public institutions of an ecclesiastical, educational, or charitable character. Chief among these is the Church of Notre Dame, the largest edifice of the kind in America, except the Cathedral of Mexico. At the founding of Villemarie, a temporary chapel of bark was built on "Pointe á Calliére," which was used until the following year, when a wooden structure was raised on the same spot. In 1654, this chapel becoming too small, M. de Maisonneuve suggested the construction of a more commodious church adjoining the hospital in St. Paul Street, on the spot where stands to-day the block of stores belonging to the Hôtel Dieu. Service was held there for upwards of twenty years. In 1672, the foundations of a more spacious edifice were laid in the Place d'Armes, and the church was completed in 1678. This lasted till 1823, when the present temple was devised, which, on the 15th June, 1829, was opened for public worship under the auspices of Mgr. Lartigue, first R. C. Bishop of Montreal. The pile was intended to be a representative of its namesake, Notre Dame, of Paris. Its towers are 227 feet

ENTRANCE TO NOTRE DAME.

in height, and contain a peal of eleven bells, unrivalled on this continent. The "Gros Bourdon" of the western tower is numbered among the five heaviest bells in the world. It was cast in London, weighs 24,780 pounds, is six feet high, and at its mouth measures eight feet seven inches in diameter. The nave of the church, including the sanctuary, is 220 feet in length, nearly 80 feet in height, 69 in width, exclusive of the side aisles, which measure 25½ feet each, and the walls are five feet thick. The church is capable of holding 12,000, and on extraordinary occasions, when chairs are used, 15,000 persons. The twin towers of Notre Dame stand out to every traveller as one of the notable landmarks of Montreal.

Other churches are so numerous that Montreal, like Brooklyn, has been denominated the City of Churches. Christ Church Cathedral, on St. Catherine Street, stands deservedly first. It is a gem of Gothic architecture, not surpassed by Grace Church, of New York. It is built of limestone, dressed with cream-coloured sandstone, and its interior fittings are in remarkably good taste. In the grounds is a monument to the memory of Bishop Fulford, one of the most distinguished prelates that ever ruled the Church of England in Canada. The Presbyterians have noble edifices in St. Paul's and St. Andrew's.

PULPIT OF NOTRE DAME.

The Methodists, Unitarians, Congregationalists and others are well represented, while the Israelites have two synagogues. The Jesuits boast of a church which is an exact counterpart of the celebrated *Gesu*, of Rome. The spirit of ambition is strong in the Catholics. The late Bishop, Mgr. Bourget, commenced the task of erecting a *fac-simile* in miniature of St. Peter's. The architect was instructed to proceed to Rome and simply reduce St. Peter's to exactly one-third of its actual dimensions and reproduce it in that fashion in Montreal. Slowly it has been growing before the puzzled eyes of the citizens, and strangers ask with wonderment what it is, or is likely to be.

Not only are the charitable institutions of Montreal more numerous in respect to population than those of any other city on this continent, but several of them belong to a high antiquity, and are intimately connected with salient events in the history of New France. The foundation, for instance, of the Hôtel Dieu, reads like a romance. When Maisonneuve offered his services to the "Compagnie de Montreal," and was named Governor of the future colony, he was sagacious enough to understand that his scheme stood in need of a virtuous woman who would take care of the sick, and superintend the distribution of supplies. Such a person should be of heroic mould, to face the dangers and privations of the wilderness. What gold could not purchase, Providence supplied in the person of a young woman—Jeanne Mance, daughter of a *procureur du roi*, near Lamoges, in Champagne—who was impelled by an irresistible *vocation* to the missions of New France. Queen Anne, of Austria, and several distinguished ladies of the Court, apprised of her merit and extraordinary resolution, encouraged her in her design; and Madame Bouillon, a distinguished lady of that period, placed means at her disposal for the establishment of an hospital. In the summer of 1641, two vessels sailed from La Rochelle, one bearing Maisonneuve, a priest and twenty-five men—the other carrying Mademoiselle Mance, a missionary and twelve men. The winter was spent at Sillery, near Quebec. On the opening of navigation in 1642, a small flotilla, consisting of two barges, a pinnace and another boat, moved up the solitary highway of the St. Lawrence, and on the 18th May possession was taken of Montreal by the celebration of a solemn mass. The two principal persons who figured at the ceremony were Maisonneuve and Mademoiselle Mance; and thus it happened that a woman assisted in the founding of this great city.

Another community has long been identified with the history of Montreal. The mission of the Grey Nuns is to assist the poor, visit the sick, educate the orphan, and enfold with maternal arms the nameless and homeless foundling. There is no charity more beautiful than theirs, and hence their popularity with Protestants as well as Catholics. The Order was founded by Madame de Zanille, a Canadian lady, belonging to the distinguished families of Varennes and Boucher de Boucherville. The old convent stood for many years on Foundling Street—named thus in its honour—opposite Ste. Anne's Market,—but had to make way for the encroachments of trade, and has since been transferred to magnificent buildings on Guy Street. The Grey Nuns have spread over the Province, and have numerous representatives in the north-west, as far even as the Upper Saskatchewan.

In the noble work of charity, the Protestant population, although numerically far inferior, has more than held its own. Notwithstanding the amplitude of its accommodation, the General Hospital was not found sufficiently large, and a good citizen, Major Mills, established another in the extreme west end, whence it derives its name of the Western Hospital. It has been said that charity differs from trade in this, that whereas the latter is always in direct ratio of supply to demand, the former reverses the rule; and the more it expands its resources, the more it finds objects of misery to relieve. The principle has held good in the case of the Western Hospital, which has been crowded from its opening day.

In 1863 a number of leading citizens, realizing the necessity of a peculiar asylum of help for the Protestant poor and unfortunate—especially the aged and feeble, who had no means of livelihood—raised upwards of $80,000, with which they laid the foundations of the institution called the Protestant House of Refuge and Industry. The dual character of the population, elsewhere referred to, has made necessary a double set of asylums for Protestants and Catholics, which accounts for the extraordinary number of these institutions, as compared with the total number of inhabitants.

GATEWAY OF THE SEMINARY OF ST. SULPICE.

IN THE CHAPEL OF GREY NUNNERY.

Chief among the educational establishments of Montreal is McGill University, whose history embraces several features that deserve consideration. Hon. James McGill, who was born at Glasgow in 1744, and died at Montreal in 1813, by his last will and testament devised the estate of Burnside, containing forty-seven acres of land, and bequeathed a large sum of money for the purposes of this foundation. The University was erected by Royal Charter in 1821, and reorganized by an amended Charter in 1852. Its

CITY HALL, AND NELSON'S MONUMENT.

endowments, exhibitions and scholarships are already respectable. The Molson Chair of English Language and Literature, the Peter Redpath Chair of Natural History, the Logan Chair of Geology, the John Frothingham Chair of Mental and Moral Philosophy, have each an endowment of $20,000. Students attend McGill not only from every Province of the Dominion, but from the United States. It counts among its professors some distinguished scholars, notably Dr. Dawson, the Principal, whose scientific reputation is world-wide. Among the affiliated institutions are Morrin College, Quebec; St. Francis College, Richmond; the Congregational College of British North America; the Presbyterian College of Montreal; the Diocesan College of Montreal, and the Wesleyan College of Montreal. Under the regulations for the establishment of Normal Schools in the Province of Quebec, the Superintendent of Education is empowered to associate with himself, for the direction of one of these schools, the corporation of McGill University. In accordance with this arrangement, the Provincial Protestant Normal School is affiliated with McGill, and for the past quarter of a century has trained teachers, especially for the Protestant population of the Province. The Model Schools attached to the institution are three in number—one for boys, one

ANCIENT TOWERS AT MONTREAL COLLEGE.

for girls, and a primary. These schools are capable of accommodating about three hundred pupils; are supplied with the best furniture and apparatus; and are conducted on the most approved methods of teaching. They receive pupils from the age of six and upwards, and give a thorough English education. There are two high schools—one for boys and another for girls—largely attended.

Montreal College and St. Mary's College are Roman Catholic institutions. The former occupies a magnificent site on Sherbrooke Street, at the foot of the mountain, and the building is probably the largest single and continuous pile in America. This institution has been intimately associated with the history of Montreal for over a hundred years. It is under the control of the Seminary of St. Sulpice, who were made seigniors of the Island of Montreal and its environs by Royal Letters Patent, in 1640. The Theological Department is specially remarkable, and has been the nursery of priests and missionaries for more than a century. Its students are from all parts. Chief among the objects of interest connected with the college are the two round towers near the gates, which tradition traces back to the early days of the colony, when they were built as outposts of defence against the red men. These towers are kept in a perfect state of preservation, as memorials of those ancient days of peril.

St. Mary's College, on Bleury Street, is under the direction of the Jesuit Fathers, and their boast is that it is second to none of their establishments on this continent, which is saying a great deal when one is acquainted with such old and successful colleges as those of Fordham, N. Y., Georgetown, D. C., and St. Louis, Mo. Their celebrated *Ratio Studiorum* is carried out to the letter, and the results deserve attention, because the methods are so different from those in vogue in our day. There is tone and style in everything connected with St. Mary's College. Strangers are received with the utmost courtesy, whether they visit the institution itself or the adjoining Church of the *Gesu*, to see its relics of saints and its frescoes.

A second Normal School for the French and Catholics, under the patronymic of Jacques Cartier, was located from its foundation in the old Government House at Chateau Ramezay, opposite the City Hall, but has since been transferred to palatial quarters on an eminence at the East End. The management is almost wholly ecclesiastical, the Principal being Abbé Verreau, distinguished as an historian and antiquarian. The Catholic Commercial Academy, off St. Catherine Street, is the only institution of the kind in the Province which is altogether under the control of laymen, and from all accounts it has met with complete success.

The Art Association of Montreal was incorporated in 1858, but for many years it had but a languid existence. The late Bishop Fulford did much to encourage its members, but the credit of having placed the society on a permanent footing is due to Benaiah Gibb, who left property, money, and a number of paintings from his own collection, to form a gallery. A suitable building has been erected in Phillips' Square, and the art gallery was recently opened by His Excellency the Marquis of Lorne and H. R. H. the Princess Louise.

While little has been done for art, less has been done for libraries. The Mechanics' Institute has a collection of books, but not at all adequate to the wants of so large a population. A movement is at present on foot, tending to the establishment of a public library commensurate with the size, wealth and culture of the city. In truth, money was left by the late Mr. Fraser, to build and furnish a public library, but for some mysterious reason, the library is still *in posse*. The Institut Canadien flourished

CHRIST CHURCH CATHEDRAL, FROM PHILLIPS' SQUARE.

for many years with a good library and reading-room, but it has of late fallen into disuse, and its books have been advertised for sale.

But Montreal is more interested in outdoor sports and in organizing amusement clubs than in art. The Victoria skating club, whose famous rink on Drummond Street was one of the first erected on this continent, has been the scene of many brilliant fancy-dress entertainments, which Royalty and nobility have graced. Those "carnivals" on the ice were first instituted here, and have since become popular elsewhere. There are three curling clubs—the Caledonia, Montreal and Thistle—with a Canadian branch of the Royal Caledonian curling club of Scotland. The Montreal curling club was founded in 1807, and ranks high in the annals of the "roarin' game." Snow-shoeing has been reduced to an art. The parent club, the "Montreal," is perhaps the most prosperous corporate body of the kind in the city. The costume is singularly picturesque—white flannel coat and leggings, blue cap with tassel—from which is derived the popular name of Tuque Bleue—red sash and moccasins. There is no prettier sight than that of the club meeting at the McGill College gates, moving up the flank of the mountain to the "Pines," and then gliding to the rendezvous at the Club House, at Outremont. The memorable torchlight procession over this route to the hospitable villa of Thornbury, made in honour of Lord Dufferin, in 1873, was a fairy spectacle which will never be forgotten by those who witnessed it. Every winter there is a sweepstakes over the mountain, a day devoted to games and races, and several tramps across country to a distance of twenty-five or thirty miles. Lacrosse is the "national game" of Canada, and in that character it had its birth in Montreal. Four or five years ago, a select team made the tour of England, and had the honour of playing before Her Majesty at Windsor. The Indian clubs of Caughnawaga and St. Regis always take part in the games, but they have long lost the supremacy which they enjoyed for centuries. There is also a golf club, established in 1873, under the auspices of the Earl of Dufferin; a bicycle club, foot-ball club, and a chess club, which numbers among its members some of the strongest and most brilliant players in the country; an active and energetic club for the protection of fish and game, as well as a society for the prevention of cruelty to animals; two gymnasia, and a McGill College athletic club, whose annual games recall many feats of skill and strength. Boating is also a favourite pastime, and there are three large yacht clubs—the Montreal, Longueuil and Lachine. A regatta in Hochelaga Basin, with the prow of the graceful little vessels steering straight as a needle for the twin spires of Varennes Church, is as pretty a sight as one could wish to see.

The turning-point in the business history of Montreal was in 1850 or thereabouts, when it suddenly manifested a tendency to expand. That change was mainly due to two causes—the Allan Line of Steamships and the Grand Trunk Railway. This leads us to speak of the shipping and the carrying-trade from the interior to the seaboard, and *vice versa*. The geographical position of the city is of course exceptional; but in order to make the most of it, it was necessary to obviate the difficulty presented by the Lachine Rapids to up-stream navigation. The only way to do that was to turn the rapids by a canal. The Sulpicians understood this as far back as 1700, when they opened a sluice, 2½ feet deep, by the River St. Pierre to Montreal, and used boats therein. In 1821 public-spirited citizens, led by Hon. John Richardson, resolved to enlarge this primitive boat canal into a barge canal. Richardson wanted it to extend from Lachine to

MONTREAL: HISTORICAL AND DESCRIPTIVE

STEAMER PASSING LOCKS, AND UNLOADING SHIPS BY ELECTRIC LIGHT.

Hochelaga, so as to avoid the current opposite the fort of St. Helen's Island and Isle Ronde, and thus make Hochelaga the real port, as Nature intended it to be, seeing that in its majestic basin the fleets of the world might moor in safety. But the opposition of interested parties thwarted this vast design, and the canal was dug only to Windmill Point, its present terminus, a distance of 8½ miles. The work was commenced in 1821 and completed in 1825. But there was more to come, because more was needed. The barge canal was not sufficient, and must give way to a ship canal. The widening began in 1843 and continued till its completion in 1849, at an outlay of over $2,000,000. With the opening of these works the commercial supremacy of Montreal was secured, because it fixed the union of ocean and inland navigation. The trade, indeed, grew to such a volume that the canal was once more found inadequate, and in 1875 another enlargement was begun, at an estimated cost of $6,500,000. This is part of a gigantic scheme for the widening of the whole St. Lawrence canal system, a work whose magnitude will be understood when we remember that from the Atlantic entrance of the straits of Belle Isle, *via* the St. Lawrence and inland lakes to the head of Lake Superior, the distance is 2384 miles, and that on that route there are the Lachine, Beauharnois, Cornwall, Farran's Point, Rapide Plat, Galops and Welland Canals, the aggregate length of which is 70½ miles; and the total lockage 536¾ feet, through fifty-four locks up to Lake Erie; also, the Sault Ste. Marie Canal, built by the United States, one and one-seventeenth miles in length, with eighteen feet of lockage. These canals make Montreal the rival of New York for the grain and provision trade of the Great West and North-west. Her facilities are great, and there is every prospect of farther and speedy development. Already, we can get on board the "Bohemian," or some other large and well-appointed steamer, at the lowest dock of the Lachine Canal, and take as pleasant a summer journey up the St. Lawrence as mortal tired of the dust and heat of the city can desire; and still on by water without a break, up lake after lake, to "the city of the unsalted seas," in the heart of the Continent. Or, we can go east as safely as west. Nearly thirty years ago the first steamers of the Allan Company were sent forth, but a series of disasters well-nigh brought the enterprise to the ground. The Company persevered, however, until now they possess one of the finest and largest fleets afloat, comprising twenty-five iron and steel steamers, to say nothing of swift and powerful clippers. These vessels ply between Montreal and Liverpool, Montreal and Glasgow, Boston and Liverpool, and Boston and Glasgow. There are beside eight or ten steamship lines employed regularly in the Montreal trade—the Dominion, Beaver, Temperley, Ross, Thompson, Donaldson, Great Western, White Cross and Gulf Ports. A French line is also in near contemplation, for next season, as well as a service with Brazil. The inland navigation is perfectly supplied. We have a daily mail steamer to and from Quebec, connecting with steamers to all the watering places of the Lower St. Lawrence and the Saguenay; also a daily line to the ports of Ontario as far as Hamilton; another daily line up the Ottawa, and a number of way-boats to all the villages and towns of the St. Lawrence and Richelieu Rivers. The port is admirably provided with wharves and basins, and farther accommodation is being prepared. Indeed, the enlargement of the harbour is one of the main questions of the future, and some remarkable plans have already been submitted to the public. All the modern

MONTREAL HARBOUR

appliances for loading and unloading are employed, and the facilities for almost immediate transhipment from freight-cars to the hold of vessels are unsurpassed. Montreal was the first port in the world lighted by electricity. The result is continuous labour. The electric lights are placed at intervals of about two hundred yards, from the mouth of the Lachine Canal to Hochelaga, so that the whole harbour is lit up. The question of harbour dues has been engaging attention, and steps have been taken to make Montreal a free port. The port is governed by a Board of Commissioners, a portion of whom represent the Federal Government, another the shipping interest, and a third part the city corporation. It is impossible to conceive of a more striking contrast than that presented by the harbour in summer and in winter. Our illustration shows that part of it near the Custom House called Island Wharf. The dock here is always crowded with ocean steamers, elevators drawing grain from barges and loading them, and vessels and skiffs of all sizes—while a forest of masts and funnels extends far down the river. The scene is one of busy labour night and day. The great river sweeps past in calm majesty, with a force that no power could arrest. But the frost king comes, and everything that looks like commerce takes flight. The river is sealed fast, till another power comes with kindly influences. The spring rains and suns rot the ice, and it begins to break. Montreal is on the *qui vive* to see it start down the river. It starts, but is usually blocked at Isle Ronde, and grounds. Then it shoves, and piles up, and the lower parts of the city are flooded. To cross with a boat at such a time is not only an exciting but often a perilous undertaking, as the cakes of ice may move or turn under the men, when of course the danger is extreme even to the most skilful ice-navigators.

The Grand Trunk Railway has been for years the main artery of the commerce of the country, and Montreal is its chief terminus. Five other lines of railway centre here—the Champlain and St. Lawrence, Central Vermont, Boston and Delaware, South-Eastern, and North Shore. The North Shore (officially named the Quebec, Montreal, Ottawa and Occidental Railway) has its central station in the eastern part of the city, on the site of the old Quebec Gate Barracks, which had to be torn down in consequence, thus depriving the city of one of its most interesting historical landmarks. This railway is the property of the local government, which is said to have expended about thirteen millions in its construction, thereby creating a debt that weighs like an incubus upon the Province.

The Montreal Board of Trade was incorporated by Act of Parliament in 1842, and consists of an Executive and a Board of Arbitrators. There is also a Corn Exchange Association, incorporated in 1863, with a Committee of Management and a Board of Review. A third corporation, the Dominion Board of Trade, received its initiation mainly in Montreal, though its annual meetings have generally been held in Ottawa. Another important body is the Montreal Stock Exchange, which holds two daily sessions, forenoon and afternoon. The scene of its operations is St. François Xavier Street, which is the Wall Street of Montreal. There all the brokers have their offices, and about noon, on certain days, the sidewalks are crowded with dealers and speculators, discussing the ebb and flow of stocks, and conducting their mysterious operations. St. François Xavier is one of the oldest and narrowest streets of the city, but it affords

TRANSFERRING FREIGHT BY ELECTRIC LIGHT.

a curious ground of observation for the visitor who wishes to form an idea of the financial importance of the Canadian metropolis. When the heterogeneousness of the population is taken into account, the city government may be said to be fairly well administered. The standing trouble is the rivalry between the East and West Ends— that is, the French and English-speaking portions.

St. Urbain is another street that may be said to be on the border-land between the English and the French-speaking population of Montreal. We see it in winter

MONTREAL WINTER SCENES.

dress, the snow cleared from the sidewalks and forming parallel lines, between which traffic makes its way much more smoothly than in summer. The snow is less of an impediment to ordinary business than is dust or rain during the other seasons

NOTRE DAME, FROM ST. URBAIN STREET.

of the year. It is a decided impediment, indeed, to the progress of conflagrations, with which Montreal used to be scourged. The department, however, is now so thoroughly organized that it is almost impossible for a fire to make any headway before it is checked. The alarm system is so perfect and the brigade so disciplined, that no conflagrations on an extensive scale have taken place within the past twenty-five years. Everything is also done to protect property in case of fire. The illustration is a spirited sketch of a salvage wagon that has just come out of the

IN ST. GABRIEL STREET.

fire station on St. Gabriel Street, and is plunging along between the lines of piled-up snow, to the spot indicated by the alarm. The duty of the men is to cover up all endangered property with tarpaulins, and to be its custodians till questions of ownership and insurance are settled.

In a first visit to Montreal, by all means let the traveller approach from the water—

from up stream, down stream, or the south shore. From all three directions the view will repay him. The river itself is so fascinating in its strength of crystal purity, so overpowering in vastness and might, that it would dwarf an ordinary city. It does dwarf every other place along its banks—Quebec alone excepted. It bears, lightly as a garland, the chain of the great bridge that binds its opposite shores with multiplied links of massive granite. The green slopes of St. Helen's Island resting like a leaf on the water, the

WOOD BARGES

forest of masts and red and white funnels, the old-fashioned hay and wood barges, the long line of solidly-built revetment wall, the majestic dome of the Bonsecours Market, the twin towers of Notre Dame, palatial warehouses, graceful spires sown thick as a field, and the broad shoulders of Mount Royal uplifted in the background, make up a picture that artist, merchant, or patriot—each for his own reasons—may well delight to look upon. To persons coming from abroad, believing Canada to be a wilderness of ice and snow, the home of Indians and buffaloes, the first view is a revelation. When they drive through any of the numerous magnificent business thoroughfares, and then round the mountain, they sometimes consider what sort of a back country that must be which supplies such a river and builds up such a city, and wonder why—in the face of such grand enterprises and unrivalled progress on the part of Canadians—they have never heard of such a thing as Canadian patriotism.

Of the three water views there is none equal to that obtained on a summer afternoon or evening from the deck of a steamer coming down stream. From the time the Indian pilot is taken on board above the Lachine Rapids, all is eager expectancy on the part of passengers who have made the journey again and again, as well as in the case of tourists who are running the rapids for the first time. As we near Victoria Bridge it seems impossible that the "Corsican" can pass under, and the question is sometimes asked whether there is any arrangement for lowering the funnels. The steamer glides along; we look up and see our mistake, and then look down upon the innocent questioner. Now the crowded harbour, the city in its fresh beauty, and the mountain in all the glory of its summer vesture, are revealed. The steamer rounds up to the Commissioners' Wharf, to discharge its Quebec passengers into the huge palace floating alongside. Land here and stroll down stream before taking a cab. You soon find yourself in the heart of French-Montreal. Here are antique barges with hay, from the surrounding country, which is being unloaded into carts primitive enough for the days and the land of Evangeline. Instead of the rush of an American city, there is an air of repose and human enjoyment. The very coasters and carters pause in their work, to exchange gossip and cheery jokes. Here, again, are wood-barges that have evidently come from a greater distance. Each barge discharges part of its load at once and places it on the wharf on racks that indicate its measurement by the cord. The purchaser can thus point out exactly how much he wants, and the barge remains calmly beside the wharf till the whole cargo is sold. A few years ago, wood and hay barges were to be found in the centre of the harbour; but the increasing traffic is pushing them farther and farther down, all the way to Hochelaga. Return to the Bonsecours. The market is a great three-storey parallelogram of cut-stone, occupying a square on the river-front, and with a stately dome and cupola. It is crowded on the forenoons of market-days, when the manners of the *habitant* can be studied to best advantage. He has come to the city with the produce of his farm or garden. Quiet, patient, courteous, he waits for customers. Sometimes, these may be his own neighbours who happen to need what he has to sell, and then he puts down his price a little. Sometimes they are from the East End—French therefore—and to them he is more than amiable, and sells fairly. But the grand lady from the West End, while receiving ample politeness, must pay full price. Still, there is good feeling between the different races and, for the most part, honest dealing. Are they not citizens of a common country, even though the Ultramontane studiously characterizes those of English speech as "foreigners"? From the market, go up the lane leading to the old-fashioned church. The lane is encroached upon by little dingy eating-houses, thrown out, like buttresses, from the walls of the church. Dingy as they are, they give a

MAIL STEAMER PASSING UNDER VICTORIA BRIDGE

better cup of coffee than either steamer or more inviting-looking restaurants. You soon reach St. Paul's Street, the street that constituted the City of Montreal at first, and now, by all means, enter the favourite city church of the *habitant*. The loud colours, the tawdry gilt and general bad taste of modern Catholicism, and the elaborate upholstery of shoddy Protestantism, are alike conspicuous by their absence. The *relicros* on the walls, the altar, the antique pulpit, remind one of a seventeenth century parish church in Brittany. We are taken back to the days of Marguerite Bourgeois, who laid the foundation-stone more than two centuries ago. Baron de Fancamp gave her a small image of the Virgin, endowed with miraculous virtue, on condition that a chapel should be built for its reception. Marguerite and the people of Montreal enthusiastically complied with the condition. From that day, many a wonderful deliverance, especially of sailors, has been attributed to Our Lady of Gracious Help. The image still stands on the gable nearest the river, and within, votive offerings and memorials of deliverances almost hide the altar. An agnostic might envy the simple faith of the people, and the statesman could desire no better race to till the soil. Every true Lower Canadian loves the Bonsecours Chapel. It symbolizes, to a race that clings to the past, faith, country and fatherland. And it is the only symbol of the kind that "modern improvements" have left in Montreal. The old Récollet has been swept away. The spoilers have spoiled Quebec. And all over the Province, quaint churches beloved by the people are being replaced by huge, costly, modern structures. In the name of everything distinctively Lower Canadian, spare symbols like Varennes and the Bonsecours!

Here, beside his church and market, in the stately commercial metropolis of Canada, the white city of America, we leave the *habitant*, with cordial recognition of what he has been and is, and with all good wishes for his future.

UNLOADING HAY BARGES.

THE LOWER OTTAWA.

CANAL AND LOCKS AT LACHINE.

THE dark-brown waters of the Ottawa at their *debouchement* below the Lake of Two Mountains divide into three channels, the two smaller of which flow north respectively of Laval and of Montreal Island, while the third and most considerable in size expands into Lake St. Louis, one of the largest lakes on the St. Lawrence. We are about to trace the course of the "Grand River" from the commercial to the political metropolis of Canada, through a region no less rich in historic associations than in its inexhaustible beauty of scenery, unchanged in the picturesque wildness of river, hill and wood, since Champlain, first of white men, adventured to explore its sombre waters; and yet, embellished with all the tokens of modern civilization and progress, its waters controlled by machinery that can lock or loose its forces, and spanned by huge viaducts through which the locomotive thunders; and farther on, as we ascend its current, directed by the skill and toil of civilized man into an open, navigable stream from city to city, its shores enriched with all that betokens agricultural plenty, while quaint church-towers and tastefully-decorated villas give the charm of human interest to scenes of such varied natural beauty.

From the wharf at Montreal we take the steamer which is to carry us up the Ottawa to our destination at the Capital. We proceed for the first eight and a half miles along the Lachine Canal amid scenery tranquil and uneventful as that of a Dutch village. Along the level banks are occasional trees and houses, whose general appearance is scarcely such as to indicate the neighbourhood of Canada's wealthiest city. Before us the canal extends mathematically straight, for the most part on a higher level than the surrounding fields, so that sometimes we can peep into the top-storey windows of the houses as we pass. Every now and then we are delayed by a lock, of which we encounter five on our way to Lachine. First the lock-gates are closed upon our steamer; then machinery is set at work which admits the water from the higher level; seething and tossing, the flood bears us up; the gates are once more opened, and after a delay of some twenty minutes we pass on. We meet endless fleets of barges, some towed by horses, some by propellors, all kinds and varieties of steamers, passenger-boats, barges, and tugs "of low degree;" all manner of nondescript craft—shapeless, heavy-laden, broad-bowed, whose native element seems to be the canal, and whose build is such that they look ill-adapted for navigation in more boisterous waters. Yet these ponderous boats have made voyages from the Far North and the Western lakes; they will float through Lake Champlain to Albany; still on, down the Hudson to New York, or on the broad St. Lawrence to Quebec. The traffic on the canal is such as in itself to give some idea of the commercial importance of Montreal. Here and there the monotony of trading-vessels is broken by the snow-white sails of a pleasure-yacht from the city; or some enthusiastic angler, absorbed in the nirvana of bait-fishing, sits in a skiff that never rocks but with the ripple of the passing steamer. There is something soothing in the intense calm of this canal navigation with which the scenery both on the canal banks and among the shipping is thoroughly in harmony. It is, as Shelley says, "a metaphor of peace." As the steamer passes between the locks, it is pleasant to go ashore and watch the canal from a little distance. The houses we pass are built with the usual high-pitched roofs of French-Canada, the slanting eaves projecting in front. All round us are the level fields extending to the foot of the canal embankment. The canal itself is invisible, and we see steamers and barges moving along, as it were, on dry ground!

At Lachine it will be well to land and stroll awhile amid the scenery of this quiet suburb of the great city, with its reminiscences of Robert Cavalier, Sieur de la Salle, and its association with so many vicissitudes in the history of the heroic and saintly founders of New France. In the words "*La Chine*" we have a record of the belief common to so many American explorers, from Columbus downwards, that through America lay the highway to the Orient, a belief which the increasing facilities of communication with the Pacific Coast will yet redeem from the list of delusions. Lachine is a quaint and picturesque old town, of some 4000 inhabitants; the houses with tall, steep gables, dormer windows and square stone chimneys; the streets gay with visitors from Montreal, a considerable number of whom reside during the summer months at Lachine, whence they come and go to their places of business in the city by the railway. Nestling among trees of immemorial growth are the parish church, and the convent, amid its high-walled gardens. The former is a handsome edifice, whose twin spires, gracefully decorated, rise high above the surrounding streets. The style is that modification of Renaissance-Gothic which the French brought from Europe, and on which French Jesuitism—the Jesuitism of the Martyrs, not of the political intriguers—has impressed the character of its glorious traditions.

Before the canal was built, Lachine was a place of greater commercial importance than at present; it was then the trading emporium for Montreal, to which was conveyed all the merchandise from the Western centres, and even the cargoes of skins and furs which the trappers of the Hudson's Bay Company had collected during the winter. Hither came, week by week, the *batteaux*, or large, flat-bottomed vessels, shaped somewhat like "bonnes," or lumbermen's boats; these arrived regularly with goods and passengers from Kingston and the head of the Bay of Quinté, and from the lake ports farther west.

The Sulpician Fathers, who were the feudal lords of the island of Montreal, were anxious to protect their new settlement of Villémarie by an outpost held from them by military tenure. Hence they gladly granted a tract of land near the rapids above Montreal to the gallant but ill-fated La Salle. He remained in possession only long enough to found a village fortified rudely with palisades, and to name it "Lachine," in accordance with the dominant idea of his adventurous life—a passage across the Continent to the Indies. After La Salle's departure, the village of Lachine conveniently situated for the carrying-trade of Montreal, continued to flourish until, in 1689, the terrible blow of its destruction by the Iroquois had the effect of overthrowing the French schemes of American conquest for a time, and reducing their tenure of Canadian soil to the space within the ramparts of Quebec, Three Rivers, and Montreal. The first aggressive march by Champlain on the Iroquois had proved not only a crime, but a mistake. This policy was that of the Jesuits and the successive Governors of New France. It consisted in converting and arming, as allies and proselytes, one Indian tribe against the other. Whatever may be thought of the morality of this policy, it might, no doubt, have proved successful, had the French only been so fortunate as to choose for their allies the more warlike Indian tribes. Unhappily, ever since Champlain's expedition up the Ottawa, he and his successors selected as their friends the feebler and less military races—the Ottawas, Hurons and Algonquins; by which step, as well as by their own repeated acts of violence, they drew on themselves the relentless hatred of the powerful confederacy known as the Iroquois, later called the Six-Nation Indians. Up to the time of the American Revolution, these savages maintained, in greater efficiency than has been known elsewhere among their wandering and disunited race, that military organization which seems the only approach to civilization of which the Indian in his native condition is capable. The Iroquois were to the Algonquins and Hurons what the Zulus are to the other negro races of East Africa. Those virtues and physical gifts which belong to savage life, and are apt to sicken or become extinct by contact with civilization, the Iroquois possessed. Their fidelity to friends is unstained by any record of such treachery as was shown by the Huron allies of Daulac des Ormeaux; their savage practices of purposed cruelty proved how much the possession of reason enabled the human brutes, who tore the scalps from their still living prisoners, to degrade themselves below the level of the wolf and bear, the emblems of their tribe. With the recklessness of a lofty ambition, the French leaders had resolved to extend the dominions of the Catholic Church and the French King far in the rear and to the southward of the English settlements on the Atlantic seaboard. In the prosecution of this grand scheme they drew on themselves the hatred not only of the Iroquois whose lands they invaded, but of the enemies of their own race and religion by whom these wolves of the wilderness were armed and hounded on. The year 1689 saw New France, under the rule of the reckless Marquis de Denonville, engaged in an Indian war along her whole line of settlements. The Iroquois had received great provocation. The Governor, by means of the Jesuit missionaries, whom he made his unconscious accomplices, had induced a number of Iroquois chiefs to meet him in peaceful conference. These he had seized and sent to France, that their toil as galley-slaves might amuse the Royal vanity. The Iroquois had scorned to revenge this perfidy on the missionaries, who were sent in safety from their camp. But a terrible retribution was at hand. Nearly two centuries ago, on the night of August 5th, 1689, as the inhabitants of Lachine lay sleeping, amid a storm of hail upon the lake which effectually disguised the noise of their landing, a force of many hundred warriors, armed, and besmeared with war-paint, made a descent upon Lachine. Through the night they noiselessly surrounded every building in the village. With dawn the fearful war-whoop awoke men, women and children, to their doom of torture and death. The village was fired; by its light in the early morn, the horror-stricken inhabitants of Montreal could see from their fortifications the nameless cruelties which preceded the massacre. It is said the Iroquois indulged so freely in the fire-water of the Lachine merchants, that had the defenders of Villemarie been prompt to seize the favourable moment, the drunken wretches might have been slaughtered like swine. Paralyzed by the horrors they had witnessed, the French let the occasion slip; at nightfall the savages withdrew to the mainland, not, however, without signifying by yells, repeated to the number of ninety, how many prisoners they carried away. From the ramparts of Villemarie, and amid the blackened ruins of

Lachine, the garrison watched the fires on the opposite shore, kindled for what purposes of nameless cruelty they knew too well. The fate of Lachine marks the lowest point in the fortunes of New France; by what deeds of heroism they were retrieved, is not the least glorious page in Canadian history.

Leaving the village of Lachine, it will be well to walk some distance along the lower road which skirts the river. Here, amid sylvan shades of pleasant retirement, we may enjoy the Lucretian satisfaction of viewing the distant rapids. Beyond the point of a long, low-lying ridge of rocky islet, the river is white with wrathful foam, and the spray clouds rise when a steamer is gallantly breasting the torrent. Meanwhile, the robins are singing from the maple trees, and the cows those optimists of the animal creation—are looking placidly forth on the rapids as if they knew that all was for the best! We pass a huge lumbering but not unpicturesque farmer's wagon, laden with grain for the mill to which the farmer's wife—a comely Canadienne, in the usual loose jacket and inevitable white hat—is driving a horse that will certainly not run away. The mill is a feature in the landscape worth observing—a quadrangular stone tower broad at the base, its lines converging at the top to support the old-fashioned, cruciform wind-sails, whose great arms move through the air like those of the giants Don Quixote assailed. Surrounded by spreading trees, and close to this beautiful river scenery, the old windmill, weather-beaten and mellowed by its seventy years' service, has an air of rustic grace not to be found in more recent and more pretentious structures. It seems that there was at one time a dispute between the owner of this mill and the Fathers of St. Sulpice, who claimed the sole right of milling on the island, and that the cause was decided in favour of the miller, who was, however, forbidden to rebuild his mill should it chance to be destroyed. Hence it was that he repaired the wooden structure by surrounding it with the stone wall which gives it its present fortress-like appearance.

From Lachine may be seen in the far distance the Indian village of Caughnawaga, where, civilized and Christianized, some five hundred descendants of the Iroquois destroyers of Lachine dream away their harmless and useless lives. This, and such as this, on other Indian reserves, is the result of all the heroism chronicled in the volumes of the *Relations des Jesuites!* By martyrdom, by endurance of privations and cruelties compared with which martyrdom might seem a merciful relief, they gained their object. They converted at last the terrible Iroquois enemy! And with what result? So much and such noble effort, only to be wasted on a race fast becoming extinct; a race which, a century hence, will have left no memorial to the Canada of the future, save where here and there our cities and rivers recall the strange music of the Indian names!

We steam along the northern shore of Lake St. Louis past the Isle Derval, a portion of the lake where the colour of the purplish-brown water of the Ottawa may be distin-

OLD WINDMILL, ON LACHINE ROAD, AND DISTANT VIEW OF LACHINE RAPIDS.

guished from the green tinge of the St. Lawrence. Of course, this is not observable under all conditions of the atmosphere, but on bright, sunshiny days, there can be no doubt whatever that this difference in colour can be distinctly traced. The dark, purple tinge characterizes the imperial river, which, from as yet almost unexplored sources, stretching to the water-shed of Hudson's Bay, from tributary rivers extending east and west and south, through many a wide-spreading lake, and over cataracts lifting their columns of spray to the clouds of heaven, past the metropolitan city of Canada, and through valleys and amid hills and islands rich in every imaginable type of nature's loveliness—here meets at last its equal—here blends its waters, though as yet distinct in colour, with its own

APPLE WOMEN AT LOCK

legitimate sister, the great lake stream of the St. Lawrence. Swiftly we steam on, crossing Lake St. Louis, where steamers are passing and re-passing, and the gay yachts of Montreal spread their white wings to the breeze. The waters of Lake St. Louis are shallow, and the shores flat, and

CANAL LOCK, AND RAILWAY BRIDGE AT STE. ANNE'S.

fringed with dusky woods, presenting no marked characteristics, except the huge guide piers erected on the way to Ste. Anne's, to mark and preserve the channel. Looming before us in the mist, we can see, as it stretches from the mainland of Ontario to the Isle of Montreal, the great bridge of the Grand Trunk Railway. In order to avoid the rapids at the *débouchement* of the Ottawa, we enter a canal close to Ste. Anne's and the abutment of the Grand Trunk bridge. This canal is about the eighth of a mile long, and has a single lock near the railway bridge. It was constructed in place of one built as early as 1816, and rebuilt in 1833 by the Ottawa Forwarding Company, who made some difficulty in admitting the passage of vessels not connected with their own business. This caused so much inconvenience, that the Legislature of Upper Canada took the matter in hand and built the present canal at Ste. Anne's.

Those sentimentalists who last century refused to see beauty in industrial buildings and works, who wept over steamships profaning the solitudes of Cumberland lakes, and could see

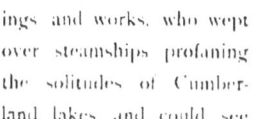

WATCH TOWER.

nothing picturesque in a building that was not a castle or at least a ruin, would determine on principle, and beforehand, that there could be nothing attractive about a mere railway bridge. Yet let those who do not refuse to see Nature, as faithfully interpreted by Art, consider how even this magnificent lake scenery is enhanced by this work, no less magnificent, of human enterprise and skill. On sixteen square towers of stone-work, each massive as the keep of a fortress, is supported

REMAINS OF ANCIENT CASTLE.

the viaduct which gives passage to Canada's most important railway. As the steamer passes under with lowered funnel, we look back on the lake and the mainland beyond it, where, far over the St. Lawrence, the summits, indistinct and dim, of the Adirondack

Mountains, mingle with the clouds. At our left are the rapids—not deep, but necessary to be avoided on account of their shallowness. Here, on rude rafts, stand the shad-fishers, ready to spear or net the fish which, visiting these rapids in shoals, come to watch for food. Poised on the precarious footing of a couple of planks fastened together and tossing on the waves, they plunge and replunge the net, not seldom bringing to light the sparkling and leaping fish, whose capture is to these poor *habitans* a source of no little gain. We pass under the bridge and through the lock, where a number of the country-folk are lounging, to greet the steamer and her cargo of pleasure-seekers. The male *habitant's* dress, if not exactly picturesque, is peculiar, and in harmony with the hot weather of August. As a rule no coat is worn; waistcoat and shirt-sleeves and loose, baggy trousers, form the whole costume, and it is *de rigeur* that both hands be kept in the trousers' pockets. The head-dress is a hat with narrow rim and high, conical top, similar to those popularly believed to be worn by magicians and witches! With them is a group of apple-women, healthy-looking dames, with short kirtles, 'kerchiefed neck, and broad, white hats. Here we find for sale green apples of last season, yet fresh and in good condition, and paper bags full of delicious grapes. Once more we disembark to stroll through the village, consisting of a group of those pretty Lower Canadian houses no poverty can make unpicturesque. In the midst of these is the church, a structure where the substratum of Gothic is varied with the features so strangely adopted from classical architecture by the art of the Renaissance. At the shrine of good Ste. Anne, the pious *voyageur*, about to encounter the perils of lumbering or river-driving, comes to pay his vows and leave his modest offering to her of whom the mediæval poet sang:

> "ANNA PARIT TRES MARIAS,
> UT PRÆDIXIT ESAIAS."

We enter the church. Jean or Baptiste is kneeling reverently. Keenly alive to the misery of parting with a cent of his hard-earned wages on all other occasions, *here* he is liberal. It is a scene that reminds one of the Middle Ages, nay, of more primitive faiths, before the ages called Christian.

Having passed through the village, we reach the ruins of a castle built to defend the island at this point, and evidently once a fortalice of considerable importance. On the brow of a hill commanding an extensive view of the lake, is a circular watch-tower, loop-holed for musketry, whose broken embrasures once held cannon controlling the landing and approaches to the castle beneath. Lower down and close to the landing-place are two castles, built after the model of fortresses of the Middle Ages—in each a lofty keep or central tower, quadrangular, without windows, save the narrow aperture through which the arquebuse of the defenders might aim securely at the lurking Iroquois without. The rest of the castle consists of high walls enclosing space sufficient to shelter the women and children of the settlement in case of invasion, and this again protected by flanking turrets. Both buildings are without ornament, save that with which Time has invested the crumbling ruins; gaunt and gray, they stand, amid the most peaceful scenes that our world can show, the memorials of a Past

BACK RIVER BRIDGE, AND SHAD FISHING.

which, though not two centuries gone by, already seems to belong to the Middle Ages! Such a fortress as this would have been proof against any artillery which raiders from the New England colonies could have brought against New France; against the Iroquois it was impregnable.

Before us, as the steamer leaves Ste. Anne's, lies the first of those expansions of the River Ottawa which so frequently occur throughout its entire course, the Lake of Two Mountains. The larger Mountain was named "Calvary" by the piety of the first settlers. In the continual presence of the terrible dangers which threatened those who, as one of them said of the Montreal settlement, had thrust their hand into the wolf's den, the founders of New France sought everywhere to impress on the land of their adoption the traces of that religion which was their chief comfort. At its summit were seven chapels—the memorials of the mystic seven of St. John's vision—the scene of many a pilgrimage, where gallant cavalier and high-born lady from their fastness at Villemarie toiled, side by side, up the same weary height.

Near this we visit the pretty village of Oka, whence the Indian occupants have been wisely removed by the Dominion Government to Muskoka. Their cottages still line the shore beneath the shade of ancient elm trees; a large cross close to the landing invites the contemplation of the pious, while summer-houses and other garniture for pleasure-making are ready for the holiday folk who crowd to this popular summer resort in skiff and steamer. To this class belong the youthful pair whom a venerable gray horse conveys—neither he nor they being at all in a hurry— along the Oka road in one of those ancient covered *calèches* used in this part of Canada. The young lady is driving; the "hood" of the vehicle covers both of them from a passing shower or from the gaze of too curious eyes.

We steam across the Lake of Two Mountains. It is an irregularly-shaped expanse of water, in length twenty-four miles, and from three to four miles wide. Calm as are these summer lakes, an experience of a sudden squall shows how the usually placid waters can be lashed into furious waves. Suddenly the sky is overclouded, the mountains on the shore seem to have withdrawn into the dim distance, the woods are swathed in mist, and quick and sharp descends upon our deck and on the waves around us the white electric rain. We meet one of those huge barges similar to those we saw in the Lachine Canal. How its heavy hulk rolls and labours while the surf breaks over it! But the strong boat is seaworthy, and the steam-tug in charge tows it heavily on.

The country on our left consists of the counties of Vaudreuil and Soulanges which, though on the Ontario side of the Ottawa, are part of the Province of Quebec. In these, as on the opposite side of the river, the French language and institutions prevail. In the seigniory of Rigaud, near the upper portion of the Lake of Two Mountains, is a remarkable mound, the "Montagne Ste. Magdelaine," at whose top is a quadrangular area of some acres, covered with stone boulders arranged by a strange caprice of nature to resemble a freshly-ploughed field—whence the place is called "*Pluie de guerets.*" From underground, the murmur as of flowing water can be distinctly heard; but all attempts to discover the cause are said to have failed, though the earth has been dug to the depth of many feet. At the foot of this moun-

LOWER OTTAWA SCENES.

ON THE LOWER OTTAWA.

tain on the lake shore, beside the mouth of the Rivière a la Graisse, is the pleasant little French village of Rigaud.

At no great distance from the north-eastern side of the Lake of Two Mountains are the villages of St. Eustache, Ste. Scholastique and St. Benoit — scenes of conflict between "Patriots" and "Loyalists" in the troublous times of '37, when passions were excited and gallant citizens were in arms against each other in feuds, which, thanks to subsequent wise government and a better state of feeling, are now happily as extinct as the wars with the Iroquois.

Near the upper expansion of the lake is the village and headland called "Pointe aux

M. GREEN BAYS, CHUTE
À VES DOGES.

Anglais," whence we look forth over the broad expanse of desolate moor, shallows and bush-covered islets in the foreground, and stretching far and wide over the horizon from the north shore, the dusky shades of the Laurentian hills, desolate and forbidding, as it were a wall between us and the fertile lands beyond them.

At Carillon the steamer's course is once more barred by rapids, to avoid which a canal has been constructed; but passengers by the mail-boat land at Carillon and take train to Grenville, a distance of twelve miles, whence another steamer proceeds without farther interruption to Ottawa. Opposite Carillon, at Point Fortune, the river becomes the boundary line between the two Provinces. At the Chute au Blondeau is another canal an eighth of a mile in length, and a dam has here been thrown across the river, which so pens back the waters that only a passage of three-quarters of a mile in length is now needed to reach the higher level above the chute. Beside the Long Sault Rapid is the Grenville Canal, excavated for the most part through solid rock, and leading to the village of Grenville, a distance of six miles. These three canals were constructed, like that of the Rideau, by the Imperial Government for military purposes. Happily, there is no prospect of their being needed for such; and even should necessity arise, their usefulness is a thing of the past, superseded, as they now are, by the opening of the St. Lawrence Canals and the Grand Trunk Railway on the front, as well as by the new lines of railway to the north, which make our intercommunication secure from any foe. Down these three rapids—the Carillon, Long Sault, and Chute au Blondeau—the lumbermen descend on their cribs of timber. Formidable as this feat looks, it is frequently accomplished by travellers who adventure in company with the raftsmen, and seldom suffer worse consequences than a wetting.

In these rapids Samuel de Champlain nearly lost his life at the commencement of his first expedition up the Ottawa from Montreal to Allumette. The forest along the river bank was so impenetrably tangled, that he and his party were fain to force their way through the rapids, pushing and drawing their canoes from one point to another. While thus engaged Champlain fell, and would have perished in the eddy of the rapids, as has many a gallant lumberman since, had he not been saved by the friendly help of a boulder against which he was carried.

The Pass of the Long Sault, on the western shore of these rapids, is memorable as the scene of patriotic self-devotion not unworthy to be compared with the achievements of a Decius or a Leonidas. In the year 1660 the French colonists of Villemarie and Quebec learned, with dismay, that a united effort for their destruction was about to be made by the whole force of the Iroquois Confederacy. Then Daulac des Ormeaux, a youthful nobleman, with sixteen companions, resolved to strike a blow which, at the sacrifice of their own lives, might break the power and arrest the progress of the savage foe. Like the Roman general of old, they devoted themselves to their doom in a religious spirit, and with the full rites of the Church in whose defence they were about to die. Where then, as now, the roar of the Long Sault Rapids blended with the sigh of the wind through the forest, they entrenched themselves, with some two-score Huron allies who, however, deserted them in the hour of danger. They had but an old fortification of palisades, which they endeavoured to strengthen. While so engaged, the Iroquois fell upon them. Through successive attacks they held at bay the five hundred painted savages who swarmed, tomahawk in hand, up to the very loopholes of the fort, only to be driven back by the resolute fire of its defenders, leaving among the heaps of slain their chief. Repulsed again and again, the Iroquois deferred the main attack till the arrival of reinforcements, who were marching on Montreal. For three days Daulac des Ormeaux and his handful of gallant followers held their post against the swarming hordes. At length, overwhelmed by numbers and exhausted by hunger, thirst and sleeplessness, they fell, fighting to the last, leaving but four survivors, three of whom, already mortally wounded, were burned at once, while the fourth was reserved for torture. But the Iroquois had paid dearly for their success. They thought no more—for a time, at least—of attacking the more formidable armaments and fortifications of Montreal. New France was saved by this deed of patriotic self-devotion. Sacred to all time should be the spot which such heroism has ennobled!

GLIMPSES OF THE LOWER OTTAWA—THE LUMBER TRADE.

At Grenville we again take the steamer, anxious to penetrate behind the wall of mountain ridge which, undulating along the eastern bank of the river, seems to forbid access to the country beyond. This is the Laurentian range, composed of that gneiss which contains the earliest fossil remains of animal life as yet recognized by geologists. We procure a canoe and a guide at Grenville, with the farther necessary equipment of a wagon, wherewith we make our way along the main road to Pointe au Chêne, on the River Rouge, above the rapids called "McGillivray's Chute." In its passage through the barriers of Laurentian hills, the Rouge courses over a continuous series of rapids to its

RUNNING THE RAPIDS.

junction, twelve miles distant, with the Ottawa. But the beauty of the scenery in this region of mountain and lake well repays the trouble of travel or portage. As we make our way among these hills, so sternly repellant from a distance, we meet fertile valleys, rapidly being cleared and made into cultivated farms. We have camped in the woods, glad of shelter, for there is a touch of frost in the early autumn air. Below, where we stand ready to launch our canoe, are the rapids of McGillivray's Chute, plunging and eddying over the wave-worn boulders; above and beyond, the calm expanse of the River Rouge, mirroring the mountain, bright with the forest foliage kindled into rich red gold colour by last night's frost, with here and there the more vivid scarlet of the soft maples. For some miles we ascend the river in our canoe, which, on our return, we have to guide through rapids, the surges foaming around us as we pass swiftly through the fretful waters in the shadow of the silent hills.

From the banks of the Rouge our canoe is carried to the shores of Lake Comandeau, or "Papineau," as it has been named after the famous leader, near whose home at Montebello its outlet, the Kinonge, flows into the Ottawa. We drive by a very tolerable road, through the hill-country, past a mountain farm at the head of Lake Comandeau. The homestead and farm buildings are log-houses; the land is roughly cultivated. Beyond it lies the lake, dark-blue in the shadow of the many-coloured hills which stretch far away into the dimness of the autumn morning. We prepare to launch upon the lake; upon the thickly-wooded shore our canoe lies turned up in the

MOUNTAIN FARM.

sun to dry, to have the seams gummed before starting. Near by is another canoe about to leave the shore, while farther off on the lake is a third midway between us and the opposite side. Beyond, the mountains, dusky green with shadowy woods, melt away into the morning mists. We launch our canoe; we speed along over the stirless water mirroring the hills and woods, amid islands aglow with the gay livery of the forest. We reach, far off, an open expanse of lake, where, amid the shallower waters, the speckled trout are wont to bask. The hills in the distance are dusky purple. Near us is an islet—the trout-fisher's favourite haunt; overhead, a huge, dome-like rock, stained with all manner of shades—blue, russet and yellow—under the encrusting lichen; at its side, high above the yellow larches, the tall pines throw their shadows over the lake. This beautiful sheet of water is about ten miles long; its surface is diversified by numerous small islands, and the mountain scenery amid which it lies gives a boldness and sublimity unknown to Southern lakes, with their low-lying shores.

Again pursuing our journey up the Ottawa, we pass L'Orignal—the county seat of Prescott and Russell Counties—at which village three of our passengers leave us for the medicinal Caledonia Springs, a distance of some nine miles inland. These springs are said to have been first indicated by the multitudes of wild pigeons that gathered

ON THE PORTAGE—LAKE COMANDEAU

near the spot. Farther on, upon the Quebec side, deep in the shadow of the elm-wood, rise the towers of what seems one of the antique *chateaux* of Old France. This is the home of Papineau, the leader, through stormy times, of French-Canadian Liberalism; one whose eloquence was as remarkable as his personal character was worthy of admiration. The feuds of those days are extinct; we can afford to remember, with pride, the virtues of one of Canada's ablest sons. The beauty of this chateau of Montebello has been worthily celebrated by Frechette in the noble tribute which his muse has addressed to the memory of Papineau.

We sail on, upon the sombre bosom of the stream, our course varied by the alternating narrowness or expansion of the Ottawa; sometimes among islands slumberous with dark verdure; anon meeting a fleet of broad river-barges laden with the piled-up lumber, and towed down stream by the steam-tugs which impart their own quick motion to the inert mass; or again steaming through wide, shallow reaches, where the solitary canoe, Canadian boat-song its familiar but beauti- ... by Moore. On ... Rivière du Lièvre a ... importance to

MONTEBELLO HOME OF PAPINEAU.

... which, through a course of 350 miles, drains an area greater in ... than ... European kingdoms. ... from the Capital we pass the mouth of the Gatineau, the mightiest

A TOW OF LUMBER BARGES.

TROUT FISHING ON LAKE COMANDEAU.

of the many tributaries of the Ottawa, which, for seven miles from its outlet, is rendered unnavigable by rapids. But we are already within the precincts of the city, and disembark, after a trip which has opened new phases of picturesque beauty in a country hitherto—however well known to commerce—but too little known to art.

NORTH SHORE OF THE OTTAWA.

OTTAWA PARLIAMENT BUILDINGS, FROM MAJOR'S HILL.

A FIRST GLIMPSE OF THE CAPITAL.

OTTAWA.

CANADA, young as she is, could furnish material for a very lively chapter on the vicissitudes of capitals. Strategically posted at Niagara, tossed backwards and forwards, shuttlecock fashion, between jealous Toronto, Kingston, and Quebec, pelted with paving-stones and burned out of their Chamber by an exasperated mob at Montreal, her legislators, thanks to the direct selection of the Queen herself, found refuge in a certain modest village-town, perched meekly on high bluffs and intervening valleys, between the spray and roar of two headlong river-falls. The town of "By" became the city of Ottawa, the peripatetic carpet-bag existence of government officials ceased, and the nomad tribes of the various departments settled down permanently under their own vine and fig-tree by the broad stream which gives its name to the spot.

But the Ottawa has a past, and to the hereditary enmity existing between two of the three great families of Indians in North America east of the Mississippi—the Iroquois and the Algonquins—an enmity carefully fostered by the greater rival powers of England and France, added to the allurements of commerce in furs, is due the important position held by this river in the life and history of Canada.

For over 160 years prior to the memorable 8th of September, 1760, when with the keys of Montreal the Marquis De Vaudreuil surrendered all Canada to General Amherst, the blood of Wolfe and Montcalm having just one year before signed the deeds which gave Quebec to England, the "Kit-chi-sippi," the "great river," as it was called by its dusky *voyageurs*, was the main route by which the store of furs, gathered through the long winter from beaver-dam and haunt of moose and otter, martin, and silver fox, found their toilful way to the big ships of the traders at Tadoussac, Quebec, and Montreal. How cruel the history of this long line of mighty waters, these ever-boiling rapids, tremendous falls, and wide-spreading lakes, is told in colours of blood in the writings of those who lived through the terrible period when civilization was making its slow, sure way into this virgin world.

To secure the valuable peltry trade, the best efforts of New England and New York, south of the lakes, and of the "company of merchant adventurers of England, trading in Hudson's Bay," were directed. New France was not behindhand, and her daring *coureurs de bois* penetrated far and wide through the vast tract between Hudson's Bay and the lakes. This, the cold North, was the great fur-bearing land, and through nearly its whole extent ran the mighty stream of the "Outaouais," as their French allies called the natives. By this noble stream, difficult and dangerous as was its course, did the Algonquins of whom they, with the Hurons, formed part—from their distant territory south of Lake Superior, hold communication with the French settlement at Montreal. Relentlessly driven from the Lower Ottawa by the systematic incursions of the terrible Iroquois, the Ottawas traversed their native woods and waters in fear and trembling. The better portion of their journey down the "Grand River," from the falls of the Chaudière (where the city of Ottawa now stands), was one of incessant danger from their traditionary foes. Up the river they were comparatively safe, for the natural difficulties of the turbulent stream made access so hard and retreat so perilous, that the Iroquois preferred to await them at the falls, or to attack them still farther below, when the most desperate fighting would not ensure safety for their hard-earned cargoes of pelts or secure themselves from the cruelest of tortures and death at the hands of their dread foes. In 1693 a three years' accumulation of beaver-skins lay at Michillimackinac, their main quarters at the head of Lake Huron, and the Ottawa was so closely barred by the Iroquois that no effort could be made to take them down. The loss of its one source of revenue was nearly ruinous to the young colony. At last Count Frontenac, the Governor, caused a strong escort to be got together, and the arrival at Quebec of two hundred canoes, all laden with furs, told that the long blockade was broken.

Up this river, in 1613, Champlain passed, in the vain hope of finding an open northwest passage to the spice lands of Cathay, till, at an Indian settlement 125 miles above the falls, he learned that his reported salt sea was a myth. Three years later he returned, passing into Lake Huron and so to Lake Simcoe, where he joined the Algonquins in a campaign against the Iroquois, the return journey from Lake Simcoe to Montreal taking forty days.

But years went by and great changes came. In 1800, Philemon Wright, farmer, of Woburn, Massachusetts, "having a large family to provide for," came, after several visits of exploration, the first of which was made four years previously, back to the foot of the Chaudière, the "big kettle," bringing twenty-five men with mill-irons, axes, scythes, hoes, fourteen horses, eight oxen, seven sleighs, and five families of women and children, together with a number of barrels of "clear pork, destitute of bone," of his own raising. For the magnificent sum of twenty dollars, the Indians withdrew their objections to his settlement, and finding that their claims to the land would not be entertained, a certain insinuating appeal for an additional thirty dollars being refused, the poor wretches quietly bowed to the strong will of the Great Father across the sea, created the invader a chief, kissed him, dined with him, and made a compact, kept thenceforward with the honesty of the uncontaminated.

Then followed a long line of busy, useful years, all tending to the improvement of his new domain. Surveys, road-making, clearings, plantings, reapings and building went steadily on, till in twenty-four years he had cleared 3000 acres and had 756 acres in grain and roots, and in 1839 died at the ripe old age of seventy-nine, the father of the town of Hull, on the north side of the river.

But the south side, whose rough, rocky cliffs had offered no attractions to the adventurous pioneer, was destined to far outshine his settlement. One of his employés, named Nicholas Sparks, was lucky enough to purchase, for a trifling sum, a large quantity of the unprized land; and when, as a strategic issue of the American troubles of 1812-15, it was determined by the Imperial Government to construct a line of canals to connect the St. Lawrence with the lakes *via* the River Ottawa, in order to afford means of communication with tide-water free from inimical interruption, Mr. Sparks sold lot on lot to the Government and to enterprising settlers, and cleared about half a million sterling. So "Bytown" arose, taking its name from the colonel of the Royal Engineers, to whom the construction of this great work had been entrusted. For some years it grew and prospered with the pecuniary aid of the military, the canal labourers, and the lumber trade—the starting of the latter having been due to the indefatigable Wright. Tradesmen, mechanics, doctors, lawyers, and all the constituents of a thriving community gathered rapidly, and in 1851 the town boasted

UNDER DUFFERIN BRIDGE.

eight thousand inhabitants, and the place still continued to grow, till in 1865 the seat of Government was transferred to it, and Bytown, thenceforward Ottawa, became the capital.

The city of to-day is a city of varied elements. There is the life of the Government and the life of the river; the race, language, religion, manners of the *ancien régime* and those of that which succeeded it, two streams of dissimilar character in source, which are content to flow in one channel amicably, but unmixed. The city may practically be said to consist of one long line of business houses, backed by ganglia of residences which extend some three miles westward to the Chaudière Falls and the city of Hull, and eastward towards the falls of the Rideau and the village of New Edinburgh, on the right bank of that river. In its centre it is known as Sparks Street, the name being taken from that of the actual founder of the settlement, where are situated the leading business and mercantile establishments.

The key to the main place of the city is a point where two converging bridges span the Rideau Canal. Standing here and looking west, one sees to the left the old "Sappers' Bridge," a solid stone structure built by the military as part of the canal works. To the right is the "Dufferin Bridge," a new, well-designed viaduct of iron, which gives access to Wellington Street, a thoroughfare of noble width, containing the handsome stone buildings of various banks, and insurance and railway offices. Fronting this street is the long, low stretch of graceful stone and iron railing with its massive gates of fine iron-work which encloses Parliament Square and the magnificent piles of the Government buildings. Immediately in front of the two bridges is the new Post Office and Custom House—a large and elegant stone edifice in the style of the Renaissance—which is one of the architectural features of the city.

Turning his back upon the Post Office and looking east, the visitor sees a broad roadway—Rideau Street—extending, on a gentle acclivity, a couple of miles. This street is lined with stores and private houses, and on either side cluster systems of streets containing residences—those on the left, sloping down toward the river, being known as

POST OFFICE, AND DUFFERIN AND SAPPERS' BRIDGE.

THE RIDEAU RIFLE RANGE.

HEAD OF THE LOCKS—RIDEAU CANAL.

Lower Town, while on the higher ground to the right lies the fashionable district, by no misnomer called Sandy Hill. Here are comfortable and often handsome and extensive villas, the more distant of which command charming views of the adjacent country and the valley of the Rideau River.

Here, also, occupying a considerable extent of ground, is the rifle range, a site of some importance, owing to the fact that it is the scene of the annual meetings of the Dominion Rifle Association, and that before its twenty targets the best shots of the country compete, selecting from their number the team which is yearly sent to contest at Wimbledon with the crack shots of Great Britain. During the week of the shooting, the city is in a state of martial *furore*; coats of red, dark-green and gray, are seen everywhere; the white tents of the association and of the different competitors picturesquely dot the ground; and the incessant crack of the rifle, the strains of military bands, the bright dresses of ladies, and the general charm of the unusual, give all the proceedings an animation for which the social world is the association's debtor. It is a widely ramified institution, practically representing all the Provinces, and is the centre of everything appertaining to military rifle practice in the country. It is also an admirable example of good organization, every detail of its work being thoughtfully brought to the highest point of perfection.

RIDEAU CANAL LOCKS.

Coming back again to the bridge, a hundred yards off on the left, with a sharp turn, runs Suffolk Street. Here we enter a section of the city almost exclusively French, with French proprietors and French characteristics; the baker becomes a *boulanger*, the lawyer is *avocat*, and *marchandises-sèches* obligingly translates itself into "dry-goods," for the benefit of the un-French world. On this street is a big three-storey cut-stone building recently purchased by Government for the purposes of a Geological Museum, the materials for which were all ready to hand in Montreal. This promises to constitute a very durable adjunct to the means of information possessed by the city. Suffolk Street contains also the French Cathedral, a large and imposing building, of the local gray-blue limestone, whose capacious interior is resplendent with gilding and wood-carving, the result of recent extensive improvements. This is the main centre of the French and Roman Catholic element. The neighbouring streets are filled with rows of small, clean and tidy cottages, whose good-natured inhabitants use the old tongue of La Belle France, and are descendants of those early *voyageurs* and *chantiers* whose traditional pursuits on the ever-beneficent bosom of the Ottawa they still largely follow.

Beyond the French Cathedral, the road approaches the river, and runs parallel with it till the Rideau is reached at a point just above the spot where it plunges in two graceful "curtains" of water to supplement the great stream of the Ottawa, forty feet below. Here is the suburban village of New Edinburgh, and here, too, is the entrance to "Rideau Hall," the local name for Government House, of which more hereafter.

Reverting to our stand at the junction of the bridges, and still turning our backs to the Post Office, there lies, on the immediate left, the entrance to the Public Gardens— a long stretch of prettily-planned walks, grass and flower-beds, with frequent rustic seats—which, though still in incomplete form, is one of the favourite summer evening lounges of the citizens. Below, runs the deep gorge through which the waters of the canal, by a magnificent series of locks, have been led to join the Ottawa, and beyond the locks rises the precipitous wooded slope of Parliament Hill; and the vast pile of the "Buildings," whose graceful outline, sharply marked out against the bright sky of the on-coming evening and the western sun, is a never-ceasing charm to the eyes of the strollers on the garden cliffs.

Crossing the Sappers' Bridge and passing the Post Office on our right, we come upon Elgin Street—whose name, as befits the capital, is a memorial of an ex-Governor— and the new City Hall, a large building of blue limestone, containing the various city offices and the machinery for carrying out the civic system.

Following Elgin Street a few hundred paces, a fine piece of open ground is met with —Cartier Square—named in honour of the illustrious Canadian statesman under whose leadership the Conservative Government for many years held steady sway. Here is the great public meeting-place. Reviews of troops, popular gatherings, the rejoicings of festival days, foot-ball and lacrosse matches, find ample accommodation. At the far end stands an enormous red-brick building—the drill shed—under whose noble span a regiment may perform its evolutions in comfort, while commodious sections are fitted up as repositories for the several arms of the militia and volunteer force centred in Ottawa. On one side of the square stands a very extensive pile of buildings in stone, of graceful design—the Normal School—one of the apices of the Government educational system of the Province of Ontario; and close by is the Collegiate Institute. In this neighbourhood is found the rising "West End" of the community. Villa residences of fine proportions and design, surrounded by well-kept gardens, have sprung up in all directions. Streets which but five or six years ago were bare fields, are now lined

MOUTH OF RIDEAU CANAL, FROM PARLIAMENT HILL.

with handsome buildings of brick and stone, and the hitherto scattered wealthy home-life of the city seems to be adopting at last the principle of segregation, which is the feature of the greater hives in all countries.

Retracing our steps along Elgin, back to Sparks Street, we follow the course of the street railway towards the Chaudière Falls, till Upper Town is left, with its busy shop-life, and passing the water-works at Pooley's Bridge, enter upon another phase of the city—the all-important element of lumber. The air becomes laden with a pleasant, healthy smell of pine-wood, and the stores we pass are filled with materials of a very matter-of-fact character—stout woollen jerseys and shantyman's boots, notable rather for great capacity for honest work than for any extreme elegance of build; huge saws, circular monsters of brobdingagian proportions, with teeth of the most appalling dimensions, and perpendicular giants of unequalled good temper, whose ungentle mission it will be to eat their placid and indifferent way through many a stout-hearted monarch of the woods; axes of the brightest; chains, "cant dogs," peculiarly-shaped instruments for canting over logs into place, and the spike-pole, the lumberman's "best companion." These, and barrels of rough-looking but most palatable pork, his staple food, form the main contents of the stores of this quarter. Life's luxuries have vanished, its realities have full possession.

As we near the saw-mills the harsh, strident buzz of countless saws is heard. This, day and night, in the "running season," is the cry of the ruthlessly-sundered logs, or the querulous gamut, up and down, which runs never-endingly, the voice of the labouring but ever-victorious saw. Upon every point of rock near the Chaudière Falls, and upon acres of massive, wooden, stone-filled embankments connecting them, to which the upper waters could be led, there have been reared the huge mill structures of the lumber kings. Flour, cement and wool have also claimed a share of the illimitable water-power. Here, overhanging a precipitous fall—there built out on mighty piles—everywhere mills. In all directions the waters have been boldly seized, cunningly coaxed, audaciously dammed up; sluices, bulkheads, slides, everywhere, everything is chaotically watery. Yet all is the very essence of order and of nice adjustment of means to ends, a very triumph of triumphant water slavery. The result is, that the greater part of the tremendous stream—here a mile broad at least—is compelled to traverse the main fall about forty feet high, and to escape through the principal channel, about 240 feet wide, across which a light but strong suspension bridge has been cleverly thrown, connecting Ottawa with Hull—the Province of Ontario with that of Quebec.

In the construction of a bridge at this difficult point the persistency of Bruce's spider has been emulated. Fifty years ago there was no bridge, and the boiling, tumbling waters of the falls a hundred yards above rushed headlong through charming tree-covered islands, in all the picturesque freedom of undisturbed nature. In 1827, when the first steps were being taken for the building of the Rideau Canal locks, and little Bytown began to look up in the world, the shot of a cannon carried from rock to rock across the whirling stream a small rope; this rope was the parent of much endeavour, of repeated failure, but of ultimate success. Finally, in 1843, the present stout structure was reared, and from its tremulous platform, in all the wild, ceaseless din of falling waters, rush of yellow, foam-covered waves and veil of misty spray, one looks at ease into the once mystic and awful, but now merely picturesque tumble and toss of living water, the famous Chaudière. Half a mile above, the long, graceful lines of a new and substantial iron railway bridge of eleven huge spans, give farther evidence of the mastery of man over this once wild spot.

On the right, beyond a broad area of brownish, gray-coloured rock, bare in the dry summer time, but covered with down-rushing water in the river-swollen days of spring, are mills and still more mills, and an immense factory for the production of matches and pails—one of the "sights" of the locality. On the left, perched high on a labyrinth of monster piles, by which the giant force of the river has been dammed up and curbed, runs a long line of big saw-mills, and entering these, the unearthly din, made up of whirr, buzz and shriek, becomes absolutely deafening. Here is the home of the saw, and anything more curiously fascinating than the aspect of the place, with its crowd of ever-busy workers, the rapid up-and-down dance of the tremendous saws, can scarcely be imagined. Set, thirty or more, framed in a row—those terrible instruments form what is called a "gate"—and towards this uncompromising combination the logs, having first been drawn from the water up an inclined plane, deftly handled and coaxed into position, are irresistibly impelled, one succeeding the other, day and night. For a moment the glittering steel dances before the forest innocent, a veritable "dance of death;" then, with a crash and a hiss, the ugly-looking teeth make the first bite, and, for five or six minutes, eat their way steadily through the tough fibre, till that which entered the jaws of the machine a mere log, emerges in the form of sawn planks, which a few more rapid and simple operations convert into well trimmed and salable lumber, ready for the piling ground and the markets of America and Europe.

The scene at night—for work continues both by night and day—is extremely novel and picturesque. Some of the lumbering firms now use the electric light, and the effect in that pure, clear glare, is of the most Rembrandt-like character. The contrast between the darkness outside, and the weird unearthly figures of the busy crowd of workers; the dark, rough backs of the dripping logs, as they are hauled up from the water, catching the reflection, and the sharp flash of the steel as it dances up and down—all contribute to make a picture of the horrible which would captivate the pencil of Doré and give Dante a new idea for a modern *Inferno*.

Amongst the novel experiences which the city offers to its visitors is the descent of the "slides," whereby the hardships of the lumberman's life become, for a few exciting moments, the attractive sport of venturesome seekers of strange thrills. The timber for

CHAUDIÈRE FALLS, AND SUSPENSION BRIDGE.

CHAUDIÈRE FALLS.

which the special provision of slides is made is no mere rough log, but has been carefully hewn square in the woods, forming great beams, destined for solid piles or massive building work. For the avoidance of the unmerciful grinding and battering on jagged rocks which passage over the falls would entail, long, smooth-bottomed channels of massive wood and stone-work have been built, leading from the high level above to the waters below, the inclination being sufficient to bring the timber safely down, carefully made up into lots called "cribs," containing some twenty "sticks" of various lengths, but of an uniform width of twenty-four feet, to fit the slide. The descent is made at a pace which, with the ever-present possibility of a break-up, gives a very respectable sense of excitement to a novice. There is but little attempt at fastening, the buoyancy of the timber and the weight of three or four of the heaviest beams obtainable being sufficient, as a rule, to hold the mass together.

Just at the head the adventurous *voyageurs* hurriedly embark, the crib being courteously held back for a moment for their convenience. Under direction, they perch themselves upon the highest timber in the rear, out of the way as far as possible of uprushing waters, and the huge mass is cleverly steered by the immense oars which are used for the purpose, towards the entrance of the chute. Ahead for a quarter of a mile appears a narrow channel, down which a shallow stream of water is constantly rushing, with here and there a drop of some five or eight feet; the ladies gather up their garments, as the crib, now beginning to feel the current, takes matters into its own hands; with rapidly-quickening speed, the unwieldy craft passes under a bridge, and with a groan and a mighty cracking and splashing, plunges nose foremost, and tail high in the air, over the first drop. Now she is in the slide proper, and the pace is exhilarating; on, over the smooth timbers she glides swiftly; at a bridge ahead passers-by stop, and wavings of friendly handkerchiefs are interchanged. Now comes a bigger drop than the last, and the water, as we go over, surges up through our timbers, and a shower of spray falls about us.

CRIB OF TIMBER RUNNING THE SLIDE.

A delicate "Oh!" from the ladies compliments this effort. Never mind; a little wetting was all in this day's march. Another interval of smooth rush, and again a drop, and yet another. Ahead, there is a gleam of tossed and tumbled water, which shows the end of the descent; down still we rush, and with one last wild dip, which sends the water spurting up about our feet, we have reached the bottom, cleverly caught on a floating platform of wood, called the "apron," which prevents our plunging into "full fathoms five." We have "run the slides." Now, out oars, and soon, striking into the powerful current which has swept over the falls behind us, we are lying moored by the side of some huge raft containing, perhaps, a hundred of such cribs as ours, and worth over $100,000, where the process of "re-making up" is going on, preparatory to the long, slow tow down the broad waters of the Ottawa to Ste. Anne, where the whole work of separation has to be gone over again. Again, too, at Lachine, the whole raft is dismembered, and the dangers of those terrible rapids must be run with no assistance from slides, before the calm bosom of the St. Lawrence can bear our timbers to the tall ships of frowning Quebec and the chances of Atlantic storms.

For us now, not unwilling to accept the hospitality freely extended to all visitors, there is the pleasant red fire of the raft to stand by, and the tin pannikins (carefully cleansed in our honour) filled from a huge and ever-simmering cauldron of blackest tea brew; there is bread, new and white enough, and vigour-giving pork and nourishing beans, all of which Jules, *chef-de-cuisine* of the craft, offers us with hospitable thought and a pleasant smile, showing his white teeth the while. Jules' dubiously agreeable mission is to fill the ever-empty forty or fifty hearty and healthy giants who compose the crew, and as they begin work and breakfasting at daybreak, the generous pots must always be ready to supply food till far on in the night. Such ponderous and much-worked machinery requires big furnaces, and the fuel must be at hand at all hours. We drink our tea and praise the bread—bringing thereby a glow of satisfaction to the brown cheek of our kind cook—and, if allowed, present a small *douceur*; then, with a hand-shake and a *bon voyage*, we step ashore and leave our craft to its fate.

This descent of the slides is a feature so peculiar to the city that all her illustrious visitors are introduced to its charms as a matter of course. The Prince of Wales, Prince Arthur, the Grand Duke Alexis, Lord and Lady Dufferin, and Lord Lorne with the Princess Louise, have all undergone the ordeal with much success and amusement, and have thereby entered the ranks of the initiated into the craft of the raftsmen. Farther than this slight playful flirtation with a difficult and dangerous life, they would not probably care to venture.

A simple, kindly-hearted, easily-amused race of men are these same stalwart sons of the forest, the rapid, and the stream. Given plenty of work and plenty of food, and having unlimited fresh air and consciences the most unburdened, the labours of the day find sufficient relief in nightly gatherings round the huge fires of the raft or shanty. Some will certainly be found who can tell a good story, dance a cunning if noisy jig, or sing one of the many quaint, childish, but often touching airs which, floating down intact from the primitive days of the early French rule, still delight the *voyageurs* of to-day. Perhaps it is the story of the *trois beaux canards*, who, swimming in the pond, are shot at by the *fils du roi*, so *méchant* with its likely but inconsonant chorus of the "rolling ball"; how the white duck fell, and

> "*Par ces yeux lui sort'nt des diamants*
> *En roulant ma boule.*
> *Et par ce bec, l'or et l'argent,*
> *Roule, roulant, ma boule roulant ;*
> *En roulant ma boule roulant,*
> *En roulant ma boule,*"

is a tale known wherever the shantyman has set foot. Or perhaps the praises of their snug halting place, "Bytown," are sung. Thus—

> "*À Bytown c'est une jolie place*
> *Où il s'ramass' ben d'la crasse ;*
> *Où ya des jolies filles*
> *Et aussi des jolis garcons.*
> *Dans les chantiers nous hivernerons.*"

Popular amongst their songs is that of the famous Marlborough, hero of *la belle nation*, by virtue of his five years' service with Turenne; and the air "*Malbrough s' en va-t-en guer-re,*" queerly surviving with us as wedded to the words, "We won't go home till morning," has startled the drinking deer of many a river bend on many a misty morning. But chief of all stands the tender "*A la claire fontaine !*" with its sad lover of the weeping heart and lost mistress, which, it is said, all the Canadian world, from the child of seven to the white-haired man, knows and sings. These are the songs which can still be heard from the brow of Parliament Hill, on the warm summer evenings, floating up from the monster rafts which, ever-gathering, lie moored at its wood-fringed base ; links are these songs, binding the river of the Past to the river of To-day.

Beyond Major's Hill, or rather at its extreme end, is Nepean Point, a rival to the big rocky promontory to the westward, upon which the Parliament Buildings stand. Here is the saluting battery, from which, on certain high " white stone " days, the curl of smoke and boom of big guns tells of a fresh birthday for the Queen, or for the young Dominion, or of the state visits of England's representatives to the Senate, or of the opening or closing of Parliament. From this, of all the many points from which the " Buildings " can be viewed, they present, perhaps, the most picturesque aspect. Sufficiently near to be taken in as a whole, and yet far enough off to be merged in the grace-giving veil of the atmosphere, their effect in the warm glow of the sun as it sets in the west is simply delightful to the painter's eye. Bit by bit their dainty towers and pinnacles and buttresses fade out in the subdued tones of evening, changing from the

WESTERN BLOCK, DEPARTMENTAL BUILDINGS.

"symphony in red" to a "harmony in gray," till moonlight makes them all glorious as a "nocturne in silver and black."

But the centre—the heart —of Ottawa lies, of course, in its Parliament and Departmental Buildings. Commenced in 1859, the first stone was laid by the Prince of Wales in 1860, and they were occupied in 1865, though much remained to be done after that date; the library and an extension of one of the blocks, the grounds, and the surrounding walls and railings, having been subsequently added. In their present form they cost fully five million dollars, and cover an area of about four acres. They form three sides of a huge square, which is laid down in grass, beautifully kept, whose fresh, green surface,

FROM MAIN ENTRANCE UNDER CENTRAL TOWER.

crossed with broad paths, stands above the level of Wellington Street, from which it is separated by a low stone wall with handsome railing and gates. Rising above this square, on a stone terrace with sloping carriage approaches on either side, the great central block, with a massive tower 220 feet high in the centre, faces the square. This building, three storeys in height, has a frontage of forty-seven feet and, like the sister buildings on either side, is built in a style of architecture based on the Gothic of the twelfth century, combining the elements of grace and simplicity which the climate of the country seems to require. A cream-coloured sandstone from the neighbouring district, to which age is fast adding fresh beauty of colour, with arches over the doors and windows of a warm, red sandstone from Potsdam and dressings of Ohio freestone, has been happily employed—the effect of colour, apart from form, being most grateful to the eye. This building contains the two Chambers—for the Commons and the Senate—and all the accommodation necessary for the officers of both Houses. The Chamber of the Commons is an oblong hall, fitted

LOOKING UP THE OTTAWA, FROM PARLIAMENT GROUNDS.

with separate seats and desks for the members, the Speaker's chair being placed in the middle of one side, leaving a somewhat narrow passage-way from which on either hand the desks of the members rise in tiers. The ceiling is supported by graceful clus-

MAIN BUILDINGS, HOUSES OF PARLIAMENT.

ters of marble pillars—four in each—and a broad gallery runs round the Chamber which, on important nights, is crowded with politicians, ladies, members of deputations and others interested, from all parts of the Dominion. The debates would be more appreciated by the public if the speakers could be better heard, though perhaps such a statement implies a compliment that should be limited to a select few of the members; but, as with so many other buildings intended for public speaking, the Chamber was constructed without reference to any principles of acoustics. Few of the speeches delivered in the House can be called inspiring. In fact, when not personal, they are prosaic. This can hardly be helped, for a Canadian Parliament, like Congress in the United States, deals, as a rule, with matters from which only genius could draw inspiration. The French-Canadian members, in consequence, probably, of the classical training that is the basis of their education, are far superior to their English-speaking *confrères* in accuracy of expression and grace of style. Even when they speak in English these qualities are noticeable. The Senate Chamber, which, with its offices, occupies the other half of the huge building, is of precisely the same architectural character, the colouring of carpets and upholstery being, however, of crimson, and the seats being differently arranged; the throne, occupied by the representative of Her Majesty, is at the far end, on a dais of crimson cloth; and in front of it is the Speaker's chair. Here the ceremonies connected with the opening and closing of Parliament take place—the former being an event of much importance—indeed, one of the leading incidents of the life of the capital. It is a pretty sight, with the gay uniforms of the military, the rich dress of the ministers, the scarlet gowns of the Supreme Court judges, and the varied toilets of the ladies. It is usually followed in the evening by the holding of a "drawing-room," at which the strict rules of etiquette which govern European assemblages of the kind are dispensed with, and any one who desires can, by complying with the ordinary requirements of every-day domestic life as to evening dress, be present, and make acquaintance with the representative of the Crown in most simple and republican fashion.

Behind the two Chambers is situated the Parliamentary Library, a building of exceptional architectural grace externally. Flying buttresses of great strength and beauty give a distinctive character to the structure, while its lofty dome is a landmark far and near. Inside it is fitted with all possible regard to convenience, the workmanship being of elaborately-carved wood, and comprising cunningly-devised recesses for reading purposes, with rooms for the librarian and his staff. In the centre is a noble marble statue of the Queen, executed by Marshall Wood. Marble busts of the Prince and Princess of Wales are prominent treasures of the room. In its chief librarian, Dr. Alpheus Todd, it possesses a head whose standing as a writer upon constitutional law is recognized in all parts of the world. The remaining buildings, on the east and west sides of the square, are occupied by the several departments of the Government, and are well adapted to meet the present requirements. The east block, which contains the office of the Governor-General and the Chambers of the Privy Council, possesses at its entrance a tower of graceful design, which very favourably impresses the spectator from Elgin Street, to whose eye it gives the first intimation of the vicinity of the buildings.

Running entirely round the three blocks of the Parliament and Departmental buildings is a broad drive, and at the sides and in rear of the library, the grounds, like those in the front, are laid out in handsome and well-planned flower-beds, with great stretches of green lawn, overlooking the cliff. Here, from a pretty summer-house erected close to the edge of the precipitous slope, a widely commanding view is afforded of the broad stream of the Ottawa to the east and west. Immense rafts are being made up in all directions; steamers and tugs ply up and down, taking big barges, laden with lumber, to the markets of the world, or toilfully working their way up the rapid current with the burden of a long "tow" of empty ones returning to the yards to be reloaded.

On the other side is the city of Hull, and farther down the river is the mouth of the Gatineau, itself a great river, whose banks are

TOWER OF EASTERN BLOCK, DEPARTMENTAL BUILDINGS.

studded here and there with queer clusters of wooden cottages, which the spring freshets annually transform into lacustrine dwellings of most grotesque discomfort. Over, far away,

"Where the sunny end of evening smiles—
Miles and miles,"

is the range of hills, the outcrop of the old Laurentians, known as the King's

Mountain, where are all manner of delightful haunts for the artist—tiny lakes and scared and moss-grown cliffs and huge boulders—places where man is yet a stranger and the whistle of the locomotive a far-distant horror of the future. The valley of the Gatineau is marvellously rich in mineral wealth—phosphates, iron ore of the purest plumbago, mica, and almost all known varieties of minerals are found, though discovery in this direction is yet in its infancy. The first three are, however, somewhat extensively mined, and only await the advent of capital to become a source of great wealth to the neighbourhood. This is a country rich, too, in prizes for the botanist and entomologist, while the river boasts of rapids and falls which would delight the eye of the painter, so gracefully picturesque are their manifold surgings and leapings.

Besides the Gatineau and the hilly range in front, the summer-house gives a view to the west far up the Ottawa till, nine miles off, the shimmer of light shows a broad surface of smooth water. Lac du Chêne is one of the many expansions of the noble river, beside which, snugly nestled, lies the village of Aylmer, a great centre for summer excursions, being only twenty minutes' run from the city by train. Below, at our feet, there runs all the way round the steep slope of Parliament Hill, a delightful winding path—the "Lover's Walk"—cut out of the hillside. A more charming stroll for man or maid, lover or misanthrope, could not be wished for. Shut off from the city life and embowered in trees, whose cool shade makes the hottest day bearable, the fortunate Ottawaite can here "laze" himself into a state of dreamy contentment. Through breaks in the foliage the silver river gleams, busy and beautiful, a hundred feet below; the white stems of the birch gracefully relieve the sombre gleam of hemlock and the fresher tints of the maple, all for him. Birds talk to him, sing to him. The oriole, with its uniform of black and orange, pauses a moment to wish him well, and a bright gleam of greenish-blue shows him the kingfisher, far too busily engaged for talk. Perhaps the momentary hovering of a tiny ball of emerald and sapphire and opal, and a sound as of an overgrown bumble-bee, shows the presence of a humming-bird; while from some near bough the "Canada bird" repeats its tenderly sympathetic note—"Poor Canada, Canada, Canada!" with most evident irrelevancy and possible chaff. From the mills of the Chaudière come the faint buzz of the saw, and the noise of the "Big Kettle," which is well seen from the "Walk." All this in the golden haze of a summer's afternoon! Who shall say that Ottawa is not beautiful?

But when the summer has worn away, and the frost in the chilly autumn nights has "bitten the heel of the going year," and the sensitive leaves of the maples, stricken to death by the first breath of winter, end their brief lives in an exquisite fever flush, making wood and hillside a very painter's feast of rich colour, Ottawa begins to prepare for the second phase of her existence, her merry winter season. Then comes the first snow fall, and soon the cheery ting-tang of sleigh-bells makes gay music for a gay white world, and the rumble and dust of her summer streets have gone for a five

GOVERNMENT HOUSE, FROM SKATING POND.

months' spell. Steamers and tugs and barges are laid up in her once-busy stream, and the sluggish waters thicken with the increasing cold till, bit by bit, the tiny ice crystals knit themselves into a solid coat two feet in thickness, and the Ottawa is bridged from shore to shore.

That the winter in Ottawa is emphatically *winter*, and no half-hearted compromise, there is not a shadow of doubt, and therein lies its charm. No vacillating slush and half-melted snow in the streets, no rain and fog in the air—all is hard and white and clear underfoot, while overhead there is the purest of blue skies, which night transforms into the most glorious of diamond-studded canopies.

Here now flock from the shores of the Atlantic, a thousand miles away; from Manitoba, the hopeful centre of the Dominion; from beyond the towering barriers of the Rocky Mountains to the Pacific Coast, three thousand miles distant; and from many a city, town, village and homestead between—the legislators of the land. The ordinarily quiet streets are busy with life, the hotels are all crowded, and the lobbies of the Parliament Buildings are haunted by those peculiar gentry who gather together round dispensers of patronage. Dances, dinners, balls and theatricals follow in quick succession. Visitors on business and visitors on pleasure come and go, and the work and play of a whole year is compressed into three stirring months; the noble piles of the public buildings are brilliant with light, while far into the night the many-coloured windows of the "Chambers" throw gay reflections on the snow outside.

The chief centre, as is fitting, of all winter hospitality, is Government House; and in the occupants of the "Hall" Canada has long had representatives of her dignity, who have worthily maintained her character as a generous and hospitable country, and the care which grudges no pains or cost to give pleasure has its own reward in the kindly feeling which invariably follows acquaintance with the simple-mannered, self-forgetting lady and gentleman who stand at the head of Canadian society.

Government House is about two miles from the city. Past the Rideau Falls, the road leads on through the village of New Edinburgh to the lodge gates. Down this road, in the winter of 1880, the horses attached to the sleigh which was conveying H. R. H. the Princess Louise, to hold a drawing-room in the Senate Chamber, bolted, overturning the sleigh, dragging it a considerable distance along the frozen ground. This accident resulted, unhappily, in severe injury to the illustrious lady. Once through the gates, a drive of a few hundred yards through a pretty bit of native woodland leads to the house. Half way up this drive the Princess has caused an opening to be cut in the woods, known as the "Princess' Vista," through which a lovely view is afforded of the broad stream of the Ottawa and the shore and distant hills beyond.

Utterly devoid of any attempt at architectural style—a piecemeal agglomeration of incongruous brick, plaster, and stone, "Rideau Hall" or Government House is at once one of the most unpretentious and disappointing yet comfortable of residences. Set in

OTTAWA: HISTORICAL AND DESCRIPTIVE

WELLINGTON STREET IN WINTER

THE PRINCESS' VISTA.

a delightfully varied area of grass, garden, and forest, comprising nearly ninety acres of land, the building presents an aspect the most commonplace to the visitor, who sees only the bare wooden porch of the doorway, flanked on the right by the tennis court (which by a charming transformation does duty as a supper-room), and on the left by the ball-room. But the pleasantness of the place lies in the yet unseen. Away back from that unprepossessing central doorway stretches a long, gray-stone, two-storied building, whose rooms look out upon flower-gardens and conservatories, and which has all those delightful surprises in the way of cosy, oddly-shaped apartments, such as buildings which have grown, bit by bit, from small beginnings so often possess.

Besides the never-ending round of balls, dinners and general entertaining, for which Government House is famous, there is the range of out-of-door fun; and here come in skating, curling, and above all, the toboggan. Out of Canada or Russia, the delights of the toboggan slide are but matters of imagination. Nowhere else can the swift downward rush into the strong, healthy embrace of the frosty air, over the glossy, white surface of the hardened snow be enjoyed; and the very best of Canadian slides—barring the somewhat dangerful Montmorency, and perhaps the glacis of Fort Henry at Kingston—is at Government House. Here, in the grounds, reared on a high mound, there rises far above the tree-tops all through the summer a huge bare structure of stout timbers, from the summit of which descends, at a steep angle, a boarded trough, ending with the foot of the hill, which winter sees snow-covered and the centre of laughter and most hearty, healthful fun. This, and two fine, smooth areas of well-kept ice, and a long, covered rink for the benefit of curlers, are among the attractions to hundreds of guests of the House through the winter season. It is a merry, jolly scene, when the rinks are crowded with skaters performing all manner of intricate figures and dances, while the sharp hiss and clink of the steel forms a cheery accompaniment to the roar and rush of the toboggan as it sweeps down with its laughing load and vanishes far away under the distant trees.

To the Canadian the toboggan is as familiar as a household word: but for the benefit of the uninitiated, it should be explained that it is a thin strip of wood about two feet wide and six or eight feet long, curled up in front to throw off the snow, the "form" being maintained by thongs of deer's sinew. Upon this a well-padded cushion or buffalo-skin is fastened, and the result is a toboggan of luxury. To be comfortable, one should be prepared—the object being to keep out the fine snow from a too intimate relationship with the body. A pair of thick woollen stockings and moose-skin moccasins over the feet, a blanket-coat of white or blue, and a tuque (or *habitant's* long cap) on the head, or one of fur well jammed down over the ears, with long, fur gauntlets, makes a capital costume. The ladies are charming in gay blanket coats of red or white or blue, or warm fur mantles, with snug white "clouds" wound coquettishly over their fur caps. Most bewitching is this Canadian tobogganning dress, bringing such piquant effect to a pretty face touched with the ripe, rich glow of health, as makes mere ball-room beauty commonplace. The toboggan is a most accommodating vehicle. Charming as a carrier of two, it is delightful with three, and four can go down on it with comfort. Having climbed to the top of the slide by a series of steps, the party prepares to descend. The garments of the gentle freight are carefully tucked in and, seated one behind the other, the steerer last, ready either with hand or with foot outstretched behind to guide the erratic craft. Letting go their hold, with the swoop of an eagle and a harsh, grating, crash and crackle, down they rush at the rate of twenty miles an hour, cutting the sharp, keen air which, in return, almost takes their breath away; bounding headlong over any irregularities in the road, past the foot of the hill in a twinkling, where a crowd of spectators stands ready to applaud success or laugh at

TOBOGGANING AT GOVERNMENT HOUSE

mishap, and flashing along the smooth white track beyond for a quarter of a mile or more till the speed slackens, and they spring up hurriedly, to leave the path clear for the next jolly party which is close on their heels. Sometimes and, indeed, frequently enough, there is a spill; the toboggan is ill-balanced, some one moves to right or left, or the preceding toboggan has scored too deep a curve in the snow, and in a moment the whole party is sent flying at all manner of queer tangents, but no harm is done. There is a good deal of laughing, much brushing off of the snow-dust,

VIEW ACROSS THE OTTAWA.

and "better luck next time." It is half the fun being occasionally upset, and, indeed, it takes some skill and much good fortune to ensure a successful run. Lord Lorne, besides building a second and loftier slide, has introduced a new charm tobogganing by torchlight—and a more quaintly fairy picture could not be desired than this affords. Hundreds of Chinese lanterns dot the trees or hang in festoons, while the long course is outlined with flaming torches, and a monster bonfire throws a ruddy glow over everything. Hot mulled wine and coffee and the music of a military band make the charm complete, and supper puts the perfecting touch to Canada's great winter pastime.

Into this merry sport, as into all others which the bright Canadian winter offers, the Princess enters with the hearty zest of her simple, unaffected, womanly nature, laughingly beguiling her more timid guests into essaying the descent with her, and successfully "taking them down." Both the present Governor-General and his predecessor, throwing the same energy into their play as into their work, have been the life and soul of rink and slide; and the natural, home-like life of the "Hall," which so many hundreds have shared, is at its brightest in these constantly-repeated gatherings.

Such, then, is Ottawa in its several aspects of social, political, and business life—the

"Fair city with its crown of towers,"

as Lord Dufferin happily styled her. Picturesque she cannot fail to be, for nature has made her so; a power she must be for good or bad, throughout the land, for her fortunes have so willed it. Holding in her midst the centred force of a whole people, and being, by virtue of her strange wild past and noble present, the link that binds the old to the new—the experience-taught, sober Old World across the sea to the fresh energy and restless vitality of this great young continent—may she prove worthy of her honours! May the bells of the capital of the Dominion ever—

> "Ring out a slowly-dying cause,
> And ancient forms of party strife;
> Ring in the nobler modes of life
> With sweeter manners, purer laws."

VICE-REGAL CHAIR, SENATE CHAMBER.

THE UPPER OTTAWA

THE attractions of the city to which the Ottawa River has given a name, its political, social, and commercial importance, lead many to limit their interest to that part of the river which lies below the Chaudière. Yet the Upper Ottawa presents an unbroken panorama of scenery scarce to be rivalled in Canada, if on the American continent; scenery that changes from the pastoral calm of unruffled river and lake, fit mirror and bath for the yet unscared Dryad of the woods, which alternate with wheat-field, farm, and village—to the torrent, whirling trees like playthings; the cascade leaping in silver shaft from the precipice; the archipelago of five hundred islets; the still, dark depth of current under Oiseau Rock; the broad, navigable stream between mountains clad with primeval forest,—to where the locomotive of the new-built railway outscreams the eagle amid the lonely hills of Mattawa. The scenery of the Upper Ottawa is, perhaps, the least known in Canada. It is still in very many places as wild, as unmarked by the presence of man, as when Champlain discovered it. Yet it is full of promise for the wealth and civilization of the future; unlimited wood-supply and water-power; land that bears the finest of cereals; marble that already decks the Chambers of our National Parliament; with hills and cliffs in whose womb lie, awaiting birth, the most useful of the economic metals. Such are but a few of the natural advantages of this part of our country.

Nor is the scenery without historic associations of interest. From the earlier times it was the great water highway of the Indian race, who knew no better road for their hunting expeditions. Its true Indian name was the "Kit-chi-sippe," of which the French

"Grande Rivière" is a mere literal translation; "sippi," or "sippe," meaning water, as in "Mississippi," and many other Indian names.

The name "Ottawa" was, according to the best Indian authorities, the appellation of a tribe of Algonquins whom the French *voyageurs* met on the river, although their real home was on Lake Michigan—the word signifying "the human ear," a tribal title. A portion of this tribe occupied the territory near Calumet and Allumette.

The modern history of the Upper Ottawa begins with the illustrious discoverer who first led the way on its waters to the great lakes of the West—Samuel de Champlain of whom mention has elsewhere been made in this work as the Father of New France and the Founder of Quebec and Montreal. An embassy from the Algonquins of the Ottawa had asked his aid in their war with the Iroquois, who, inhabiting what is now New York State, were a kind of pre-historic Annexationists in their desire to add to their own country what is now Canada. It was, all through, Champlain's policy to make the Algonquins subjects, converts and soldiers, against the Iroquois heathen. And when a Frenchman of his party, named Vignan, who had passed up the river in the Algonquin canoes, returned, after a year in the Upper Ottawa region, with a wonderful story of a great lake at the source of the Ottawa, and of a river beyond it that led to the ocean, Champlain was captivated by the tale. All the gold of India and the spice islands of the Orient seemed brought within the reach of France. On Monday, the 27th day of May, 1615, he left his fort at Montreal with a party of five Frenchmen including Vignan and a single Indian guide, in two small canoes. Carrying their canoes by land past the rapids, they glided in the tiny egg-shell ships that were freighted with the future of Canada's civilization, over the tranquil depth of Lac du Chêne, till the cataracts of the Chats, foaming over the limestone barrier stretched across the lake, confronted them as with a wall of waters. Undaunted by a scene still, as then, terrible in its wild sublimity, they pressed on, toiling with their canoes over the portage to where Arnprior now stands; thence over the Lake of the Chats to what is now Portage du Fort. Here the Indians said that the rapids—those of the Calumet—were impassable. They entered the broken hill country through a pine forest where a late tornado had strewn huge trees in every direction. In the painful toil of crossing this *débris*, they lost part of their baggage. Long years afterward a rapier and an astrolabe, or astronomical instrument for observing the stars, were found in this region: the date on the astrolabe, corresponding to that of this expedition, showing it to be a veritable relic of Champlain. Past the perilous impediments of this portage, they crossed Lake Coulange to the island of the Allumette. There a friendly chief named Tessonet received them. While at his camp, Champlain discovered that Vignan had deceived him, and had never been farther up the river than the camp of Tessonet. Champlain pardoned the impostor, whom his Indian allies wished to kill with torture. He then returned to the fort at Quebec, and in his frail vessel once more crossed the ocean to France. Here he met with some encouragement, and returning with supplies and missionary priests, Champlain set out a second time on the Upper Ottawa with a single Frenchman and ten Indians, till he reached the Indian camp at Allumette. Thence, twenty miles of navigable river stretched before him, straight as the bird flies, between the sombre hills. Passing the rapids—the Joachim and the Caribou, the Rocher Capitaine and the Deux Rivières—they reached the term of their voyage on the Ottawa at its junction with the Mattawa. Thence they made their way to Lake Nipissing and the great Western Lakes. A score of years afterwards, successful in all the great exploits he had undertaken, this strange compound of adventurer, statesman, soldier, saint and scholar, died at Quebec, on Christmas Day, 1635.

To Champlain, discoverer of the Upper Ottawa route, traders and mission priests succeeded as civilizing agents. A fur-trading company was formed by merchants in France, whose *voyageurs* and *coureurs de bois* penetrated far up the river among the friendly Algonquins. Important mission stations were formed in the Huron and Simcoe regions, the road to which was by the Upper Ottawa. It is impossible to read of the marvellous labours and sufferings of those missionaries without feeling the admiration due to brave men. One missionary died at a slow fire, his neck circled with hot axes, his head in mockery baptised with boiling water, praying for his torturers to the end. Father Jogues, having survived torture and mutilation, returned to France, where he was greeted as a martyr for the Faith. All Europe rang with his praise. In the Royal Palace the Queen—Anne of Austria—kissed his dismembered hand. But he would not be stayed from returning to his work in the wilderness. Another was found dead in the woods. He was kneeling; his hands clasped—frozen while he prayed! Apostolic devotion met with Apostolic success. The blood of the Jesuit martyrs has been the seed of the Roman Church on the Upper Ottawa. In every town and village, even to far-off Mattawa, the Roman Catholic church is one of the largest; the Indians continue firm in its fold. Regular visits are paid each winter by mission priests to the shanties; few Christian congregations are more devoted to their clergy or more attentive to religious worship, than these rough, French-speaking lumbermen, many of whom are of half-Indian descent.

To the fur-trade of the French merchants succeeded, after the English Conquest, the rule of the Hudson's Bay Company, whose forts and outposts have been receding, as a higher form of industry supplants the traffic of the hunters. Now the trade, *par excellence*, of the Upper Ottawa, is that of lumber, for which the river is the main artery in Canada. In fact, this industry has assumed a first place in our commerce; the vast forests along the river margin are peopled every season by armies of lumbermen; and the Ottawa floats the wealth thus secured on to the sea-ships that bear it to every haven in the world.

For nine miles above the Chaudière the Ottawa is so broken by rapids as to be

TIMBER BOOM, FITZROY HARBOUR.

unnavigable. A steamer plies between Aylmer and Fitzroy Harbour, on the Ottawa side of the Chats rapids. The passage along the expansion of the river, called Lac du Chêne, affords a view of the pleasant village of Aylmer. On either shore the country side betokens advanced civilization—gardens and farm-lands stretching far and wide. On the Ottawa side a quaint old wooden church marks, in the township of South March, the settlement of descendants of military officers of the Anglo-American War of 1812-15. On the Quebec side is the village of Quio, at the mouth of the river of the same name, where the steamer calls. In the background are the dark outlines of the Laurentian Mountains, their nearer slopes covered with dense woods. The scenery now is as wild as when Champlain first adventured on these waters. Landing at Pontiac, from a group of log-houses whose primitive roughness is not ill-matched with the scenery, we see in the distance the gigantic limestone barrier which here crosses the river, and the far-off column of cataract-spray from the largest of the Chats rapids. The steamer touches, at Fitzroy Harbour, a point in the scene well worthy of study, and where we get one of the best views of the Chats. The little village is out of sight—insignificant and poverty-stricken—but from the hill which hides it we see the walls of precipice, island and cataract, which stretch across the entire Ottawa, like the bridle of stone with which the genii in Eastern fable were bidden to curb some mighty river! At the left side, on the Fitzroy shore, is the mouth of the River Carp, which winds its tortuous way from the pleasant pastures of Hazeldean, near Ottawa; and a semi-circular strand, strewn with logs, ends in a point covered with dense, low verdure.

THE CHATS, FROM PONTIAC.

Near us, two fishermen are shoving off a boat; it is of the kind called a *bonne*, or "good girl." These boats are much used by lumbermen. Flat-bottomed, invariably painted red, and shaped something like a "scow." It is well to hire one of them and push into the lake so as to get a thorough view of the waterfalls. These are generally counted as sixteen; in reality, we observe many more, and as we get nearer, realize the fact that the entire strength and stress of the Ottawa is bent on forcing its way over this barrier of limestone precipice. Sometimes it takes the opposing rampart by storm, surging over it in a sudden charge, foamless and sprayless, an unbroken dome of water; then, as its first force is spent, and it has lost its spring, it begins to plunge, surging and seething round the rocks that interpose to break its course, and hurling downwards the logs it has carried in its current, like missiles against a foe. Or, as we glide beneath the overhanging cliffs, we see how, from some narrow opening at the summit, a rocket-like, lance-shaped shaft of clear white water leaps alone into the abyss below! Between the cascades, the rocks appear like separate islands, where the thirsty cedars and willows cling with serpent-like

THE CHATS FALLS.

roots to the water-hollowed stone; maple and birch brightening the sombre pines, and veteran firs, gaunt with years, keeping guard. And through all, in a thousand unseen channels, we feel that the river-flood is spreading the secret of its fertilizing power. Most remarkable of all, however, is the largest of the "chutes" or waterfalls; it is that whose white spray, rising high over the outline of the wood, we saw from Pontiac—a pillar of mist, which but for its purer whiteness, might be mistaken for one of the columns of bush-fire smoke in the country around.

On a closer view we discern, on either side, the shelving or sharpened masses of bare brown rock, to whose sides and summits the cedars cling as for dear life, clutching with their spreading roots all available vantage-ground. Far above, where the wind wafts aside the curtain of dim-blue vapour, we can see the torrent sweep, at first without impediment or break. But in the centre, black against the snow-coloured cataract, rises a mass of rock—a miniature fortress—secure in the midst of the turmoil. Breaking upon this, like cavalry against an army it cannot shake or shatter, the pride of the cascade is humbled. It divides into two torrents, in whose career all shape and outline is lost in a fury of foam, in waves that hurry they know not whither, turning to and fro the logs that fleck their course, and fully realizing the grace and bounding ease of the tameless wild beast from which these waterfalls were not inaptly named.

As a means of direct communication between the portions of the river above and below the Chats, a slide has been constructed at considerable expense by the

QUIO, FROM THE CHATS.

Canadian Government. Beside this the slide-master's house is built, a good view of which may be seen from Fitzroy Harbour. After examining the waterfalls, and especially the largest chute, the Niagara of the Chats, it is pleasant, while close to its reek and rout, to look towards the Quebec side from the strip of waters to the "Everlasting Hills" in the far distance; the charm of the perspective is enhanced by jutting point and island, beyond which are the church-towers and house roofs of the French village of Quio.

The origin of the name "Chats" is doubtful. Some say it is a translation of the Indian appellation, it being a habit of the early French *voyageurs* to adopt the Indian designations; others, that it was so called from the number of wild-cats found in the neighbouring woods; while a resemblance that might well have suggested the name is seen in the cataracts with extended claws, in rifted rocks like the fangs of the *felinæ*, in the hissing, spluttering and fury of the descending cascades. But above that region of noise and terror, the "Lake of the Wild-Cats" is tame, with talons sheathed and tempestuous passions hushed. Through the clear, exhilarating air, the sun is strewing gold upon the stirless water, except where the steamer glides with a track of swaying jewels. The sky is imaged in the ultramarine of the lake, or rather, of the river, which here expands so broadly that a faint blue mist veils the woods on the Quebec shore. This expansion extends nearly to Portage du Fort. Arnprior, on the south shore, is a place of some importance, from its lumbering establishments and its quarries of beautiful marble, of which the shafts of the columns in the Houses of Parliament at Ottawa are formed. Beyond and above us, wind, with slope ever-changing, never monotonous, the dark-purple undulations of the Laurentian Hills.

Near the end of the lake we notice an enormous boom stretching across the river. On the Quebec shore is the dwelling of the boom-master, whose duty it is to see to all things pertaining to the effective working of that important key to the lumberer's treasury. The boom seems closed against us; but as our steamer, the "Jeannette," approaches, the boom-master's assistant, who has been on the look-out for us, walks airily along the floating boom, narrow as it is, and opens a kind of gate. We pass through, and steam onward under the shadow of a steep hill covered with forest, the haunt of bears and lynxes. Here the river parts into several narrow channels, which run between small islands of white stone. The current is very rapid; at the high water of spring no steamer can breast it, but now our little craft makes way gallantly. As we pass close beneath the miniature cliffs, we remark how their rocky sides are scooped and tunnelled, sometimes in the most curious shapes and mimicries of human art. As a rule, the markings are longitudinal, and resemble those which a comb would make if drawn along the surface of a fresh-plastered wall. The farthest of these islets is called Snow Island. To the river-drivers descending the stream in the spring, the mass of white rock looks like a huge drift of snow.

The steamer lands us at the little village of Portage du Fort, at the foot of the series of rapids down which, from over the falls of the Calumet, the Ottawa thunders. The road, up hill and down gully, which replaces the portage path of ancient days, even now suggests the difficulties which caused this carrying-place to be called "Portage du Fort." Before the construction of the railway, this bit of stage-road was an important link in the chain of Upper Ottawa communication; but now it is little used except by the river-drivers and the few inhabitants of the villages at either end. We pass a pretty little Gothic church perched on the hill which overlooks the Portage du Fort rapids. It belongs to the Episcopalians, and is built in rigidly-correct early English style; there are some good memorial windows, gifts of the Usburne family who owned the mills, which have since been transferred to Braeside, near Arnprior. The river between Portage du Fort and the Calumet is only navigable by the lumbermen's boats descending the current in the high waters of spring-time. Even to these, this part of the Ottawa is dangerous, and is the scene of many fatal accidents. Where the river winds under the Portage du Fort church, its course takes a sudden turn, at the northern angle of which there is a projecting arm of sharp-pointed rock, partially submerged by the spring flood-tides. Woe to the birch canoe or even the stouter-ribbed *bonne* carried, by incautious steering, too near the " Devil's Elbow." Over nine miles of uninteresting hilly road we drive to Bryson, a thriving village close to the Calumet Falls, where we hire a canoe with an Indian—or rather, half-breed—to propel it. He is most painstaking in his endeavour to carry us to every point of interest. Strangely insecure as these most capsizeable of craft appear on first acquaintance, one soon gets to like them. The motion is gentle, and they glide over the water like a duck. The canoe brings us to a point where, by ascending a portage track up the hill, we get close to the Grand Chute. This track is much worn. As we reach the summit of the hill, the guide bids us pause beside a mound covered with stones and fenced by a rude railing. The railing and a rough attempt at a memorial cross have nearly all been cut away by the knives of visitors—not in desecrating curiosity, but in veneration for the sanctity of him who sleeps beneath! It is the grave of Cadieux.

In the days of the early French explorations of the Upper Ottawa, there came to this region of the Allumette and Calumet, where Champlain himself had been so kindly received by the chiefs of the Ottawa Indians, a French *voyageur* named Cadieux. No one knew why he had quitted Old France; but though he could fight and hunt as deftly as the oldest *coureur de bois*, Cadieux also knew many things that were strange to these rough children of the forest. He was highly educated. Especially could he compose both music and poetry, and could sing so that it was good to hear him; and he wooed and won a lovely Indian maiden of the Algonquin Ottawas. Their wigwam, with those of a few of her tribe, stood near this very spot, close to the Great Fall of the Calumet. Once upon a time, they were preparing their canoes to go down with their store of winter furs to Montreal. All was peace in their camp when, on a sudden, the alarm was given that a large war-party of the dreaded Iroquois were stealing through the woods. There was but one hope left. Cadieux, with a single Indian to support him, would hold the foe at bay, while his wife and her friends should launch their canoe down the rapids. It was quickly done. The canoe was committed to the boiling waters of the cataract, the skilful Indians paddled for their lives, and the wife of Cadieux, who was a devout Catholic, prayed Ste. Anne to help them. From eddy to eddy the canoe was swept, and still, as she bounded on, the Indians saw that a figure seemed to move before them to direct their course—a form as of a lady in mist-like, white robes. It was Ste. Anne, protecting her votaress! And so they all made their way safe to Montreal, thanks to the good Saint.

But poor Cadieux did not fare quite so well. Instead of invoking a saint, he was carefully taking up his position behind one tree after another, every now and then shooting an Iroquois. These subtle warriors, not liking to fight what they supposed to be a considerable force, withdrew. But the comrade of Cadieux was slain, his home destroyed, and after some days Cadieux himself died of exhaustion in the woods. Beside him was found, traced by his dying hand, "*Le Lament de Cadieux*," his death-song, which the *voyageurs* have set to a pleasing but melancholy air. It is much in the style of similar "Laments," once common in Norman-French, and is still a favourite at the shanties and on the river. Our guide, who did not look on the above-given legend from the point of view of "the higher criticism," and who had a pleasing voice, sang the song as we stood beside the grave. The French lumbermen and Indians still come here to pray—to do this brings good luck on forest and river—and the trees all around are carved with votive crosses, cut by the pen-knives of the devout among the lumbermen.

We descend through the wood, observing, as we pass, another enormous timber slide. Again we take our way through the woods and down to the beach, where we hear the roar, before indistinct, of the rapids. A little farther on we reach the spray-drenched, slippery rocks, and the greatest of the Upper Ottawa waterfalls, the Grand Chute of the Calumet, is before us.

Those who have most fully analyzed the impression made by such cascade scenery as the Chats, will feel that it is made up of many distinct impressions of the various forms of falling water. In observing this, the largest of the seven chutes of the Calumet, one is struck with the unity and breadth, as well as the sublime beauty, of this cataract. To those who have eyes to see and hearts to feel, it is true with regard to the beauty of form in falling water, as in all other aspects of scenery, that Nature never repeats herself. Her resources are inexhaustible. It is only the incurable cockney who can say, "Sir, one green field is like all green fields!"

In the background is a semi-circle of dark cliffs, gloomy with impending pines. It is cleft in the centre, where, from a height of sixty feet, through foam and spray, and echo of conquered rocks, the main body of the river rushes down. At its base a promontory of black and jagged granite throws into relief the seething mass of whiteness. At some distance to the left of this, and nearer to where we stand, a second torrent of volume equally vast, dashes, white as a snow-drift, through veils of mist. To the right, where the wall of cliff approaches us, a single thread of silver cascade, as furious in its fall, circles and pulsates. In the centre is a vast basin—the meeting of the waters—which rush and drive hither and thither, as if they had lost their way and did not know what to do with themselves. It is a spectacle not to be paralleled in any other waterfall we know of, not excepting Niagara: this vast sea of cataract, this lake of foam, with its setting of cliff, brown in the shadows, purple in the light, and parted in the foreground by the immense masses of ribbed and stratified rock over which the mad passages of water triumph with a supreme sweep and a roar that scares the solitude, as, free at last, they madly career along the lesser rapids to the deep below. Wild and desolate, indeed, are these black and foam-sheeted rocks amid which we stand; no living presence near, but the fish-hawk hovering, with hoarse scream, over the torrent.

FALLS OF THE CALUMET.

Above the Calumet Rapids, as the steamer is no longer running and there is no marked feature in the river scenery to repay canoeing, it is best to drive back to Portage du Fort and proceed by stage to Haley Station, on the Canada Pacific. The country is exceedingly broken and hilly—the same geological formation that we see at the Calumet Falls. Over this country Champlain toiled in what he has described as the most trying part of his Upper Ottawa expedition. The natural difficulties of the rugged hillside track were then enhanced by pine forest, impenetrable on either side of the narrow portage path, which was in many places blocked up by fallen trees, the *debris* of a late tornado. But like the Prince who made his way through the enchanted forest to the "*Belle au bois dormante*," Samuel de Champlain pressed on through all obstacles to where the Future of Canada called him. His journals record the loss of some portion of his baggage at this part of his route. As we have mentioned, an astrolabe has been found in the neighbourhood, no doubt a relic of this memorable adventure. A journey of thirty miles brings us to Pembroke, the county seat of Renfrew. This thriving town is not yet half a century old. Its founder, "Father" White, came to the place in November, 1825. Its prosperity was secured by the growing lumber trade. It is now a progressive but by no means picturesque semi-circular array of buildings in the rear of the railway bridge, and at the confluence of the river Muskrat with the Ottawa. On all sides are piles of lumber, and Pembroke is scented afar off by the odour of fir, pine and cedar, as surely as Ceylon by "spicy breezes." There are no buildings worthy of remark except the Court House and the Catholic church—a large but unornamented structure of cold-gray stone, which stands on the highest ground in the centre of the town. Presently we start in a small steamer, similar to that in which we travelled on the Lake of the Chats, noticing the vast quantities of timber afloat in a boom at the mouth of the Muskrat, and a large wooded island near the town, used only as a pleasure resort. With woods and villages indistinct in the distance, Allumette Island lies on the opposite side of this expansion of the Ottawa, which takes the name of the Upper Allumette Lake. We pass on the Ontario side the mouth of Petawawa River, one of the largest lumbering tributaries of the Ottawa, by which some of the best timber is floated down. Its length is one hundred and forty miles, and it drains an area of two thousand two hundred square miles. The Upper Allumette presents much the same features which have been described in the Lake of the Chats, an equally beautiful expanse of water, fringed with dense woods of oak, poplar, birch and maple, while the tall pines everywhere lift their rugged tops above the sea of verdure. The land on either side is said to be excellent and fairly settled, producing quantities of grain and cattle for the use of the lumber shanties. Formerly pork was the staple food of the shantymen, but fresh beef is now found to be healthier for the men, and the cattle are easily driven over the portage, where to carry barrels of pork was endless labour. The Allumette Lake terminates at the Narrows—so called not because the river is narrow, but because there is but a small channel navigable. In this, as we pass, soundings are taken with a pole, the steamer stopping while it is being done. Here we enter an archipelago of seemingly numberless islands covered with beech, birch, poplar and cedar; and, in the fall season, the pleasantest time of year to make this expedition, lit with lustre of the regalia which the woods assume, to wave farewell to departing summer. It is pleasant to sit on the steamer's deck and watch her glide, with her boat duly in tow astern through these bright waters, "from island unto island," each rising around us in turn, the fresh green of its cedars nestling on the water and contrasting with the scarlet of the soft maple, the yellow of the birch, the young oak's garnet and the larch's gold. Though but little known in comparison with the Thousand Islands, the Narrows of the Upper Ottawa are, in the opinion of most who have visited both, far the more beautiful. And the Narrows has the advantage of being as yet unprofaned by the noise and *impedimenta* of vulgar tourists

At the end of the Narrows is Fort William, till lately a Hudson's Bay Company post; the steamer stopping here, we land. The building formerly occupied by the Company is now a store, supplying a large extent of farm country. As we stood watching the entrance of a very primitive road through the bush, and mentally wondering what manner of horses or vehicles could adventure therein, the question was solved by the appearance of a farmer's wagon on its way to the Fort William store, which is also Post Office and commercial centre to the region. The horses were as fine, large-built and strong as one could wish to see; the driver quite at his ease in managing them, and with ample leisure to pay attention to the rosy-cheeked, laughing-eyed lasses who sat with him. One of these lasses will probably, at no long time hence, keep house through the winter months, while that young man and that team are away in the shanties, earning good pay for the dear ones at home.

From this point, that part of the Ottawa called Deep River begins, where, pressing against the base of the mountains on its northern side, the stream stretches on for twenty miles—deep, dark and navigable. The bluff of this mountain range which we first encounter is called the Oiseau Rock. The front is precipitous; a plumb-line could be almost swung from the summit to the base, where, as the steamer passes quite close, we see the dark openings of caves, said to have been used by the Indians as places of sepulture, which have never been explored. The name "Oiseau Rock" is taken from a legend, common to the folk-lore of every nation, of an eagle having carried off a papoose from an encampment to its eyrie on the summit, whence it was rescued by the mother. These cliffs should be seen by moonlight, which may easily be done by any one inclined to take boat on a fishing excursion from Des Joachims. Then it is that, gliding beneath the cliff which rises sheer above us with its gray lights and sable shadows, we learn to know the giant precipice, where nothing that has not wings has climbed.

The mountains, after leaving Oiseau Rock, are of a more convex shape, and are

SCENES ON THE UPPER OTTAWA.

covered with woods. The pines and firs become more frequent. Dark patches of umber-coloured verdure formed by them alternate on the hillsides with the gayer array with which the forest-nymphs have vested the trees as a farewell tribute to summer. At no time in the year can this scenery look so lovely, and nowhere can the matchless beauty of Canadian autumn forests be seen so perfectly as where these hills are mirrored in the river.

At the head of the Deep River, and under the shadow of these wood-covered mountains, is a wharf with a cluster of outbuildings, and on the slope of a neat

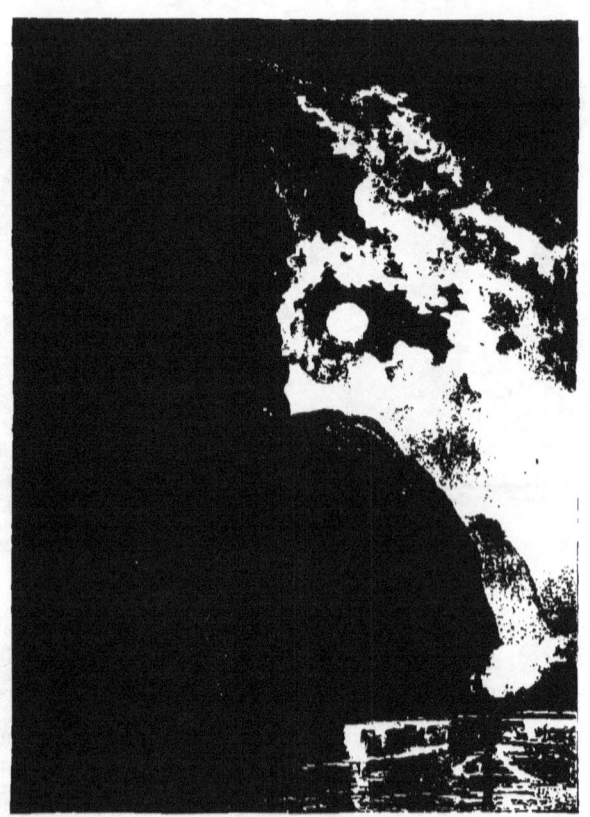

OISEAU ROCK.

green-swarded ascent, a house, something like a Swiss chalet, with a double veranda running all around it. This is our destination—the Hotel Des Joachims. Here it is well to rest awhile, to be lulled to sleep by the roar of the rapids close by;

DES JOACHIMS LANDING.

to be waked by the sunshine lighting up the green, gold and scarlet of the Joachim forest-hills.

As the Joachim rapids are impassable, we drive by stage over the portage to the river-bank above the rapids, where a canoe may be hired to Mackay, a station on the Pacific Railway. Though inferior in beauty to the Deep River scenery, the stream here is over 300 feet wide. The aspect of river and banks is of the same character, and the swift, silent canoe voyage has its charms. At Mackay's the bank has a lower level, and is covered with boulders great and small, of water-rounded gneiss. The name Mackay is taken from a farm-house near by, the only habitation until the Pacific Railway station was built. Here, we find the place positively crowded with lumbermen and railway labourers. All day they swarm to and fro, gang after gang arriving by the incoming trains. All night they sing, shout and dance.

The best way to see the Upper Ottawa scenery from this point is from the cars of the Pacific Railway, which for some distance here run along the summit of a steep hill sloping directly down to the river. The scenery is much the same as at Deep River. We pass the Rocher Capitaine and the outlet of the Deux Rivières, and early in the afternoon are landed at the Pacific Railway station at Mattawa. Nothing could be more wildly desolate than the aspect of this village. In the shadow of silent hills the Ottawa widens beside it, to receive the waters of the river which gives the place its name. This was the goal of Champlain's explorations of the Upper Ottawa; by yonder dark stream he turned his dauntless course to the westward lakes. The village of Mattawa is the most primitive, perhaps, to be seen in Canada. The people have no taxes, no politics, no schools; all these blessings, no doubt, will be theirs in time.

It is easy to get a large canoe and go up the river to one of the beautiful lakes that form part of it. These are of small width and great depth of water. The banks are of steep and dun-coloured granite. Here in these dense shades of impenetrable verdure—here, where even the lumberman never comes—all is desolate as when Champlain found it; desolate as it was, before civilization commenced with the first savage who invented a stone-hatchet; as it has continued since the mysterious era when life began, when the first fish shot through these dark waters, when the first wolf howled for food within these forest solitudes.

Mattawa will always be a depôt for the lumber trade, and probably, as the shanties move farther on, may to some extent take the place of Pembroke, and a more distant Ultima Thule, that of Mattawa. The streets are irregular, blocked with huge granite or gneiss boulders, causes of stumbling and offence to man and beast. But there are several merchants with good supply of wares, who certainly have no reason to complain of hard times.

Mattawa is the nearest to civilization of the Hudson's Bay Company forts. We were shown their stores, where are treasured a goodly stock of valuable furs and skins, from that of the silver fox, most rare and valuable of all, to those of the mink, lynx, and muskrat. The supply of furs, we were informed by the Company's agent, is at present very great. This is because of the thriftlessness of the present race of the young Indians, who kill the animals required for breeding. He thought the fur-trade was not likely to last above a century as a traffic on any considerable scale. The Indians too, he thought, were not likely to last much longer. In former times the Hudson's Bay Company would not traffic with them for liquor; but now all sorts of unprincipled traders bring the fire-water for which the Indian hunters are sure to keep up the demand—till death enforces prohibition.

From its far-away sources in the chain of lakes and swamps which feed also the Saguenay, the St. Maurice and the Gatineau, the Ottawa comes, bringing through the deep waters of Lake Temiscamingue the spoils of great forests of pine, which for years to come will keep up the supply of those vast rafts of spars, logs and timber, which have been meeting us all the way from Quebec. The Pacific Railway from Mattawa will continue its construction westward by the old Trapper's route, past Lake Nipissing and north of the inland seas of Huron and Superior.

www.ingramcontent.com/pod-product-compliance
Lightning Source LLC
Chambersburg PA
CBHW031739230426
43669CB00007B/409